RELUCTANT REPRESENTATIVES

BLACKFELLA BUREAUCRATS SPEAK IN AUSTRALIA'S NORTH

Canis Xavier was a fireman in the early Northern Territory public service under Commonwealth administration before Northern Territory self-government in 1978. This frontispiece photograph is reproduced from the Annual Report of the Northern Territory of Australia 1965–66 (Department of Territories 1968: 60) with the permission of the Commonwealth Government of Australia.

Photographing him again, a later annual report claimed that Canis Xavier was 'the first Aboriginal in the Northern Territory made a permanent fire officer' (Department of the Interior 1971: 40–1).

Photographic reproduction by Christine Cummings, Canberra.

RELUCTANT REPRESENTATIVES

BLACKFELLA BUREAUCRATS SPEAK IN AUSTRALIA'S NORTH

ELIZABETH GANTER

Australian National University

PRESS

Centre for Aboriginal Economic Policy Research
College of Arts and Social Sciences
The Australian National University, Canberra

RESEARCH MONOGRAPH NO. 37
2016

ANU PRESS

Published by ANU Press
The Australian National University
Acton ACT 2601, Australia
Email: anupress@anu.edu.au
This title is also available online at press.anu.edu.au

National Library of Australia Cataloguing-in-Publication entry

Creator:	Ganter, Elizabeth author.
Title:	Reluctant representatives : blackfella bureaucrats speak in Australia's north / Elizabeth Ganter.
ISBN:	9781760460327 (paperback) 9781760460334 (ebook)
Series:	Research monograph (Australian National University. Centre for Aboriginal Economic Policy Research) ; no. 37.
Subjects:	Aboriginal Australians--Government relations. Torres Strait Islanders--Government relations. Aboriginal Australians--Politics and government. Torres Strait Islanders--Politics and government. Representative government and representation--Australia. Australia--Politics and government--Citizen participation.
Dewey Number:	323.0420994

Cover design and layout by ANU Press.

Cover photograph: Sarah Nelson, *Shifting sands*, 2008. Acrylic on canvas, 125 x 146 cm. Photograph by Karen Brown Fine Art, Darwin; reproduced with the permission of the artist.

This work is dedicated to Aboriginal and Torres Strait Islander public servants and their communities, for a future in which they have greater choice of representation.

And to my brother, who thought deeply and imaginatively.

John Robert Ganter
1958–2016
Vale

Contents

List of figures

List of tables

Preface

'That won't take you long!' was the light but rueful refrain of some Aboriginal and Torres Strait Islander senior public servants in the Northern Territory, on hearing I wanted to interview them for this research. There were indeed few of them, relative to the Northern Territory's Aboriginal and Torres Strait Islander population. In the face of continuing indicators of socioeconomic disadvantage in their communities, why had so few Aboriginal or Torres Strait Islander people joined government departments? After all, government develops the policies and designs the programs that fund the organisations that deliver the services to their people.

The very idea of an Aboriginal or Torres Strait Islander senior public servant remixes the usual counterpositioning of coloniser/colonised, government/Indigenous people, actor/acted upon. Something new is suggested. One interviewee who had been drawn into the public service through the vague enticements of Indigenous employment policies in the sprawling, racially divided and intricately networked desert town of Alice Springs told me:

> We're not only seen as statespersons for government, we're also seen as statespersons for our people.

Statespersons for *both* government and his people? Kel, as I call him, went on to explain:

> We're not owned by this mob, we're not owned by that mob.

'Government' and 'our people' were distinct mobs, but they were both potential audiences for these 'statespersons'. This seasoned Aboriginal senior public servant knew his family and country and had lived most of his life in and out of his much-romanticised dry desert town; yet he felt disowned, his identity suspended between 'this mob' and 'that mob', government and community. Hearing Kel's words in the cool, comfortable office that belied the tensions of his role, I wondered what part issues of belonging and identity played in the relatively low numbers of Aboriginal and Torres Strait Islander senior public servants.

This book is informed, enlivened and inspired by my 2007 interviews with past and present Aboriginal and Torres Strait Islander public servants in Australia's Northern Territory. The interviews were no doubt coloured by unfolding political events. Just as our conversations began, the Australian Government declared an emergency intervention in the Northern Territory's remote Aboriginal communities—so the words quoted in this book came from people at a particular place in a particularly heady time. Then again, policy change has been one of the great constants in Australian Indigenous affairs. The issues raised by the interviewees could well resonate for Aboriginal and Torres Strait Islander employees in other times, places and work settings—indeed, for all with a stake in building more responsive and more democratic government. But the extent to which my interviewees' experiences are transferable beyond the Northern Territory is a matter for Aboriginal and Torres Strait Islander public servants to consider. If this book generates interest in the issues that lie behind Indigenous public sector employment policies, for those who develop them and for those who participate in them, I will have met my mark.

A word about myself. I had lived in the Northern Territory since 1984, and at the time of the interviews I had been a senior public servant in the Northern Territory Government for some 20 years. I was known in the Northern Territory community and could orient myself in the physical and political geographies of my informants' working lives. I had visited many of their communities and knew some of their families through genealogical research in my earlier work on land claims. This shared history deepened our conversations, but it sometimes divided us. For some, I had been—still was—the galling white middle-class colleague from elsewhere. This may be so, but I treasure our continuing association.

Setting up the doctoral research that underpins this book required substantial legwork and attention to ethics. The recruitment process approved by The Australian National University (ANU) Ethics Committee had been designed with personal invitations in mind, but the Northern Territory Government's Aboriginal and Torres Strait Islander employment statistics only reported position levels and departments. Privacy laws prevented the Commissioner for Public Employment or any department from releasing employee names. Indeed, the Commissioner for Public Employment had no central record of the names of Aboriginal and Torres Strait Islander employees. The integrity of the research relied on the appearance and reality of my independence from the government, but I needed permission to approach public servants personally. Thanks to championing by my industry adviser, Dennis Bree, the Northern Territory Government opened its doors to the research without asking for more than the protection of employees' privacy and a copy of the final thesis. Department chiefs accepted the terms: employees could be interviewed in departmental offices and meeting rooms during working hours without having to report their participation more officially.

Once these assurances were in place, I drew on collegiate relationships with a few Aboriginal and Torres Strait Islander public servants for the first interviews. The social field revealed itself organically as I was steered towards an informal network of present and past employees. That an interviewee had been a Northern Territory Government employee at any time was straightforward enough to become a necessary condition of participation. Employment in a senior role was less easily established without an interview. If someone was referred to me, I asked for an interview. Prospective participants had time to consider the aim of the research and conditions of participation before we got to the point of invitation. Invitees were given advance notice of the questions before signing their consent. Interviewees chose the time, place and method of recording and were free to withdraw their participation at any stage, without explanation.

Despite the warnings, it took the best part of a year to set up and record 76 semi-structured, conversational interviews. Each interview was as long as it needed to be—usually one to two hours. We met in interviewees' fluorescent-lit air-conditioned offices and under corporate artworks in meeting rooms. Some preferred my quiet office amid the tropical frangipani at the ANU North Australia Research Unit in Darwin or the corkwoods and buffel grass of the Desert Knowledge Precinct in Alice Springs. Some nominated coffee shops or their homes, where we were memorably interrupted by a topical interjection from one interviewee's house painter. Some of the very few interviewees who had moved interstate agreed to the telephone. One tracked me down on a return visit to the Territory. I felt inhabited by the interviews, hearing them, replaying them later, transcribing them, checking the transcriptions and listening again. The stories were of lives and careers different from my own, but they were made strangely familiar by the corporate history and bureaucratic language we shared.

The interviewees' identities have been protected. Pseudonyms are used throughout the book. Departmental functions are renamed to avoid recognition. At the request of interviewees, the terms Aboriginal and Torres Strait Islander are used when referring to them in preference to the generic 'Indigenous'. Torres Strait Islander connections are only specified where interviewees emphasised those connections and where specifying them does not reveal any identity. Of course, some interviewees will recognise their own stories. Some have chosen to reveal their identities since the research, indeed a few have expressed interest in archiving their interviews for future public access. While I welcome that project, the original consent agreements protect all interviewees from any breach of privacy on my part. This condition is essential to the quality of the research and the relationships on which it depends, as the Northern Territory is a small place in which identities are easily revealed.

One person should be named here, although not as an interviewee. The Northern Territory community was devastated by the loss of a beloved friend and colleague when Karmi Sceney, a senior Aboriginal public servant who came from the Tiwi Islands, was killed in a light plane crash along with her husband and two Ethiopian daughters in 2012. I had first met Karmi, then Karmi Dunn, when we both worked in the Office of Aboriginal Development in 1992. Karmi went on to become the elected chair of the Aboriginal and Torres Strait Islander Commission's Yilli Rreung Regional Council before returning to the Northern Territory Public Service some years later as a senior consultant on Aboriginal education. Hers was a voice like no other. Karmi pushed the Northern Territory Government from the inside, calling out inconsistencies in policy, in particular inadequacies in Aboriginal schooling, and urging her people to be more active participants in government. When I re-entered the Northern Territory Government with the new title of Dr Elizabeth Ganter in 2011, Karmi was a critical friend and advocate for this research.

Initially wary, Karmi blazed my trail at the postdoctoral presentations and executive seminars that followed. Karmi urged me to go harder and further in communicating the work, and her terrible and untimely death committed me to publishing my findings.

The book manuscript would not have been started without a Research Fellowship with the ANU Centre for Aboriginal Economic Policy Research (CAEPR). Thank you to Matthew Gray, then director, for inviting me in; to later director, Jerry Schwab, for so generously supporting the publication; and to Frances Morphy, for unflagging editorial support throughout. Thank you to Julie Lahn and Nick Biddle for collegiate engagement on their related project about the Australian Public Service and to Janet Hunt, Katie Curchin, Inge Kral, Boyd Hunter, Marisa Fogarty, Denise Steele, Tracy Deasey and all other CAEPR colleagues for their interest, encouragement and friendship. Thank you very much again, always, my partner Will Sanders, for your constancy and intellect, and for showing me how writing can sing.

Most importantly, I acknowledge the interviewees. Without their trust, their stories and their marvellous sense of theatre, this book would never have been worth writing.

I also acknowledge the Northern Territory Government for my unique and privileged career as social anthropologist and policy executive. My years in the Northern Territory Government taught me everything a public servant needs to know, and set up an enduring research partnership. I acknowledge the Northern Territory History Grants Program for early funding. I acknowledge and thank the Northern Territory Commissioner for Public Employment, Craig Allen, and Commission staff for their generous embrace of this research and its findings.

For reasons of privacy, I cannot name the many outstanding public service colleagues, in the Northern Territory and in Canberra, whose frank insights and imaginative support of my academic work have contributed so much to this project, in early and recent times. I acknowledge every one of you and will happily sign your book.

The PhD research on which the book is based (Ganter 2010) was sponsored and supported by the Desert Knowledge Cooperative Research Centre and sat within the overarching Core Project, 'Desert Services That Work: Demand Responsive Approaches to Desert

Settlement'. This project analysed the interplay between the supply and demand for services to desert communities (see Moran et al. 2009). Thank you to Mark Stafford Smith, Jocelyn Davies, Mark Moran, Patrick Sullivan, Sarah Holcombe, Ruth Elvin and later Nora Devoe, for helping my crossover into research. Although independently conceived and investigated, the contribution of my research to the larger Desert Knowledge Cooperative Research Centre project was to question and complicate the assumption of government as supplier and Aboriginal and Torres Strait Islander people on the demand side, only ever the consumers of government services. In a representative bureaucracy, the presence of Aboriginal and Torres Strait Islander public servants not only generates demand from within the nooks and crannies of government, but also involves Aboriginal and Torres Strait Islander people on the supply side.

I am deeply indebted to Professor Tim Rowse of the ANU History program for his dedication to this project as my PhD supervisor, not to mention our meetings since as civilians (coffee then, whiskey now). I am very grateful to the other panel members, Professors Richard Mulgan and Diane Austin-Broos and Mr Dennis Bree of the Northern Territory Government, and to Professor Ann McGrath for taking on the roles of panel chair and submission-day photographer so enthusiastically at the end. I am also grateful to Francesca Merlan, Tom Griffiths, Nicholas Brown, Marian Sawer, Emma Kowal, David Martin, Julie Finlayson, Doris Kordes, Karen Downing, Christian O'Brien, Kristal Coe, Danielle Spruyt, Bentley James and Nicole Everett for astute observations and support at various stages of the project. I am beyond grateful to Melissa Lovell, Katie Curchin and Penelope Marshall for exposing this social anthropologist to the treasures of political theory.

I am also indebted to the examiners and manuscript reviewers whose comments and encouragement helped shape this book. Thanks to Suzanne Dovi for improving my political theory and later welcoming me to Tucson, Arizona, and to Tess Lea for helping refine my anthropology. Thank you very much, Rolf Gerritsen and an anonymous reviewer, for your compliments and suggestions. Your reviews improved my scholarship.

I want to thank June Hings for her linguistic insight, Darryl Howe for his perceptive reading of the draft, Christine Cummings for her artistic guidance and photography, Sarah Dunlop for the word, and Toni Warburton for whispering the original abstract out of me when it seemed out of the question. Jennie Renfree and Chris Capper deserve a very special mention, as do Derek Farrell, Janice Warren and Karen Edyvane for their contributions many and varied on the Darwin front. And my parents, Patricia and Derrick Ganter, for on top of everything else granting my sister Wendy and me the privilege of their care.

Now to Sarah Nelson. I met Sarah in the Northern Territory Department of Community Development in 1986. Sarah is an Anmatjerre woman from Stirling Station, also known as Wilora (meaning 'sandy country') in central Australia. In the many years since she quietly left the public service, Sarah has been friend and family. She is now a soaring artist, and I thank her very much for her generous permission to reproduce on the front cover her beautiful representation of the shapes in the sand.

Finally I acknowledge my two sons, William and Frankie Braybon, who lost their father to cancer in the early stages of this book. I salute their bravery and resilience and the memory of John William Braybon, who never gave up.

1

'Just bums on seats'?

Introduction

> How can you make decisions about Aboriginal people when you can't
> even talk to the people you've got *here* that are blackfellas?

This question was posed by an Aboriginal senior public servant in
2007. She was imagining a conversation with the Northern Territory
Public Service in Australia's north, whose invitation to Aboriginal
and Torres Strait Islander people to join its departments forms the
backdrop to this book. Counterposing 'Aboriginal people', the
ubiquitous problematic policy subject, with the idiomatic 'blackfella'
who is 'here' in government, her question resists the simple narrative
that those who call themselves 'blackfella' can only live in the bush
and have policy done to them. Telling us that 'blackfellas' may be
present but not feel heard in the administration of government, her
question alerts us to complex tensions for Aboriginal and Torres Strait
Islander public servants in the Northern Territory of Australia.

Sarah, as this speaker will be known, was telling us that Aboriginal
and Torres Strait Islander public servants share a racial identity
with their policy subjects and service recipients. Many have history,
family and land in common with the communities they serve. More
often than not, the aspects of identity they share with the Northern
Territory's disadvantaged Aboriginal population make them attractive
to a public service seeking to appear more representative of the
people it serves. Sarah was reminding us that the public service is also

1

attracted to Aboriginal and Torres Strait Islander public servants' education, skills and experience, the qualities that set some apart from their people and make them members of the rising Indigenous middle/ professional class. Sarah warned:

> You have a pool of Indigenous people and you have a group of whitefellas sitting there talking about blackfellas' issues—without even engaging you! ... So that's why I question whether we're just numbers, we're just *bums on seats*.

Sarah's admonishment to government was in the tone of an old and familiar employment relationship. But we all know that old and familiar relationships can involve neglectful assumptions. Reporting 'bums on seats' or Indigenous employee numbers assumes that the mere presence of Aboriginal and Torres Strait Islander public servants will bring about their meaningful contribution to government. In the words of one of Sarah's colleagues: 'It's a start: If they're [we're] not there, then you got no basis to do anything.' This colleague was voicing the 'politics of presence', the view developed by representation theorist Anne Phillips that the presence of minorities in enough numbers will eventually change the content of politics (Phillips 1995: 25). Sarah was insisting on a more substantive kind of representation—that she must not only speak as a public servant but be heard, if her people are to be taken into account.

Speaking as an Aboriginal or Torres Strait Islander employee presents dilemmas. Some are reluctant to be seen as representing their people in changeable policies and programs. The question, 'What do Aboriginal people think?', may be directed vaguely towards an Aboriginal or Torres Strait Islander employee if there is one present in a meeting. How should he or she speak in reply? Public service ethics call for objectivity. The issue may call for local knowledge. The community may benefit from that knowledge. Yet this employee may feel constrained by knowing that he or she is not authorised to speak for his or her community and that he or she, privileged by well-paid employment, is not representative of the entire Northern Territory Aboriginal and Torres Strait Islander population. This employee will feel a weight of responsibility, knowing that there ought to be properly representative external bodies, unconstrained by government, speaking for their people. This isolated representative of the dispossessed and disadvantaged may feel that even if he or she accepts the well-intentioned, everyday invitation to represent an Indigenous viewpoint, the nuances of answering will not be heard.

At such moments, an Aboriginal or Torres Strait Islander bureaucrat must choose between undesirable alternatives. To stay silent is not to participate in the terms of employment, and possibly turn down the opportunity to assist a community. To speak is to relinquish control over the information, to open oneself up for misinterpretation and be seen to acquiesce in a one-sided relationship between the government and Aboriginal and Torres Strait Islander Australians. Either way, one may be misheard. Whichever choice, the speaker is always situated somewhere in the social complex and, through speech and writing, participates in the construction of 'others' (Alcoff 1995: 100–1).

The choices available to the members of minority populations when they are in positions to speak or act on behalf of others have been captivating British and American political theorists for decades. These are the dilemmas of representation, or in the words of the famed representation theorist Hanna Pitkin, 'the making present *in some sense* of something which is nevertheless *not* present literally or in fact' (1967: 8–9, italics in original). For some Aboriginal bureaucrats, meeting this everyday expectation is not as easy as it sounds. The 1967 work of Hanna Pitkin and subsequent analysts tell us why this is so. Through an elegant and insightful literature, Anne Phillips, Jane Mansbridge, Melissa Williams, Suzanne Dovi and others went on to refine our tools for understanding descriptive representation, or the representation of groups on the basis of likeness. In theoretical terms, the key question is how the descriptive representatives of historically dispossessed groups participate in the substantive representation of issues.

This book draws the nuanced vocabulary of political theory into the Indigenous public sector employment context in Australia, applying arguments developed for the electoral sphere to the fine-grained and unpredictable research data elicited through interviews with bureaucrats. We are concerned here with informal representation, where the sources of authority are messy and unclear. We are not concerned with formal principal–agent representation, where the principal's authority binds the agent and the agent's accountability is enforced, for example, through voting. We are concerned with the subtleties and nuances of informal representation 'in some sense', in this case through employment in bureaucracies that seek to be representative of the populations they serve—so-called *representative* bureaucracies.

This book is about how and why 'bums on seats' *do* representation, even if they do it reluctantly.

Beyond tokens and advocates

The idea of *representative* public servants, particularly representative Aboriginal and Torres Strait Islander public servants, conjures the possibility of other, less clearly articulated, accountabilities than those contained in the terms of public service employment. At times, Aboriginal and Torres Strait Islander people in official roles have been characterised as 'advocates', whose radicalism compromises them as public servants. Alternatively, Aboriginal and Torres Strait Islander officials have been characterised as 'tokens', who compromise their communities through a greater obligation to the public service.

Outspoken Charles Perkins, the first Aboriginal Australian to become a senior Commonwealth public servant, personifies the advocate through his biographer, historian Peter Read (1990). Perkins was a civil rights campaigner in Australia in the 1960s, organiser of the famous Freedom Ride around the state of New South Wales against racial discrimination in 1965. Perkins was appointed an Assistant Secretary in the Commonwealth Department of Aboriginal Affairs in Canberra, the national capital, in 1973. Deputy Secretary in 1979, Perkins was the Australian Public Service's single Second Division (senior executive) statistic from 1973 to 1981. In these positions, Perkins was counselled repeatedly for public challenges to his minister and secretary. He was cleared of any wrongdoing, appointed Secretary of the Commonwealth Department of Aboriginal Affairs in 1984 and sacked by the minister in 1989 when his advocacy of an Aboriginal organisation was seen as a serious conflict of interest (Read 1990: 290–301). Charles Perkins was seen as speaking for Aboriginal Australians and as partisan in favouring their interests over other notions of the public interest.

In his own account of his early career, Perkins tells us he had experienced firsthand the policies that controlled Aboriginal lives at the Bungalow in Alice Springs where he had lived as a child with his mixed descent Arrernte mother. Perkins tells us he later felt 'gazed upon' by senior departmental colleagues, rather than genuinely involved, until the moment he spoke up and fell out with the bureaucracy: 'I was no longer the messenger boy in the office' (Perkins 1975: 172). Perkins describes 'shattering, demoralising' experiences on joining the public service: 'I worked through papers and memos which told me what to do ... the bureaucracy swallowed me up' (1975: 109). He thought himself seen as 'too emotional' and saw many Canberra-based officers as 'cold, hard statues'. He wrote: 'I could not penetrate their armour' (1975: 158–9). Perkins emulated what he saw in his mentors by learning to 'say one thing and do another' (1975: 159).

The influential Australian historian CD Rowley may have had Charles Perkins in mind when he suggested that the first Aboriginal public servants, 'hoping to be received as the representatives of their people must have been dismayed to find themselves cogs in the bureaucratic machine' (Rowley 1978: 207). Lorna Lippman, campaigner for Aboriginal rights in the 1960s and 1970s, revealed her commitment to this view of government in her depiction of 'former Aboriginal radicals' who are 'in government employ, *thus effectively silenced*' (Lippman 1979: 188, emphasis added; see also Bennett 1989: 102–3). Whereas advocates rail against the strictures of bureaucracy, tokens accept them. Some say tokens 'sell out'. Tokens or sellouts benefit from Aboriginality's symbolism without accountability or commitment to distinct Aboriginal interests. Anthropologist Michael Howard gave us this characterisation in his study of Nyoongah–state relations in southwestern Australia. He described Nyoongah people employed in the 'bureaucratic brokerage niche' as disconnected from their communities, 'seeking refuge' from political involvement and creating an 'isolated elite' (1981: 116–8), witlessly 'co-opted' and without 'real power' (1981: 144). For Howard, the token bureaucrat's self-account was merely 'false consciousness' (Howard 1982: 95) and the token's brokerage a form of 'indirect rule'. At around the same time, anthropologist Lee Sacket characterised Aboriginal bureaucrats as the successors to 'White go-betweens', 'far from typical' Aboriginal people who 'owed their prominence to their being the most assimilated of their people' (Sackett 1983: 405). In her later exploration of relationships between the Rembarrnga people and local cattle stations in the Northern Territory, anthropologist Gillian Cowlishaw made a similar critique when she portrayed 'insiders to the state' as 'go-betweens' who may at best 'occupy their positions temporarily and uncomfortably' (Cowlishaw 2004: 65–6).

By always opposing state agency and Aboriginal and Torres Strait Islander interests, both the token and advocate characterisations draw on a limited theory of government and limited aspirations for Aboriginal political identity. The state and the vision for Aboriginal political identity are one-dimensional. The Aboriginal public servant either takes on the system from the inside and leaves as a shining hero, or stays in some uncomfortable and shaming twilight zone, over-promoted and ineffectual. Whereas the advocate is seen to exercise political agency, the token is only afforded state agency. The advocate represents too much; the token represents too little. One engages in political stand-off while the other becomes the state. Either way, state interests are positioned as antithetical to Aboriginal political interests.

This book proposes that the political identity of Aboriginal and Torres Strait Islander public servants is formed by their relatively autonomous relationships to multi-sited portfolio interests. All sites within the state do not support the same imperatives and all who work in them are not in unison. To see the state as a one-dimensional, unpeopled entity is to fall for the 'state effect', a term coined by insightful political theorist Timothy Mitchell for the mistaken belief that government departments are the repositories of objectivity, impartiality and independence (Mitchell 1999). Those who rail against the subjectivities and inconsistencies of government fall for the state effect just as much as those who more obviously uphold them by reproducing the government's self-account. This book seeks to bypass both problems by more detachedly observing government through the personal, off-the-record accounts of those who try making it work.

My starting hypothesis is that somewhere between representation that is too much and representation that is too little, there must be representation that is about right—that is good enough. What would that representation look like in the public service? In the view of American normative political theorist Suzanne Dovi (2007, 2002) the relationship between representative and represented is key and central to 'good' political representation. Good elected representatives seek to know and be known by their constituencies and to interact with them fulsomely. They seek opportunities to explain themselves and to hear from those they represent. Good representatives need historical connection and a sense that they share the aims of those who are absent. Dovi proposes we judge descriptive representatives by the same standard. For Dovi, good descriptive representatives need 'strong mutual relationships with dispossessed subgroups' (2002: 729). These relationships need to be based on 'mutual recognition' (2002: 735–8).

In his study of the interaction of race and class in African-American electoral politics, African-American political scientist Michael C Dawson found that 'the *more* education one had, the more likely one was to believe that blacks were economically subordinate to whites, and consequently, the more likely one was to believe that one's fate was linked to that of the race' (Dawson 1994: 81–2, italics in original). Dovi drew on Dawson's 'linked fate' to argue the importance of 'shared aims' in the relationship between descriptive representative and those they represent (Dovi 2002: 738). Both should respect each other's relationship to the group. Both should be inclusive, and not be too quick to declare others inauthentic (Dovi 2002: 737). Dovi argued later that 'good representatives' should keep 'unjust excluders' at a distance (2007: 161–2). Otherwise some would be excluded again—this time, at the hands of their own people. This was Howard's general assumption for the subject communities of his token Nyoongah bureaucrats.

Dovi's work offers more sophisticated analytic tools than the simple narratives of advocacy and tokenism. Many of the Aboriginal and Torres Strait Islander people who participated in the research did not see falling out with their employers as useful to communities, nor were they silent participants in policies and programs. They did not hesitate to raise tough issues and they tried to be inclusive. Some asserted that being in positions of responsibility called for competency *and* accountability to those who looked to them for help, whose fates they believed they shared. In the bureaucratic context, this might be as good as representation gets.

This book does not assume that it is only ever tokenistic and politically compromising when descriptive representatives align their interests with government. In 1970, HC 'Nugget' Coombs described 'the Government services' as an arena in which Aboriginal leaders could 'work quietly to build the foundations on which political action

7

will rest', warning that Aboriginal leaders 'need not, indeed should not, all of them be in the forefront of political action' (cited in Rowse 2000: 78).

A decade later, away from the centres of national policy discourse at The Australian National University's North Australia Research Unit in the tropical city of Darwin, Dr Peter Loveday also saw the potential in government employment. Loveday was interested in the relationships that lay behind Aboriginal contributions to the public service. Observing the challenges of service delivery during the early years of Northern Territory self-government, Loveday advised that 'aboriginalising' the public service may mean more than having 'someone ... with a black skin to do white things'. A member of an Aboriginal group, he explained, 'may now be in a preferred position, compared with others in his group' (Loveday 1982: 111). Political scientist Rolf Gerritsen (1982), Loveday's colleague, looked back at the group when he observed the differential effects of power deriving from internal and external sources in Aboriginal community politics. Loveday took these ideas a step further when he looked beyond the group to acknowledge the 'unofficial, unpublic and officially unorthodox' ways (1983: 2–4) in which the presence of Aboriginal people was influencing public service administration. With local Aboriginal researcher Raelene Cummings, Loveday went on to test the 'stereotypical racist contrast between "real" Aborigines and "burnt potatoes"' through interviews with 43 Northern Territory Aboriginal and Torres Strait Islander public servants in the late 1980s. A 'burnt potato' is black on the outside and white on the inside, and uses his or her Indigeneity for personal privilege. If, as Loveday tells us, illness had not cut the work short, the project might have stimulated earlier attention to the tensions of representing for Aboriginal and Torres Strait Islander public servants (Loveday & Cummings 1989: 4).

Since the 1980s, research into the complex politics and potential of Aboriginal and Torres Strait Islander contributions to the public service has been sparser. Surveying Aboriginal and Torres Strait Islander health managers in 2000, John Wakerman and colleagues saw the tensions they reported experiencing as cultural rather than political (Wakerman et al. 2000: 25–6, 39–43). Applying an economist's perspective, Boyd Hunter argued the role of 'discrimination' in employment disadvantage in the Australian labour market, though commenting on the difficulty of isolating and measuring discrimination factors empirically (Hunter 2005: 79). Two studies of the subjectivities of white bureaucrats showed that ethnographic research could bring deeper empirical insight. Tess Lea's fine ethnography of 'helping white' bureaucrats in the Northern Territory who were 'learning to govern' Indigenous health, found them 'hyper-privileging the contributions and presence of Aboriginal colleagues who operate in brokerage positions' (Lea 2008: 182). Emma Kowal's subsequent, powerful ethnography of liberal intervention found 'White antiracists' who could not tolerate radical difference (Kowal 2008: 346; Kowal 2015). Lea and Kowal's studies invited the consideration of parallel urges among Aboriginal and Torres Strait Islander public servants, and revealed the viewpoints of some in my interviewees' collegiate group.

More recently, Steven Larkin has taken up the political dimensions of Indigenous public sector employment in his doctoral examination of racist attitudes in the Australian Public Service, drawing on his perspective as an Indigenous senior executive (Larkin 2013). Anthropologist Julie Lahn has pointed to the need for further research into the representation of Indigenous people in professional occupations and engagement with work in urban locales more generally, including the relevance of ideas about an emergent Indigenous middle class (Lahn 2013). Finally, Biddle and Lahn (2016) have just released a study of the Australian Public Service that will be discussed in Chapter 6.

My theories and methods will build on these approaches, and will situate Aboriginal and Torres Strait Islander employees both as officials in structures of governance and as obligated members of communities.

To understand the interviewees better, to discover how they saw their representation, we need a working theory of bureaucracy.

A working theory of bureaucracy

One view of the bureaucracy is that it is an impartial, technical and politically neutral machine divided into departments by the portfolio interests of elected representatives. Each department develops policies and runs programs that cascade down into a myriad of tiny actions by a multitude of public servants who only ever see a fragment of the whole picture. This is the Weberian view. From the outside, this is a familiar image.

Another view portrays a more enlightened public service. This public service understands that knowledge is partial. This view might resonate better with many who are on the inside. Public servants might agree with the accountability theorist, Richard Mulgan, that the idea of the public service as impartial, technical and politically neutral is 'a useful myth, a graphic metaphor', for ensuring the public service remains a stable instrument of democratically elected government (Mulgan 1998: 13). Public servants well know that before decisions are made, proposals must be drafted. If drafts are to see the light of day, public servants have to persuade other public servants of their value. Email by email, meeting by meeting, proposals are revised, reiterated and revisited. One authority for the discretionary/deliberative view of the public service, American political theorist Henry S Richardson, tells us that public service departments are in fact mandated to be discretionary and partial under the general legislative conditions that grant them the autonomy they need to do their work. If bureaucrats could not use their judgement in the development and implementation of policy, nothing would ever be achieved (see Richardson 2002).

These two views are the rational/technical and discretionary/ deliberative faces of the public service. They are in tension, yet both are true. The exercise of discretion in the public service, its weighing of things, is governed by an ethos that asks bureaucrats to be fair and impartial in that weighing by acknowledging their partiality.

The idea of representative bureaucracy is that the presence of individuals from particular social groups will make a bureaucracy reflect them, like a mirror. The aim of a representative bureaucracy is to improve the work of government by exposing that work to a variety of perspectives. It is through the interaction of 'situated knowledges', it was observed by the political theorist, Iris Marion Young, that 'self-regarding understanding' may shift to 'comprehensive understanding' (Young 2004: 20). This shift relies on the discretionary/deliberative view of the public service. A socially diverse bureaucracy can only improve the work of government if bureaucrats from socially identified categories bring themselves into their work. So, representative bureaucracy accepts the premise that bureaucrats are influenced by their social identities (race, gender, class or other characteristics). The aim of representative bureaucracy is to make the bureaucracy more impartial, fairer as a whole, by recognising that individual public servants are prone to the partialities that come with their social categories, and that all individuals are susceptible to some level of identity-based self-interest.

If the best possible objectivity comes from acknowledging partiality, then by implication an Aboriginal or Torres Strait Islander public servant may be there to speak, at times, as an Aboriginal or Torres Strait Islander person. That person's merit may include some notion of making his or her voice heard as an Aboriginal or Torres Strait Islander person. In practice, though, it is not easy for those licensed by their social categories to speak for particular interests. Public servants from other social categories may believe that their own views reflect a broader notion of the public interest, and may not judge the expression of Aboriginal or Torres Strait Islander views as meritorious. Aboriginal and Torres Strait Islander public servants must not only be representative of social diversity but must also uphold the rational/technical view of government administration. They must compete within its ranks and its rules. Like all public servants, their terms of engagement must include upholding the appearance of impartiality in government.

The passive/active distinction

The passive/active distinction is central to the theory of representative bureaucracy. Passive, or descriptive, representation refers to the mirroring of a population in a demographic sense. Active, or substantive, representation refers to the responsiveness of government, through processes that are more discretionary and engaged. Applying the distinction to the public service as a whole, Kenneth J Meier, an American political scientist known for his efforts to prove the theory of representative bureaucracy, described bureaucracy as 'passively representative if it looks like a given segment of the population' and as 'actively representative if it advocates the interests of a given segment of society' (Meier & Hawes 2009: 270).

Whose view of likeness, whose view of interests? The distinction between passive and active representation is clear enough in theory, but it doesn't hold up in practice. Even in the 1970s, Samuel Krislov argued that representative bureaucracy was not realisable in fact, because employee characteristics could not ever really prevail over the rational/technical purpose of bureaucracy (Krislov 1974: 136).

American researchers tried to identify the conditions under which minority representatives were most likely to represent the interests of their communities—for example, when they were working together on issues affecting their interests (Thompson 1976: 203) or when they were in service delivery roles (Thielemann & Stewart 2003). As Meier and Hawes summarised the research in 2009, the relationship between passive and active representation was still correlative rather than causal (Meier & Hawes 2009: 274).

The case for representative bureaucracy was weak. Building on Coombs' insights in the 1970s, Peter Wilenski, Chair of the Australian Public Service Board from 1983 to 1987, encouraged the Australian Government to be more responsive to underrepresented sections of the Australian community. To strengthen the argument for internal diversity, Wilenski proposed a distinction between representing and contributing. Speaking of the 'least powerful interests' in the Australian Public Service: 'Their role is not to "represent" (in the sense of "*argue for*") the case of a particular group but rather *to make a contribution* to decision-making which reflects the values and background of the group from which they are drawn' (Wilenski 1986: 222, emphasis added). What if those values gave rise to dissident views? What if others did not include these 'least powerful interests'? Between arguing and contributing, or advocating and influencing, said one of the interviewees for this research, 'it's a fine line'. Wilenski's distinction does not help us understand how this line works in practice. To lessen the risk of losing representative voices in departmental priorities, Wilenski's solution was to 'require administrators to be far more explicit about their value premises' (Wilenski 1986: 63). But as the American empiricists had already demonstrated, the ideological grip of values was strong, and organisational socialisation made it hard for administrators to be explicit about their values. Charles Perkins had experienced these hard realities. With the benefit of hindsight, we may see that his lasting contribution to the Australian Public Service was his lone, jarring, argumentative voice.

The research into representative bureaucracy gives priority to the public administration account. In so doing, it largely forgets the represented. The research into representative bureaucracy does not ask important questions about the relationship between descriptive representative bureaucrats and their identity groups, and how these bureaucrats reconcile their identity with the rational/technical view of the bureaucracy. The passive/active or mirror/agency distinction, as it is also known, is useful enough for the purposes of public administration, but the more nuanced vocabulary of political representation meshes better with the interviewees' deliberations over what to say and do about their people in the myriad moments of everyday work. Theorists of political representation are more comfortable analysing political content and behaviour, using the terms descriptive and substantive to distinguish between what representatives *stand for* and what they *stand up for* through speech and action. Ultimately, substantive representation is about the crystallisation and representation of group perspectives. We will apply the finely honed theories of political representation to understand more about how this plays out between bureaucratic representatives and their represented.

A final note on my general approach. This book presents public service language and behaviours—including the very idea of representative bureaucracy—as artefacts of the government project, not self-evident truths. Readers are invited to suspend their judgement of government: not to be disapproving of the discretionary, partial administration of democratic government but to acknowledge these less acknowledged aspects of the work of public servants. Of course public servants bring identity to their work. Of course bureaucracies that strive to be representative encourage particularised populations to bring identity to their work. Of course this sets up tensions within the public service; of course there are workplace politics. Of course the tension between active representation and the principle of impartiality is not limited to representative bureaucrats. Representative bureaucracy creates the appearance of an impartial state by singling out the members of certain social groups for particular kinds of representation. As we shall see through the interviews, if those seen as representative argue with that identity, representative bureaucracy contains and limits their representations. Deeming that some public servants are representative of ethnicity, gender or some other politically relevant attribute might imply to the unwary observer that public servants who are not so identified are impartial. That too would be to fall for the state effect.

One hundred hours of speech

The interviews, conducted between July and December 2007, yielded a substantial body of data—100 hours of speech and nearly 2,500 pages of transcription, recording the encounters of 76 individuals with hundreds of public service projects since Northern Territory self-government in 1978. The effect of the presence of the researcher, a white middle-class educated southerner and former colleague, cannot be underestimated. But our discussions were frank, and the interviewees were open to having them. These were professional bureaucrats with confident views. While they did not form a group in the sociological sense of a coherent and self-referring entity, the lives of these 39 men and 37 women converged on a career detail. This was that they had all worked in the administration of the Northern Territory at some point in its self-governing years. Many knew each other. Some were in each other's stories.

The interview questions explored the nature of the interviewees' work, how influential they believed they were as public servants and the situations that created conflicts for them. Most of the interviews were held in Darwin, the Northern Territory's humid, developing capital and the central headquarters of most departments. Darwin is at the north of the Northern Territory, the so-called 'Top End'. Other Top End interviews were held in Katherine, three hours' drive south from Darwin and in Wadeye, a large Aboriginal community that was once the Catholic mission of Port Keats, an hour's flight southwest of Darwin. In desert Central Australia, the interviews were in Alice Springs, 1,600 km south of Darwin, and in the small multiracial town of Tennant Creek. One interview was held in Ntaria, the old Lutheran mission of Hermannsburg west of Alice Springs amid the gracious white gums of the wide, winding, dry Finke River bed.

About the interviewees

The interviewees reflected candidly on their careers, personal histories and sources of identity, contextualising their accounts in work events. When invited to characterise their relationship with the Northern Territory Government, the answers ranged all the way from the quirky 'platonic' to the accusatory 'poison cousin', which in Aboriginal terms is an avoidance relationship among close kin. Edith, who came from a Top End local language group, explained 'poison cousin' to mean:

> Part of the same things, like they can sit in the car, but they've got their backs to each other; there's no touching.

'Poison cousin' is a rich and telling metaphor for the relationship between some Aboriginal public servants and their government. This was a strong cultural reference. But generally speaking, the interviewees were uncomfortable with public service colleagues assuming they would make culturally distinct Aboriginal contributions. They preferred to watch and learn to participate in public service cultures. While acknowledging their embeddedness in the norms of public service workplaces, many still felt racially and culturally different. Even so, it was a clear theme of the interviews that Aboriginal culture was a matter for them to raise and discuss, and not other public servants.

Often, the interviewees referred to their absent constituencies as 'the remotes'. Remoteness is relative. For example, the entire Northern Territory is described in national policy as remote and regional. For the interviewees, 'the remotes' was mostly shorthand for the 40,000 Aboriginal people who lived in rural-remote communities. Sometimes, 'the remotes' was used synonymously with 'the non-compliant with government programs'. But as the interviewees also knew, many traditionally oriented remote community dwellers are compliant policy and program subjects who work to benefit their communities. And the non-compliant behaviours associated with itinerant populations in urban areas, reflecting government policy settings, are challenging government in new ways. When referring to 'the remotes', did the interviewees simply mean, 'not us'? Even this interpretation would be too simplistic, as we shall see that many had come from remote places themselves. Because some were actively engaged in making Aboriginal and Torres Strait Islander people more present in the public service, 'the remotes' could also have referred to future employees.

Pinning down the absent in bureaucratic representing will lead us to consider whether the absent were imagined, just as the state is imagined, as an abstraction that is only given form through representation.

Pitkin tells us that descriptive representations are 'renderings of an "original" in a medium different from it' (1967: 72–3). The representative is like but not the same as, the represented. The likeness cannot go too far without losing the element that makes it representation. That element need only be a matter of extent, or the relationship of part to whole. The interviewees fulfilled the basic definition of descriptive representatives by being part of, but not the whole of, the Northern Territory Aboriginal population and by coming from some, but not all, communities and regions. They were *like* the represented in this sense, but they were *not* the very problematic policy subjects, the disaffected, program-non-compliant others that some of the programs they administered were trying to reach. The experiences of Northern Territory Aboriginal people in the protectionist and assimilationist policies of the past had been intensely dislocating, but had bestowed educational and employment advantages that now fitted some for public service professionalism. Between many Aboriginal and Torres Strait Islander public servants and the rest of their population, there was not only a relationship of part to whole, but also of social differentiation through historical circumstance.

If representativeness is not typicality, the representative might *improve* the 'typical' likeness of the represented by emphasising those characteristics most 'relevant for reproduction' (Pitkin 1967: 87). This is an important idea, because not all characteristics of the Northern Territory's problem population might be deemed 'relevant for reproduction'. Bureaucratic representation might selectively reproduce the comportments of social compliance—work ethic, sobriety, parental responsibility and policy acquiescence— to encourage the Northern Territory's problem population to adopt certain behaviours. Some interviewees gave accounts of modelling such behaviours and exhorting their less compliant communities to follow suit, effectively appropriating the aims of government in what the postcolonial scholar Homi Bhabha calls the 'final irony of partial representation' (Bhabha 1984: 129). Although relevant observations were incidentally made by some community-based interviewees, the research on which this book is based did not set out to test the views and reactions of the represented. The research was designed to elicit the views of those representing, understanding absent communities through the constructions of their representatives.

This is not a study of the loyalties of front-line officers and counter staff who deal directly with the public, the 'street-level bureaucrats' of Michael Lipsky's work on the culture of direct service (Lipsky 1980)—although some interviewees did meet that description—but on the experiences of those whose service was more indirect due to the responsibilities of seniority. This is a study of public servants who were closer to creating, naming and funding services than delivering them, who worked at the nexus between operations and policy and who had some discretion to make active representations in their departments. The closer public servants are to the top of hierarchies, the more the community expects them to be accountable and the more is invested in the appearance of impartiality and fairness. The more senior the officer, the more likely it is that his or her written words will not be changed by someone who is above them in the hierarchy.

This research follows the Northern Territory Government's definition of a senior public servant, from middle management to the executive and senior executive levels.[1] The interviewees were typically middle managers, although some were executives and senior executives. From middle management upwards, public servants may work in close proximity to executives and senior executives, and will be judged by others for their operational efficiency and strategic thinking. They might represent the government publicly. Their networks are both internal and external. They often have staffing and budget responsibilities, and they are expected to convey impartiality by reconciling diverse perspectives.

Fifty-three of the total 76 interviewees had been employed at a senior level at some time since Northern Territory self-government, but the other 23 also had interesting and relevant things to say. Ten of the 53 senior-level interviewees were or had been employed at executive or senior executive levels of the Northern Territory Public Service.[2]

---

1   In 2007, the definition of senior for statistical purposes in the Northern Territory Government equated to Administrative Officer level 7 or above or equivalent in other salary streams. Above Administrative Officer 7 was level 8, after which the executive levels began. The current pay progression, which was introduced in 2011, starts seniority a little higher at Senior Administrative Officer 1 (SAO1), or the equivalent of the former Administrative Officer 8.
2   The executive- and senior executive–level interviewees were very thinly spread across departments. For reasons of confidentiality, they are generally discussed together and as part of the larger senior cohort.

Most interviewees were in their 40s and 50s, but their ages ranged between the 20s and 60s. The only significant demographic difference between the senior and non-senior group was that there were more women (30) than men (23) among the 53 senior-level interviewees. While half the interviewees had not completed high school, more than half had achieved post-school qualifications later in life. Not having completed high school had not prevented anyone's entry into the public service. Having tertiary qualifications had not been the deciding factor in their promotion, as a higher proportion of non-senior than senior interviewees had university degrees. Of the total group, 46 were in the Northern Territory Public Service in 2007 and 30 were former employees.

Table 1 organises the 76 interviewees by their senior/non-senior status and whether they were currently in the Northern Territory Public Service or were former employees in 2007.

Table 1: Seniority by Northern Territory Public Service (NTPS) employment status

		NTPS employment status in 2007 76 interviewees		
		Current NTPS	Former NTPS	Total
Senior/non-senior	Senior in NTPS at some point in career—'senior'	34	19	53
	Never senior in NTPS—'non-senior'	12	11	23
	Total	46	30	76

Source: Author's research.

From before the time of Northern Territory self-government until 2001, the Northern Territory was governed by a Country Liberal Party majority. The first Labor Government was elected in 2001. The interviewees had commenced employment fairly evenly across these political periods. Of the 46 interviewees who were in the public service in 2007, 19—more than 40 per cent—had been recruited before 1990 and six had 30 years' continuous service. That there had not been more attrition over the decades suggests that quite a few careers had endured the political upheaval of the Northern Territory's only change of government. But if there was a core of longer serving Aboriginal and Torres Strait Islander officials in the Northern Territory Public Service, it is difficult to put a precise character or figure on it.

If a public servant was still in the service in 2007 after more than a decade of employment, it meant that he or she had stayed in place over different political periods. This could indicate a commitment to stay. In this category were 31 interviewees, but there were few clear successors to those whose long careers were coming to end after 30 years of self-government.

Considering the Northern Territory's tight social and professional networks, it is conceivable that the 53 senior-level interviewees constituted a significant proportion of those who had *ever* worked for the Northern Territory Government as a senior public servant. But this book is fundamentally about the people behind the numbers. Working for the Northern Territory Government meant participating in the government of their place. This was expressed as some kind of right, entitlement or even obligation. Even though the public sector dominates the Northern Territory's relatively small employment base, working for the Northern Territory Government was more than just a job. Many who stayed thought of themselves as role models to others. We shall explore the criteria by which political theorists judge descriptive representatives to be good representatives and by which the interviewees judged themselves, but this book will not judge them. The approach we take will be descriptive and probing, and will place the highest value on critical self-reflection by the participants.

Through the instrument of Labor's 2002–2006 Indigenous Employment and Career Development Strategy, the Northern Territory Government recognised that disadvantaged Aboriginal and Torres Strait Islander people were not present 'literally or in fact', and sought to remedy that absence by soliciting the advice of those who were more able to fulfil the requirements of merit selection for public service positions. Like the invitations that followed, and like Indigenous public sector employment policies elsewhere in Australia, the Northern Territory Government's invitation to Aboriginal and Torres Strait Islander people contained no foretaste of the tensions within the very idea. The invitation was upbeat: join us, let us count you, contribute to policy and decision-making and reap the rewards of long service.

So Indigenous employment policies ask Aboriginal and Torres Strait Islander people to help build the evidence base for a representative bureaucracy. Beyond the obvious material security of their positions as public servants, we shall consider the extent to which Aboriginal and Torres Strait Islander employees could also make a plausible case to themselves that they were doing something worthwhile for the Northern Territory's Aboriginal and Torres Strait Islander population.

Guide to the book

We shall see that the Northern Territory Government's invitation to Aboriginal and Torres Strait Islander people is quite ambivalent. No democratic government can invite people to contribute to the public service on the basis of their social identity without potentially placing them in tension with their professional obligations as public servants. At the same time, once it has acknowledged significant plurality among those it governs, no democratic government can afford not to make the invitation.

The invitation to Aboriginal and Torres Strait Islander people to participate in the administration of the Northern Territory contains the expectation that once present in the public service, they will do some kind of representing. Hanna Pitkin dared her readers to 'capture an instance of representation' (Pitkin 1967: 1), but a fork in the disciplinary road limited subsequent research to the electoral sphere. By staying in the public administration account, those who tested the idea of representative bureaucracy also spoke among themselves. Ideas about *doing* representation that might have predicted tensions in the public service did not stray in. Theorists of political representation tended to find the (oversimplified) state bureaucracy an unlikely site for legitimate representation (for example, John Dryzek 1996: 479–80) and those in it simply victims of cooption (see Michael Saward 1992). American theorist Susan Bickford acknowledged the 'intuitive possibility', as I do, that 'citizen identities can be enacted' within the state context (Bickford 1999: 92; see also Cooper 1995). But most of the theorists who went on to venture into non-electoral spheres only looked as far as mechanisms for citizen participation at the outer edges of the bureaucracy, for example John Dryzek's development of the idea of 'discursive' representation (Dryzek & Niemeyer 2008).

Some theorists are now untying representation from electoral processes and moving beyond the descriptive/substantive distinction. One example is Saward's later development of representation as a 'precarious and curious sort of claim about a dynamic relationship' (Saward 2006: 299; see also Saward 2009), in which the 'representative claim' works to constitute the community that is the subject of representation. Another example is Andrew Rehfeld's recasting of the dilemmas of political representatives as those of public decision-makers (Rehfeld 2009). The tension between needs and wants, which we will see was a central tension for the interviewees, is often at the core of difficult policy decisions. We will test these insightful developments through the interviews.

Having reconfigured the state from an amorphous monolith to a series of sites with which employee/citizens engage with discretion, we can now see something that is of central importance for building more representative bureaucracies. This is that public service employment may legitimately produce instances of political representation. This point was acknowledged by feminist theorists Marian Sawer, Sophie Watson, Anna Yeatman and Hester Eisenstein when they used the terms and tools of political representation to understand the role of government employment in the advancement of feminist political agendas in Australia in the 1970s and 1980s (Eisenstein 1996; Sawer 1990; Watson 1990; Yeatman 1990). Australian Indigenous feminist intellectuals have tended to disassociate themselves from white middle-class feminist agendas, arguing that these agendas mask white women's racial privilege (for example Moreton-Robinson 2000: 32). But it is unfortunate that the feminist theorists' insights into gender representation did not spark analysis of the distinct issues raised by Indigenous representation through government employment. In 2001, when Sawer called for 'thicker', more descriptive accounts of parliamentary representation in Australia (Sawer & Zappalá 2001), anthropologist and historian Tim Rowse observed in the Australian literature the assumption that Aboriginal people living traditional lifestyles had limited capacity for democratic participation. Rowse traced this assumption to narrow concepts of representation and a divergence between the disciplines of social anthropology and political science in Australia (Rowse 2001).

The cost has been high. In spite of our reliance on the contributions of Aboriginal and Torres Strait Islander people to the government bodies that are responsible for the substantive representation of Australian Indigenous affairs, we know too little about the roles Aboriginal and Torres Strait Islander people play in them.

This book will show how a representative identity may be formed in the vagary and indeterminacy of administrative discretion. Indigenous employment policy invites Aboriginal and Torres Strait Islander people to be present in departments and, once there, to conjure the absent by participating in policy development and problem-solving. When they spoke of representing the intended beneficiaries of Aboriginal-specific policies and programs, the interviewees were active representatives in the sense of defending their portfolios. When they revealed other audiences for their work, they implied other kinds of representing. In this book, the question of who is representing whom is always relevant and the answer is always context-dependent. Representation is a relationship, and it cannot be easily relegated to the inside or outside of departments. Bureaucrats are citizens, and some straddle the inside/outside divide through their communities and organisations. Descriptive representatives do not have geographic constituencies like electoral representatives do, but there are implicit membership criteria. As the political theorist Melissa Williams observed (1998), these can include memories of historic dispossession.

We shall hear in the interviews that just being present and talking about it entangles senior public servants in the efforts and tensions of governing. This book will not take their descriptions of programs and responsibilities as self-evident truths but as ideas that all public servants learn to voice about the nature and causes of problems, what is to be done and who should do it.

Representative bureaucracy could be quite confounding from the point of view of many Indigenous Australians. Representative bureaucracy's invitation contains the contradiction: we embrace your statistic, but we cannot necessarily embrace you. We shall see that self-identifying Aboriginal or Torres Strait Islander public servants were granted some of the privileges of inclusion, but rarely that of serving non-Indigenous populations. Through the interviews, we shall see much more besides. No assumption is made that a public service career would either intensify or erase an Aboriginal or Torres Strait Islander person's connection to their absent constituencies. The interviews assumed that competent and professional Aboriginal or Torres Strait Islander senior public servants might have enduring relationships with, even political commitments to, other Aboriginal or Torres Strait Islander people that they might exercise responsibly and with due attention to the other ethics of public service besides representation, just as other public servants might do in relation to other constituencies.

Sarah, the interviewee whose words opened this chapter, could justifiably believe herself licensed to speak for her community. This would be especially so if her employer held enlightened ideas about the merits of social identity and actively sought to understand Northern Territory Aboriginal people more fully. What are Sarah's options if she does not feel heard? She might speak more assertively, running the risk of strident advocacy. She might speak less, abandoning the opportunity to contribute her social identity and feeling token. She might find some other frame of reference. The political theory shows that one can never only be an employment statistic. One is inevitably an agent of an imagined absent constituency. Can one choose not to represent others? Who descriptive representatives are (their representativeness) obliges and commits them to certain kinds of speaking (their representations) in relation to others (the represented). The interviewees will show us that their very identities obliged and committed them to actions that were sometimes beyond their choice.

The issues raised in the book are relevant to wider debates about the problems of minorities and their relationships with government. If readers find my approach descriptive, or perhaps parochial, that is the nature of ethnography. It is my contribution to a body of theory and debate in minority–government relations that has largely drawn on experiences outside Australia. That literature has skimmed too lightly over politics in the public service. I hope my selective application of sophisticated theories of representation to the everyday world of my interviewees will inspire further scholarship into minority–government relations, including representative bureaucracy, and embolden Aboriginal and Torres Strait Islander public servants in Australia.

The book will progressively situate the interviewees in their geographical, historical and political context. The Northern Territory is part of Australia's vast northern frontier, with over 1.4 million square kilometres covering nearly one-fifth of the Australian mainland. The Top End of the Northern Territory, where Darwin and Katherine are, encompasses northern wetlands and tropical savannas. These graduate southwards into the hot, dry deserts of Central Australia through Tennant Creek and Alice Springs. The Top End and Central Australia depict commonly recognised points of geography and administration. Idiomatically, there is no 'south'. Northern Territorians reserve that term, sometimes disparagingly, for the more populous cities and regions of south, southeastern and southwestern Australia, where they feel that people sometimes forget or misunderstand Australia's far north.

Chapter Two spans 100 years of government effort to attract and report on the numbers of Aboriginal and Torres Strait Islander employees across the Northern Territory landscape. This effort intensified when the Northern Territory achieved self-government, but the invitation for Aboriginal and Torres Strait Islander people to participate in government is one of long standing. It has also been one of long-standing ambivalence, and this ambivalence set the tone for the response. The research found that participants were in orbit between government and non-government roles. Their mobility in and out of the public service created a 'turnstile ticker' effect, as one interviewee said, that kept the Indigenous public sector employment statistics reasonably stable but made targets elusive.

In Chapters Three and Four, the interviewees tell how they accepted the Northern Territory Government's invitation to help make it more representative of their people. We will hear how and why they accepted the invitation and what limits they placed on their acceptance. We will explore the dilemmas that made them reluctant to speak as representatives. Read together, these two chapters give a sense of the workplace issues that initially compel, but ultimately turn some Aboriginal and Torres Strait Islander public servants away, which they do either by leaving the public service for a while or staying 'under the radar', as one interviewee described her subtle withdrawal.

Chapter Five presents the interviewees' reframing of the invitation to speak by describing themselves as role models. We will hear the intriguing ways in which role models represented Aboriginal people to government, and how some strong and committed Aboriginal senior public servants purposefully represented the government to their communities. We will look at the life issues and political conscience that motivated such moves, and explore more fully the dimensions of the relationship between those present and absent from the administration of government.

Chapter Six sums up the research and its significance for those trying to build public institutions that better reflect the Aboriginal and Torres Strait Islander populations they mean to serve. We will move beyond the theory to understand role modelling as political representation—a move by Aboriginal and Torres Strait Islander public servants who wanted the government to see their people in a better light. The book concludes with some suggestions as to how government could build better relations with Aboriginal and Torres Strait Islander Australians through public sector employment. These suggestions are ventured cautiously because in truth, better relations with Aboriginal and Torres Strait Islander Australians can only be built directly with them. Through the interviews, this book will tell you that.

2

The Northern Territory's turnstile ticker

Representative bureaucracy is a relatively recent policy in the longstanding invitation by successive governments for Northern Territory Aboriginal people to participate in the administration of their population. Interviewees urged me time and again to follow the numbers. One man who had been watching the government's relationship with Aboriginal organisations in Central Australia for a long time, described Indigenous employment as a 'turnstile ticker'. It was not easy to find a consistent storyline in periodically revised categories of employment and reset baselines, but the interviewees' general unease with the government's decontextualised, over-optimistic reportage suggests we will find underlying issues, perhaps continuities, if we look hard enough over a significant timeframe.

Aboriginal people were used as labour in the earlier administration of Australia's Northern Territory, but their work was menial under the policies of Aboriginal protection and assimilation that characterised the period of Commonwealth control before Northern Territory self-government in 1978. The Commonwealth administered the Northern Territory for some 66 years before self-government, involving many Aboriginal people in operational roles that were cast as so minor that these staff were excluded from public service privileges and conditions. The events of this era were formative of the family histories, political identities and work ethics of the interviewees, as many were the children and grandchildren of the domestic labourers, railway workers and police trackers of the Commonwealth's early administration.

The Indigenous employment numbers narrate the historic, still-remembered relationship with government that lies at the heart of Aboriginal political identity in the Northern Territory—Edith's 'poison cousin'. But Edith also said about the Northern Territory Government and its relationship with Aboriginal Territorians:

> We're all married to each other now. We're all intertwined.

Edith was referring to a history in which people of mixed descent were incarcerated and trained for employment in 'half-caste' institutions—the Kahlin Compound in Darwin and the Bungalow in Alice Springs—under early protectionist policies. Some interviewees were first- and second-generation descendants of the very people who had supplied the labour for government departments and the households of key officials in these not-so-distant times (Department of External Affairs 1919: 44). 'Government employment' was seen as the exemplar for less reputable private employers—but this was not employment in today's terms. There was little choice and there were no private wages.

A number of the interviewees were moved as 'half-caste' children to new homes on Melville and Croker Islands by patrol officers employed by the Native Affairs Branch under the Commonwealth's expanded World War II presence. After the war, the Northern Territory Administration oversaw an elaborate machinery of settlements, missions and 'town' employment in which Aboriginal and Torres Strait Islander people, including 1,000 redundant Army recruits, were occupied in many forms of government labour. However, when the Northern Territory Administration took stock of government employment in 1949, there were only around 60 Aboriginal trackers and other assistants (Wilson 1998: 87; Northern Territory Administrator 1949).

The number of Aboriginal people in government employment nearly doubled over the next decade, as the definition expanded to include traineeships in hygiene, hospital and medical, teaching, domestic, catering, welfare, surveying and patrol work on government settlements and missions. In the 1960s, the number briefly skyrocketed then fell. Three thousand Aboriginal people were recorded as 'employed' on government settlements and missions

(Department of Territories 1964: 50) until the introduction of equal wages made that categorisation unsustainable for the limited financial capacity of the Northern Territory Administration (see Rowley 1971: 307). By 1966, the figure for government employment again excluded remote settlement workers and had fallen back to 300 (Department of Territories 1966: 57).

After decades of drawing Aboriginal people into menial labour, the Administration had drawn a line between 'employment', which was for those recruited into the administrative bureaucracy, and 'training', which was for those in the service delivery machinery of settlements and missions (Department of Territories 1968: 62). This distinction was expressed in two full-page portraits published by the Northern Territory Administration in 1968. One was of Canis Xavier, the fireman in this volume's frontispiece who had already served four years with the Northern Territory Public Service.[1] The other, Zoc Mulda, from the remote settlement of Haasts Bluff, was photographed at an oxywelding class in Darwin. Canis was about to be paid award wages, whereas Zoc was in training (Department of Territories 1968: 60–1).

Through the 1967 Referendum, the Australian public gave the Commonwealth a clear mandate to make special laws and policies for Aboriginal and Torres Strait Islander people in the Australian states and the Northern Territory. Many thought there should be a reconsideration of Aboriginal affairs, as Aboriginal and Torres Strait Islander people were now free to participate in government on a more equal footing. But Charles Perkins' rise through the public service was a rarity, as past policies had not prepared many Aboriginal and Torres Strait Islander people for the opportunity of public service careers.

Perversely, it was just as the Commonwealth nurtured the first national institutions of Aboriginal self-determination and land rights that it began ceding control of the Northern Territory to self-government.

---

1   There had been a Northern Territory public service since the early Commonwealth administration, which expanded and contracted relative to Commonwealth departments until Northern Territory self-government. This pre-self-government Northern Territory public service took on the Fire Brigade in 1965.

The original 10 per cent

During the final years of Commonwealth administration, arrangements in the Northern Territory gave the Commonwealth the opportunity to draw on Aboriginal employment in the Northern Territory as the nation's first evidence of a socially diverse Australian Public Service. In the spirit of Aboriginal self-determination, the Australian Public Service treated Aboriginal and Torres Strait Islander employees with renewed numeric diligence and a new racial respect, inviting departments to contribute to an annual survey of Aboriginal and Torres Strait Islander employees in 1973. The survey drew on the newly accepted definition: 'a person of Aboriginal or Torres Strait Islander descent who identifies as an Aboriginal or Islander and is accepted as such by the community with which he is associated' (Australian Public Service Board 1975: 2).

In 1973, 450 Northern Territory-based Aboriginal and Torres Strait Islander employees were recorded. In 1974, the number swelled to nearly 1,500 with the absorption of 1,039 formerly exempt municipal workers, hospital attendants and teaching assistants into the Australian Public Service 'Fourth Division' after full wages were awarded to those on training allowances in Northern Territory settlements. Many were temporary employees (Australian Public Service Board 1975: 3–4, 6; Rowley 1976: 369). In evidence to the Parliamentary Joint Committee on the Northern Territory, a Commonwealth representative calculated the Territory's Aboriginal public sector employment rate at 10 per cent, omitting the original 450 (which would have increased the percentage) and setting the 1,039 settlement workers against a base figure of 11,000 Northern Territory-based Australian Public Service employees (Joint Committee on the NT 1974: 2559). For the entire history of the Northern Territory Administration, these settlement workers had been excluded from the full provisions of the Australian Public Service Act. Now they were celebrated (see also Briggs 2008).

In time, after a few hundred local employees had trickled into Northern Territory Aboriginal councils and associations, the Commonwealth handed over some 1,100 Aboriginal and Torres Strait Islander employees to the Northern Territory Public Service. This left just over 100 Aboriginal and Torres Strait Islander staff forming a concentration of 'Third Division' clerical workers in the Commonwealth Department of Aboriginal Affairs in the Northern Territory (Australian Public Service Board 1980: 5). The Northern Territory Public Service had inherited a nascent representative bureaucracy through responsibility for the delivery of services to remote communities (Australian Public Service Board 1976: 5).

Target practice in the early years of self-government

In the early years of self-government, Northern Territory politicians sought to carve out a unique future for the region. HC Coombs was encouraging the machinery to support a more responsive and socially diverse Australian Public Service (see Coombs 1977), but Northern Territory policies were reactive to, rather than cooperative with, national approaches. The Australian Parliament was concerned with the capacity of the incoming administration to manage the Territory's demographic and cultural complexity, and the architects of the policies and structures of Aboriginal self-determination were cautious about the Territory's capacity to be a vehicle for Aboriginal empowerment.

The original state of mind

The Northern Territory was to be the site of sparkling new bureaucratic machinery: 'a vision splendid of a bureaucracy based on merit', as the *Canberra Times* satirised it for the nation's delectation on the eve of self-government (Juddery 1978). The Northern Territory Public Service was cavalier with established practices in the pursuit of a Territory-style public service. Among those taking up the reins of self-government, the mood was ebullient and rebellious. The Public Service Commissioner asked Chief Minister Everingham to 'let us of the N.T.P.S. have a go to develop something different and more dynamic than the tired bureaucratic machines in the States and the A.P.S.' and promptly amalgamated the unskilled and clerical divisions, which made school completion unnecessary to an individual's rise to the top (PSCNT 1978).

Beneath the swashbuckling allusions to a new inclusiveness, the vision was predominantly for the employment of settler locals. Aboriginal people formed 25 per cent of the Northern Territory's population, but the Northern Territory's original and permanent population was barely in the picture. Territory officials preferred to employ the white settlers who had arrived during the period of the Northern Territory Administration.

The political economy of Northern Territory self-government presented deep challenges, and the Northern Territory Government was affronted by the continued presence of the Commonwealth in local affairs. Through the Department of Aboriginal Affairs, the Commonwealth continued to administer community development programs in remote areas, leaving the Northern Territory Government to deliver health, education and policing services across the Northern Territory's complex geography, while without full responsibility for Aboriginal affairs. The Commonwealth had secured legislated land rights for Northern Territory Aboriginal people in 1976, which placed a major limit on some of the aims of self-government, and the Northern Territory Government often presented itself as the adversary of traditional claimants who were represented by Commonwealth-funded land councils. Aboriginal Territorians were being enticed into a seemingly more benevolent political relationship with Canberra, while the Northern Territory Government provided a convenient scapegoat for the difficulties and costs of remote service delivery.

When Prime Minister Malcolm Fraser asked the Northern Territory Government to fund training positions for Aboriginal people over and above the staffing transfer, Chief Minister Everingham asked for 'concrete evidence' of the Commonwealth's commitment to the Northern Territory by demanding the Commonwealth supply the positions 'prior to transfer' (Everingham 1978: 1). Behind the scenes, Everingham pushed his bureaucracy long and hard for imaginative proposals to improve Aboriginal employment and training. Departments deliberated over how they should engage with Aboriginal people to achieve it (Everingham 1979). In 1980 Everingham set Aboriginal employment targets of '10 per cent by 1982, 15 per cent by 1985, and 20 per cent by 1990' as the public service contribution to a Five Year Program to improve remote communities. The Program also aimed for the 95 per cent 'Aboriginalisation' of government works (Everingham 1980: 3075–6) (PSCNT 1983: 24; see also OAL 1983: folio 262).

The race back to 10 per cent

The 10 per cent target must have seemed safe enough for a public service of 11,000 staff that was still waiting for 1,100 Aboriginal and Torres Strait Islander Australian Public Service staff to transfer in with self-government. But Everingham's 15 and 20 per cent targets were ambitious. After the transfers, an internal survey located 1,137 Aboriginal and Torres Strait Islander employees, who formed 10.5 per cent of the public service establishment of 10,879 legislated positions (OAL 1983: folio 262). But the establishment figure inflated the percentage by providing a smaller base than the 'actual' workforce of around 14,500 allowing for staff turnover, leave and other variables (PSCNT 1983: Appendix A). Also, in 1983 the Northern Territory Public Service establishment excluded government authorities like the Northern Territory Teaching Service, Electricity Commission and uniformed police force (OAL 1983: folio 256). Both restrictions on the base figure were about to change, as these authorities were soon incorporated into the public service establishment figures. Comparison against the 'actual' workforce was to become the convention from 1985.

When calculated against the larger workforce figure, 1,137 Aboriginal and Torres Strait Islander employees formed just 7.8 per cent of the Northern Territory Public Service. Everingham's targets had become even more ambitious. They were doomed for definitional reasons alone, but in the face of public service growth they stood even less chance. On whatever calculus—the inflated 10.5 per cent or the more realistic 7.8 per cent of the larger workforce—with only 37 more Aboriginal and Torres Strait Islander employees than the 1,100 inherited with self-government, there was no apparent justification for Everingham to tell the Commonwealth that his government was 'ahead of its targeted percentage' in Aboriginal employment in 1983 (Everingham 1983). Target-setting quickly went out of fashion, although it would later tempt new political actors.

'Are you a radical black?'

By 1983, Aboriginal and Torres Strait Islander public servants were working as teachers and teaching assistants, health workers, police aides, rangers, community workers, essential services operators and liaison officers (OAL 1983: folio 256). Some Aboriginal and

Torres Strait Islander public servants also assisted with centralised employment and training. Through some of these officers, departments made sporadic but significant efforts to encourage the active representation of Aboriginal community interests.

Two such efforts will be described here. Through archived memoranda and the observations of the interviewees who were involved, we shall see how both efforts ran afoul of other priorities in the end.

The first is the story of a small cohort of Aboriginal Liaison Officers in the Department of the Chief Minister who became known as the government's 'eyes and ears'. When voting enrolment became compulsory for Northern Territory Aboriginal people soon after self-government in 1979, the government had a new incentive to capture the hearts and minds of the Aboriginal constituency. Intent on establishing trust with Aboriginal constituents, the Department of the Chief Minister had begun recruiting a local Aboriginal field force in the Office of Aboriginal Liaison. Through these specially recruited local Aboriginal people, its 'eyes and ears', the Office was asked to 'facilitate a close contact' between the government and Aboriginal communities (Department of the Chief Minister 1979: 2; Deputy Director-General & Director Office of Aboriginal Liaison 1981: 4). The Aboriginal Liaison Officers were asked to 'encourage an understanding by Aboriginals of their responsibilities within the Northern Territory community' (Department of the Chief Minister 1979: 2).

The Aboriginal Liaison Officers were part of the wider cohort of field workers across the departments who were assisting building relations of trust with Northern Territory Aboriginal people. But the Aboriginal Liaison Officers were special messengers. A consultant described their role as 'provider and receiver of information, perhaps on controversial subjects' (Cross Cultural Communication Consultant 1980: 4). The visibility of these officers was crucial for a program of representative bureaucracy that was both passive and active, as we can see in the consultant's advice that 'a number of factors related to personality, appearance, cultural affiliation, etc. ... determine the level of trust that an officer can achieve as an individual' (Cross Cultural Communication Consultant 1980: 4–5).

Matthew had been one of the government's 'eyes and ears'. A Commonwealth transferee, he remembered being asked when he applied for the role in 1978: 'Are you a radical black?' In his interview, Matthew laughingly attributed getting the job to his quick assurance: 'No, I'm just a simple family man'. But the question is interesting. The interviewer might have finished the question '... like Charles Perkins?' The invitation for active representation was not an invitation for external advocacy, as Matthew well knew. But the interview panel's question about Matthew's personal politics acknowledged that these Liaison Officers had some discretion to act beyond departmental control. The question is also poignant, because it turned out that one of Matthew's supervisors had been involved in the removal of his baby sister to a 'half-caste' home many years before. Matthew had asked for, and received, a private apology. Matthew held no grudges. The job suited him. He felt understood and mentored. He had found the question about his personal politics revealing and amusing rather than offensive, as he summed up this period in his long and loyal public service career:

> That's the best job I ever had. They utilised each and everyone's talents.

Matthew called the time of the Office of Aboriginal Liaison the 'golden years for Aboriginal people'. These early days had set the tone for Northern Territory Aboriginal people to be embraced as the colleagues and agents of self-government.

'Eyes and ears': A sacrificial upgrading

A review of the Office of Aboriginal Liaison in 1981 found that Aboriginal Liaison Officers had been 'thrust into the field without sufficient training' and 'suffered from growing pains'. There was clearly an intention that the officers would 'move into higher managerial and/or executive positions' (Deputy Director-General & Director Office of Aboriginal Liaison 1981: 11), but the reviewers reported that 'some critics in Government' felt the Liaison Officers 'do not communicate effectively' and 'do not play a sufficient role in some issues'. The Office had acquired a propagandist reputation in some sectors, particularly with the Aboriginal Land Councils, with whom the Territory Government had waged ideological battles over Aboriginal land and other rights-based claims. Arguing that the government was benefiting from a service that made the Chief Minister 'indirectly accessible' to Aboriginal communities 'through individual Liaison Officers', the reviewers recommended that the Office be dismantled (Deputy Director-General & Director Office of Aboriginal Liaison 1981: 13).

The retiring director defended the Aboriginal Liaison service, arguing that the government's public opposition to traditional land ownership had compromised it. He advised 'particular patience and encouragement to overcome disadvantages which characteristically often inhibit the rapid or spectacular progress of Aboriginal officers' (Director Office of Aboriginal Liaison 1983). But the Liaison Officers did not survive a second review in 1983, and it was decided to 'upgrade' their positions to bring in 'Aboriginal content at more senior levels' (Acting Director Office of Aboriginal Liaison 1983: 6). A handwritten note to the Chief Minister explained that the upgraded new positions were needed 'to get better Aboriginal input into policy making and implementation' (Office of Aboriginal Liaison 1980 [1983], underlining in original).

Ironically, the decision put Matthew and his colleagues out of a job. Matthew and some others moved into other departments, as there was no ready market of local Aboriginal people who could compete with other applicants for the senior positions.[2] Advertising for the new positions was mulled over at length, and eventually approved in November 1983. In the end the advertisement was anodyne and impersonal, hardly inspiring of the Aboriginal involvement in high-level policy formulation that had been fought all the way to the top and had sacrificed careers: 'Aboriginal people are encouraged to apply' (Deputy PSCNT 1983).

What notion of representation sat behind these reforms?

The first review of the Office of Aboriginal Liaison suggested that senior Aboriginal public servants should provide a consultative mechanism within the public service. Noting that 'Aboriginal people remain under-represented in the labour force', it was recommended

---

2   Within two years, the Office of Aboriginal Liaison had been subsumed into the Department of Community Development. Here, the field force was rebuilt as the Northern Territory's Office of Local Government.

as an important step in 'improving consultation and communication' that the government 'take concerted action to ensure that Aboriginal people are encouraged, and equipped to move into positions of influence within government' (Deputy Director-General & Director Office of Aboriginal Liaison 1981: 18). The second review criticised a national representative body, the National Aboriginal Conference, for failing to represent Aboriginal communities, and the Northern Territory's Land Councils for having 'too narrow' a charter. Aboriginal Council Presidents' Conferences, which brought Aboriginal council members together with government ministers and public servants on a regular basis, were seen as 'ad hoc' and as promoting 'localised or parochial issues'. Through the files, community issues were downplayed in favour of 'the upgrading of a genuine policy capacity', which was clearly intended as the selective representation of interests agreeable to the government. The assumption was that disbanding the Aboriginal Liaison Officer service would not reduce Aboriginal representation in the government 'if we are able to attract Aboriginal impact at a higher level in policy formulation' (Deputy Director-General 1983: 3). Unlike Aboriginal Liaison Officers, the proposed Aboriginal Advisory Bodies would 'of their own volition advise Government of Aboriginal concerns', 'avoiding localised issues' and attending to 'real policy matters' (Acting Director Office of Aboriginal Liaison 1984: 3, underlining in original).

The Aboriginal advisory bodies were never established. In the absence of such bodies, there was clearly a working hypothesis among some in the bureaucracy that Aboriginal senior officials would actively fill the representational void through the representation of their communities in government and the representation of government in their communities. But the Aboriginal Liaison Officers had scattered or left.

'A pretty political statement': A sacrificial downgrading

The second story of active representation records the fate of another small cohort—this time, of more senior Aboriginal public servants. In 1984, the Public Service Commissioner invited the '12 most senior Aboriginal employees' across the service to join a working party. The working party was to develop ways to assist Aboriginal staff 'to apply with equality with other Public Servants for promotion' and prepare the public service 'culturally' for an increased number of Aboriginal and Torres Strait Islander employees (Scott 1985: 198). Aboriginal training officers were employed to organise and deliver courses in letter and report writing, 'interviewing results', time management, motivation, job applications and assertiveness (PSCNT 1984: 20; see also PSCNT 1981).

By 1986, the Commissioner had established an all-Aboriginal enclave of local recruits. This small unit had the remit to encourage 'upward mobility' for Aboriginal and Torres Strait Islander employees in the public service (Aboriginal Development Division 1986). Its services included personnel grievance counselling and 'interview panel membership'. The unit ran very specific training courses: telephone techniques, 'practical public speaking' and 'graphs in the work place' (PSCNT 1987: 27). An interviewee who developed these courses had felt her responsibility to the trainees keenly:

> If they didn't ring in by a certain time like 8.30 or 9, we had a car, once we'd know we'd go out and we'd wake 'em up ... we just were hard on them ... if we believed they were slack, we'd say, 'You're treating us as Aboriginal people in here, what the hell are you going to do when you're out there?'

This interviewee had concluded her warning to the trainees: 'We're not going to let you give Aboriginal people a bad name.' Behind these efforts was a growing industrial voice. Instances are apparent in archived file notes, as when some members of an advisory committee to the Public Service Commissioner who worked in the unit recorded their objection to being told they could not use the colours of the Aboriginal flag in promotional material for the training courses (Advisory Committee to the PSCNT 1985). Over time, successive restructures and transfers downgraded the unit. On hearing plans of a final restructure that threatened to separate their underpinning practical knowledge from the policy aspects of their role, the industrial unrest reached a peak and the staff staged a walkout. Around 10 staff arranged alternative employment for themselves, announcing their departures simultaneously. The director was the last to resign, at which point the 'staged departure', as an interviewee called it, was made public. By the time of the restructure, there was almost no team left.

The 'downgrading' was discussed in the Northern Territory Parliament. In an interview in the *Northern Territory News* in 1988, the outgoing director described herself as 'dedicated to the task of finding paths of independence for urban and remote Aborigines'. Analysing the event, Loveday and Cummings suggested that the staff's actions should be understood in the light of the fact that 'early directives had outlined an activist and reforming role for the Branch' (Loveday & Cummings 1989: 5–6). As an interviewee in 2007 recounted the event:

> We were getting so successful they wanted to split it into policy and operational. And we fought nicely. You know what? The reason we were successful is because we actually do know ... exactly what's needed ... We made a pretty political statement.

A note of advocacy and sense of shared interest are conveyed by this interviewee's reference to an understood 'we'. In seeking a mirror of the Northern Territory sociality, the Northern Territory Government had encountered active representation in a public dressing down by its own protégés. In refusing to participate in the restructure, these public servants were defending the value of Aboriginal networks and connections at senior levels of the public service.

Mirror, mirror ...: Steady numbers

After these early entanglements, the quest for the public service to mirror the Northern Territory's Aboriginal population was haphazard. Invitations for active representation can be identified, but they were more enigmatic. Aboriginal and Torres Strait Islander employee headcounts were carried out with varying degrees of enthusiasm. No approach was fully realised, and none completely disappeared. These were not clear pathways to known destinations but winding trails with occasional offshoots, some dwindling to nothing, others overwritten by successive bureaucrats trying to animate Aboriginal and Torres Strait Islander participation in the public service.

A statistical vacuum

The Northern Territory Government joined the general trend towards a hollowed-out public service in the 1990s. In the absence of a sector-wide policy, departments took the approach of grooming individuals for seniority. Under new legislation in 1993, the Public Service Commission became a kind of consultant to a newly consolidated public service, eventually subsuming its satellite authorities into a single legal entity. Chief Minister Steve Hatton introduced a policy of mainstreaming Aboriginal service provision, holding that 'those most expert in the delivery of particular services should provide them to all Territorians, taking into account the special needs of different communities and people' (Hatton 1992: 7). From the mid-1990s, it was up to departments to interpret this requirement through their own plans for Aboriginal employment and career development.

The quest for a representative mirror and improved Aboriginal training and career development continued through the efforts of the more diligent departments, such as the Office of Aboriginal Development and the Department of Education's Aboriginal Development Branch. Between 1995 and 2000, departments put in place various programs to support Aboriginal employment, including organisational exchange programs, cadetships, new apprenticeships and community partnerships. With a brief to work across the government to improve service delivery through better government–Aboriginal relations, the energetic Office of Aboriginal Development boasted 36 per cent Aboriginal and Torres Strait Islander staff one year (Office of Aboriginal Development 1996: 39). Working on some of these initiatives, several interviewees spoke of feeling that a baton had been passed to them by former Aboriginal colleagues. Relay teams of Aboriginal and Torres Strait Islander public servants cut their teeth on Aboriginal employment policy, moving between the Commissioner's office and departments.

One interviewee called the 1990s a period of 'huge opportunities but no commitment'. There were certainly opportunities through public service growth. From 14,000 staff in 1993, by 1999 the Northern Territory Public Service was again nearing a 15,000-strong workforce. Northern Territory Aboriginal people were not measurably sharing in the opportunities of this growth, although by now they formed more than 25 per cent of the population.

What did this interviewee mean by 'no commitment'? The Office of the Commissioner for Public Employment, as it was now known, did not monitor employee numbers over these years. Sector-wide Aboriginal and Torres Strait Islander employee surveys were twice attempted, each time resulting in a 'low response', it was reported, which 'illustrated the complexities involved in self-identification'. There was a vague promise of 'additional emphasis over the next year' (OCPE 1997: 33). Some key departments were uncomfortable with programs that acknowledged social diversity in the public service. Indeed, one department expressed the view that the achievements it had reported in Aboriginal employment were the direct result of 'there being no distinction between Indigenous and non-Indigenous programs, thereby minimising the "them" and "us" attitude' (OCPE 2001: 22). Another interviewee commented that this lack of recognition and relationship was the 'policy gap' of the period. She said she had felt shame on realising that the Aboriginal community, even within the public service, had seen her as personally representing this 'policy gap'. She observed that some Aboriginal colleagues had distanced themselves from the public service during this time: 'A lot of them tended to step into community organisations and have time out ... and work in an environment where you sort of like the frameworks around you.'

But in the eyes of many, the leadership program supporting the careers of Aboriginal and Torres Strait Islander men had been an outstanding success. 'The Kigaruk', as it was called, was rare in its open recognition and encouragement of Aboriginal and Torres Strait Islander identity and difference. An interviewee who had helped set up the program described its purpose as 'for Aboriginal men to get through their glass ceiling'. He noted that before the Kigaruk, the Northern Territory Public Service used to have 'all these little Indians ... we hadn't sort of moved past the concentration of entry-level trainees'. The Lookrukin program for Aboriginal and Torres Strait Islander women soon followed. Some interviewees were able to exploit these programs to build executive careers. One who had done so summed up the secret of his success as 'patience, pragmatism, practicality'. The logic of executive success for a committed Aboriginal careerist was 'to lose a few battles to eventually win the war', he said. This interviewee worked for:

> The ideal of seeing some equity in our population, seeing Indigenous people with the same life expectancy or seeing Indigenous children with the same opportunities that other kids have.

He added: 'I think I'd give the game away if I lost sight of those goals.' For this Aboriginal senior public servant in 2007, public service seniority was 'where the real power is'.

The 1990s had produced an articulate and committed professional strategist. But, more than two decades after the sacrificial upgrading of the government's original 'eyes and ears', and more than a decade after the sacrificial downgrading of those defending practical knowledge, there were precious few senior Aboriginal and Torres Strait Islander employees.

2001: Back to the future

The Territory's first Labor Government arrived to a statistical vacuum. A new Commissioner for Public Employment reset the Indigenous employment baseline, calculating his endowment as 725 Aboriginal and Torres Strait Islander employees or 4.6 per cent of the Northern Territory Public Service (OCPE 2005: 9). Treating this figure as an undercount, those implementing the Indigenous Employment and Career Development Strategy of 2002–2006 set about correcting it by encouraging more Aboriginal and Torres Strait Islander employees to self-identify (OCPE 2008: 27).

The 2002–2006 Strategy aimed to improve 'business outcomes' and address 'the economic and social costs associated with low levels of employment amongst Aboriginal & Torres Strait Islander people' (OCPE 2002: 3). 'Skilled and knowledgeable Indigenous people' were required 'in appropriate numbers at all levels' of the Northern Territory Public Service. The Strategy aimed 'to address the critical under representation of Aboriginal & Torres Strait Islander people within the Northern Territory Public Sector workforce'. The Strategy eschewed the diffidence of previous governments, listing foremost among its intended outcomes 'increased numbers' and the '*adequate representation* of Indigenous people at all levels within the Northern Territory Public Sector to enable *effective contribution* to policy and decision making affecting Indigenous people' (OCPE 2002: 7, emphasis added).

The *Cooee* newsletter advertised professional development opportunities to Aboriginal and Torres Strait Islander staff and the 'Indigenous Employment Tool Kit' provided a 'model for community engagement' (Ah Chin 2006: 21, 25). Biennial reports enumerated Aboriginal and Torres Strait Islander employees by agency, level and gender. The Strategy claimed steadily increasing numbers of Indigenous employees. From its putative 4.6 per cent baseline in 2002, the Strategy reported 7.6 per cent Indigenous employment in the Northern Territory Public Service at the end of 2006 (OCPE 2007: 7).

The Strategy invited both numbers and contributions, but only seemed interested in the numbers. It certainly introduced a new note of Indigenous recognition into the Northern Territory Public Service through the encouragement to self-identify. But like so many previous attempts, it too trailed off to an uncertain close when a new Commissioner replaced its champion and wondered what to do next.

This was the situation during the interviews in 2007.

Doubting 'increased numbers' of Indigenous employees, one interviewee described the Labor era as a period of 'more people identifying'. 'To be as honest as I can,' this person said, 'I think the increase in the numbers overall is a mixture of actual increase and just better data integrity.' Although a sponsored evaluation of the 2002–2006 Strategy also pointed to an increase (Vemuri 2007), the longitudinal data do not suggest there had been any significant increase in the number of Aboriginal and Torres Strait Islander employees. Taking the 2007–2008 Indigenous employment figure of 7.8 per cent as an end point, Table 2 shows that the number of Aboriginal and Torres Strait Islander employees had only barely increased—by just over 100, from 1,137 to 1,250, in the 25 years between 1983 and 2008. Against public service staffing overall, the 2008 ratio of Aboriginal and Torres Strait Islander employees had simply returned to the 1983 ratio.

The same Indigenous employment rate after 25 years suggests an unshakable ratio. After a long history that we have seen was deeper than self-government, by 2007 the Northern Territory Government's invitation to Aboriginal and Torres Strait Islander people to join the public service had resulted in hardly any increase in their numbers.

If the overall rate of Indigenous employment had not changed, had anything else?

The figures in Table 2 suggest that the proportion of Aboriginal and Torres Strait Islander employees who were in administrative roles nearly tripled between 1983 and 2005, from 15 to 42 per cent of total Aboriginal and Torres Strait Islander staff. This may be explained in part by the trend towards generic administrative classifications, as the vast majority of Aboriginal and Torres Strait Islander employees were still in community roles as Aboriginal health workers, community police officers, assistant teachers, and interpreters (OCPE 2004: 18). But Table 2 also tells us that 64 Aboriginal or Torres Strait Islander senior public servants had self-identified and were reported to be at their desks in December 2005, and that between 1983 and 2005 the proportion of Aboriginal and Torres Strait Islander staff who were in senior positions had multiplied from 1 per cent to 5.8 per cent. Sixty-four was a tiny cohort, and this cohort only constituted 2.2 per cent of all senior staff in the Northern Territory Public Service, but it was there.

There is no doubt that the Northern Territory Government had inherited an incipient representative bureaucracy from the Commonwealth in 1978. Since that original bequest, the total proportion of Aboriginal and Torres Strait Islander employees had barely increased by 2007, the year of the interviews. But as we have seen, through the scarring battles that followed self-government, the number of Aboriginal and Torres Strait Islander employees who were in administrative roles, and who were at senior levels, had grown.

Table 2: Indigenous employment rates in the Northern Territory Public Service (NTPS) 1978–2008

| Year | 1983 Survey | Indigenous Employment and Career Development Strategy 2002–2006 | | | | | 2007/08 Annual Report |
		2002 Estimate	2003 Sept	2004 Dec	2005 Dec	2006 Dec	2008 July
Source		(OCPE 2005: 9; OCPE 2008: 27)	(OCPE 2003: 4, 8, 16)	(OCPE 2004: 22, 25)	(OCPE 2006: 7, 9, 18)	(OCPE 2007: 7)	(OCPE 2008: 27)
No. Indigenous employees	1,137 (OAL 1983)	~725	788	1,006	1,119	1,170	~1,250*
NTPS workforce	14,552 (PSCNT 1983)	14,600	15,492	16,236	15,387	15,378	16,000
% Indigenous employees	7.8%**	~5%	5.1%	6.2%	7.3%	7.6%	7.8%
No. administrative (% of Indigenous)	170 (15%)	?	?	381 (38%)	467 (42%)	490 (42%)	?
No. senior (% of Indigenous) (% of NTPS senior)	11*** (1%) ?	6 (0.8%) ?	12 (1.5%) (1.2%)	52 (5.2%) (1.8%)	64 (5.8%) (2.2%)	?	?

* 1,250 is 7.8% of the NTPS workforce of approximately 16,000 in 2008. The Office of the Commissioner for Public Employment figure of 1,380 Aboriginal and Torres Strait Islander employees in 2007–2008 (2008) does not reconcile with the percentage.

** 10.5 per cent of the NTPS establishment (OAL 1983).

*** In 1993, the cut-off was at 'A5', which is equivalent to the Administrative Officer level 7 in the classification system still current in 2007.

Source: Author's summary (OCPE 2003, 2004, 2005, 2006, 2007, 2008; OAL 1983; PSCNT 1983).

A longstanding and ambivalent invitation

The interviews began within days of the Australian Government declaring the Northern Territory Emergency Response, also known as the Northern Territory Intervention, in July 2007, following a report on child abuse in Aboriginal communities (Northern Territory Board of Inquiry into the Protection of Aboriginal Children from Sexual Abuse 2007). Arguing that the Northern Territory Government had presided over a failure of policy and service delivery, the Australian Government passed special legislation imposing new controls over Aboriginal lives by controversially suspending the *Racial Discrimination Act 1975*. The Intervention cast a spotlight on Aboriginal dysfunction—child abuse, substance abuse, 'rivers of alcohol'—singling out the Northern Territory's remote communities. On the day of the announcement on 21 June 2007, Minister Mal Brough described a three phase military-type strategy of '(1) stabilisation, (2) normalisation and (3) exit' (Brough 2007). Protectionist policies found renewed purchase with the Australian public, but this time Aboriginal and Torres Strait Islander leaders joined the debate. The intense contestation, between the Commonwealth and the Northern Territory, between Indigenous and non-Indigenous Australians, and within the Aboriginal and Torres Strait Islander community, permeated an astonished Northern Territory Public Service during the interviews. Two former government executives who had worked for the Commonwealth and the Northern Territory over the previous 25 years released a book depicting services to Northern Territory communities as part of a 'failed state in remote Australia' (Dillon & Westbury 2007: 30). Many bought into the rhetoric of failure.

In 2007, under the scrutiny of the entire nation, the Northern Territory Government announced the Generational Plan of Action. For the first time, there was a 20-year vision for Aboriginal affairs. Through the Generational Plan, titled 'A Better Way of Doing Business', Chief Minister Clare Martin set Indigenous employment targets for the first time since Everingham's targets. They were the same as Everingham's—10 per cent in five years (this time, by 2012) and 20 per cent in 10 years (by 2017) (Northern Territory Government 2007: 17–18). The Generational Plan introduced a new aim, that Indigenous employment rates would reflect local demographics. This would mean 'Indigenous Territorians informing the Northern

Territory Government of their aspirations and needs, the Northern Territory Government listening and Territorians and the Northern Territory Government taking action together' (Northern Territory Government 2007: 21). As in 1983, the Generational Plan committed the Government to setting up an advisory body to advise the Chief Minister and the Indigenous Affairs Advisory Council.

Through the Generational Plan, the longstanding invitation to Aboriginal and Torres Strait Islander people to participate in the administration of the Northern Territory continued, seemingly oblivious to the historical revisionism. The Northern Territory Government continued to invite Aboriginal and Torres Strait Islander people into its confidence and its ranks. But appealing as this might have been, after a generation of ambivalence it would take more than promises of localism and listening to turn the numbers around.

Employees in orbit

Reading the report that 64 Aboriginal and Torres Strait Islander senior public servants were at their desks at the end of 2005 sparked my curiosity. Who were the people behind this statistic? Trying to find them in 2007 opened an apparently closed social field into something more fluid when my criteria for participation in the research expanded to include any Aboriginal or Torres Strait Islander person who had been a senior Northern Territory Government public servant at any time since Northern Territory self-government. The method of personal referral snowballed to reveal a social network of past and present senior public servants—162 in all. Informants were constantly pointing to those who had left the Northern Territory Public Service.

Nearly 40 per cent of the referrals were to former employees, and more than half of these former employees were now employed by non-government organisations in receipt of public funds to deliver services to Northern Territory Aboriginal communities at arm's length from government departments—the so-called 'Indigenous sector' (Rowse 2002, 2005). They were working in Land Councils and in Aboriginal health, housing, legal, research and community organisations. Some sat on the boards and committees of these organisations as their primary occupation. Some worked in Indigenous-focused or Indigenous-owned businesses. Some owned businesses. It turned out that nearly 60 per cent of the final interviewee group of 76 had been employed in the Indigenous sector at some stage of their careers.

When our long-time watcher of the government's relationship with Aboriginal organisations in Central Australia called Aboriginal employment a 'turnstile ticker', he implied there had been frequent entries and exits. The research corroborated this observation. The flow of staff between the Northern Territory Public Service and the Indigenous sector went both ways, as more than 50 per cent of those who were in the Northern Territory Public Service in 2007 had been employed in the service on a separate previous occasion. It is also the case that more than 50 per cent had worked in the Indigenous sector in-between their public service entries. While the group was mobile into other sectors as well—non-Indigenous organisations, Commonwealth departments (particularly the former Aboriginal and Torres Strait Islander Commission), other state governments, the broader research and private sectors and electoral politics—the pool of potential interviewees foreshadowed what was later confirmed in interviews. This was that the Indigenous sector was the dominant alternative to the Northern Territory Public Service as a source of employment for Aboriginal and Torres Strait Islander careerists.

Of the former employees, 10 had become senior elsewhere. Some of those still in the service who were non-senior had tried unsuccessfully for promotion, whereas the 10 who had risen to positions of seniority elsewhere had developed public profiles and a level of voice they had not achieved as public servants. Seven were running Aboriginal organisations or businesses, and three had public identities as the members or chairs of boards or as community leaders. They were all in the Indigenous sector.

A professionally mobile group was in some kind of orbit between the public service and its publicly funded, arm's length organisations. Only nine interviewees had *only ever* worked for the Northern Territory Government.

The Office of the Commissioner for Public Employment had noted a high staff turnover rate and acknowledged a 'churn' factor (OCPE 2009: 78–80), but had not reported the level of mobility found in this research. No core of longer serving officials had emerged since self-government, but was there a core of officials in orbit? Seniority seemed like a closed circuit, with the same people moving around departments and in and out of the public service. Half those recruited between 1990 and 2001 had left by 2007. Of the 33 senior Northern Territory public servants interviewed in 2007, another 10 had left by 2010. At that stage, one had returned. More have since returned, and more have left. Again, the government's less politically constrained partner in service delivery, the Indigenous sector, was a common destination. Given Aboriginal senior public servants' clear interest in participating in the government of their place—by way of entitlement, as one interviewee said—it is important to understand what made them reluctant to stay. By moving into the Indigenous sector where they could occupy roles that more clearly sanctioned advocacy, it is conceivable that some were seeking to resolve the ethical ambivalence of their roles as public servants.

The interviewees had all been engaged in some way or another by the invitation to contribute to the Northern Territory Government, and their experiences of a complex policy history are etched into the interviews. So are their doubts and triumphs as participants in the public sector employment programs that gave them careers. We shall see that issues of identity loomed large for them, and that a number who had become dislocated from their ancestral country had found a way back to that country through public service work. Some spoke of fostering arrangements—their own or their antecedents'—through policies of child removal, describing themselves or their ancestors as 'Stolen Generation'. This was a reference to the 'Bringing Them Home', also known as the 'Stolen Children', inquiry into the extent and effects of the policies of child removal for Australian Indigenous people (Human Rights and Equal Opportunity Commission 1997). A number of interviewees had personally been fostered or adopted under these policies, two of them into missions in the 1950s. 'Mixed up culture' was the name one interviewee gave to the generational effect of these policies. Most had acquired 'Stolen Gen' as a family identity through a parent or grandparent. We can see this in Bruce's account:

My grandmother is Stolen Gen but her sisters were a lot older when they were taken and we still maintain some of our practices. I don't speak the language but I know words and that, but they did. They could speak fluent language and my aunt gave a lot of evidence for [a land claim]. They're all gone now.

Bruce was a well-known local man with a mixed ancestral geography. His connections now extended between Darwin and Alice Springs.

Some interviewees had assisted others to self-identify to achieve the public acknowledgement of what had previously been for many employees a more private ethnic identity. That process relied on Aboriginal and Torres Strait Islander employees knowing each other, because privacy laws inhibited direct inquiries. A Central Australian interviewee who evidently did not know everybody mocked the privacy restriction:

> We weren't allowed to target Indigenous employees—you can't get any direct answers, so virtually I had to sit in a hospital foyer saying, 'Did you go to NAIDOC [the National Aborigines and Islanders Day Observance Committee]? Can I talk to you?'

Another interviewee took the process more seriously, explaining the delicacies:

> I was really acutely aware that I was often seen as a government employee and what that meant, so we had a really big job of trying to be as clear and as honest and as up front as we could be when we were talking to them about why we were asking that question ... that if we knew where Indigenous people were, we could really develop strategies around that ... the older people, they were saying—hang on, hang on, last time you asked that, my sisters and brothers were taken away from me ...

What did it mean for an Aboriginal or Torres Strait Islander person to be seen as a government employee—and what did it mean for a government employee to be seen as an Aboriginal or Torres Strait Islander person, in the Northern Territory? The interviewee who spoke these words sounded confident of the benefits of self-identification, but she later spoke of doubts. Enthusiastic agents of Aboriginal and Torres Strait Islander employment policies continued to have diverse encounters with the practicalities of implementation well beyond the 1980s.

The Northern Territory Government's Indigenous employment program has most certainly drawn on both notions of mirror and agency. By 2007, how was it faring on population proportionality, with 7.8 per cent Aboriginal and Torres Strait Islander employees in the Northern Territory Public Sector workforce? There were approximately 60,000 Aboriginal and Torres Strait Islander people in the Northern Territory, and they formed a very significant proportion at 31 per cent of the total population. So the public service was nowhere near proportionately representative of the Aboriginal and Torres Strait Islander population of the Northern Territory. In 2010, the Northern Territory Government reported that Indigenous employment was 8 per cent of the public service, suggesting for the first time a significant increase in Aboriginal and Torres Strait Islander employee numbers (1,600) in a workforce approaching 20,000 (OCPE 2010). In 2015, as we will see in the concluding chapter, the Indigenous employment rate had only increased to 9 per cent.

Achieving proportionality would struggle against the geographic distribution of the Northern Territory's Aboriginal and Torres Strait Islander population. Only one-third of Aboriginal and Torres Strait Islander people live in the larger multiracial urban towns where government is centred and where most other Territorians have settled. Two-thirds live in the smaller rural-remote communities that are scattered across a large expanse at various distances from these larger multiracial urban towns. The smaller rural-remote communities range in population from approximately 1,600, in the case of Wadeye, down to single families in some of the many very remote homelands that dot the landscape. These populations are highly mobile within their service delivery regions.

Achieving proportionality would also struggle against the low socioeconomic status of these populations. The Northern Territory accounts for 10 per cent of Australia's Aboriginal and Torres Strait Islander population, but a much larger proportion of those who live in Australia's remote areas. The Northern Territory's remote Aboriginal communities are often seen to encapsulate Australia's remote area problem. From the Prime Minister's latest reports on closing the gap in Indigenous socioeconomic disadvantage between Indigenous and non-Indigenous Australians, we can see from the results for remote and very remote areas that Northern Territory Indigenous people would rate lowest on many indicators (Commonwealth of Australia 2016; see also Commonwealth of Australia 2015). This is a low rating indeed, as Australian Indigenous people as a whole rate poorly against most socioeconomic indicators. Aboriginal and Torres Strait Islander people have for many years been, and still are, overrepresented in the criminal justice system with worsening rates of youth detention and adult imprisonment, as well as high rates of chronic disease, hospitalisation, child neglect, mental health issues and suicide. Literacy and numeracy rates remain well below national averages, and most indicators worsen with remoteness (Steering Committee for the Review of Government Service Provision 2014).

Against such overwhelming odds, the precise public sector employment ratio hardly matters. What matters more is an understanding of the people who constitute the public sector employment statistic and the kind of representing they do. How is it practically possible in the Northern Territory for Aboriginal public servants to contribute to government policies and programs *as Aboriginal people*?

The office environment in the Northern Territory Public Service celebrates informality, egalitarianism and a 'can do' attitude. In this hail-fellow-well-met culture, the laughter is contagious. Many workplaces exude the infectiously warm, casual inclusiveness that is often presented as the Northern Territory's own. On emerging from their offices to attend meetings, busy executives may change course to converge on the sound of laughter or wish someone a happy birthday over sausage rolls and the ubiquitous Australian tomato sauce. Formality is lampooned. The Northern Territory Public Service seems to welcome Aboriginal and Torres Strait Islander employees with open arms, conveying sensitivity to the possible objection that it is a largely white bureaucracy populated by north-migrating southerners. Departments try to acknowledge the original inhabitants of a vast expanse who have long been the subjects of government administration. Aboriginal public servants are invited to improve their people's odds by joining the Northern Territory Government, which since the granting of self-government has been the biggest employer in the economy and for many, the main game in town.

What happens when blackfella bureaucrats speak?

3

Accepting the representative invitation

Merely being dark-skinned is enough to raise questions like 'Where are you from?' or 'Do you identify?'—as a public servant of Indian origin cheerily informed me when I was mistakenly led to him as a potential interviewee. This person had evidently added to someone's perception of a public service representative of Aboriginal and Torres Strait Islanders, even though he was not one. Conversely, an Aboriginal or Torres Strait Islander public servant can be perceived to stand for Aboriginal and Torres Strait Islander people without any action or acknowledgement on his or her part. But it is only when considered from the perspective of others that descriptive representation is passive. From the perspective of those who do it, descriptive representation is not passive. If someone self-identifies, even though that act is private, he or she has participated actively in their representation. Given the interviewees' general belief that most Aboriginal and Torres Strait Islander public servants self-identify, most must bring personal agency into the earliest moment in the construction of their representative identity within the public service.

This important observation calls into question the passive/active distinction in the theory of representative bureaucracy. Bureaucratic representatives are always active agents, in one way or another—never really 'just bums on seats', despite the preoccupation with numbers in Indigenous employment policies.

As more-or-less active agents in their public service destiny, from where do bureaucratic representatives draw their authority? The sources of their authority are less obvious than those of electoral representatives, for whom candidate-selection and voters make it very clear, or those of official government representatives instructed by their minister or department. Having an Aboriginal and/or Torres Strait Islander identity is one source of authority for an Aboriginal or Torres Strait Islander public servant. Remember we are interested in representing that is informal, extempore and unsanctioned; this representation draws on a loose sense of authority and engenders a loose sense of accountability. The ambivalent invitation of Indigenous public sector employment programs makes the public service a rich site to study informal representation. How does one accept an invitation when it is unclear how that acceptance will be valued? An ambivalent invitation might provoke an ambivalent response. After self-identifying, an individual might draw on his or her identity in other ways. To accept the invitation is to enact a representative identity through ordinary moments in the working day, and embark on a course with no definitive end point. Acceptance may be conditional, circumstantial and momentary.

Self-identification is not passive, but it is a weak form of representation on its own—a toe in the water, a gesture towards, but not the full realisation of a representative role. To realise a representative role is to draw on one's identity more purposefully. Acceptance is like taking a swim in the sea. The procedure is unremarkable but by the end, you are changed. First, the invitee tests the water by self-identifying—it's just a tick in the box. If the invitee draws on that identity by speaking for others, he or she plunges in. The experience may be bracing or lukewarm. As quickly as the body finds out, it adjusts to new knowledge. Full immersion is not for everybody. But those who stroke buoyantly into the depths will be choosing from a repertoire of styles that merge so well with their work practice that they will in effect, with barely a ripple, have accepted the invitation to represent others.

A toe in the water: Depicting likeness

> If I was talking to another Aboriginal person I would say my grandfather is [a language name], he was born on [a particular] mission and my grandmother was born in [another location] and taken to [a different] mission … But if I was talking to somebody that wasn't of Aboriginal descent, I'd say I was born in [a capital city] but raised in [another state] and then spent from high school onwards in the Northern Territory.

Rose was speaking of the adjustments she made when explaining her identity in the social world. On recruitment to the public service, the first opportunity for interviewees to reveal their presence as the member of an Indigenous category was to tick the non-compulsory box in MyHR, the web-based personnel management system. The next opportunity was in annual reviews. This was how public servants indicated if they were Aboriginal, Torres Strait Islander, both Aboriginal and Torres Strait Islander, or 'non-Indigenous'. Ticking one of the first three options generated their inclusion in the Indigenous employment statistics.

Of the 53 interviewees from senior levels in the public service, 50 had self-identified as a matter of personal policy for the duration of their employment. This chapter is mainly about these 50 self-identifying senior interviewees. Among them, 47 had identified as Aboriginal, two had identified as Aboriginal and Torres Strait Islander, and one had identified as Torres Strait Islander. Thirty-one of the 50 self-identifying senior interviewees were in the public service in 2007.

Why self-identify? 'Because it's who I am' was a common reply: 'I am Aboriginal/Torres Strait Islander/both.' Acknowledging their racial identity was the primary reason. Many nominated as a secondary reason to help build the quantity of Aboriginal and Torres Strait Islander employees, by confirming their presence in government.

Acknowledging race: 'We're never black enough'

Naming the place or language from which you are descended, if you know it, is a common part of communicating an Aboriginal or Torres Strait Islander identity. All but two of the 50 self-identifying senior interviewees knew and named their place and language of origin.

This also speaks of your family history, because the movements in that history will have framed your identity. Interviewees traced their families' movements from their places of origin with clarity: they put names, times and historical contexts to the movements of their ancestors and the policies, intermarriages and employment opportunities that had built their identities. As for Rose, identities were not fixed but contextual and adjustable.

Table 3 distinguishes the 50 self-identifying senior interviewees by two criteria they presented as important: whether they were local to the Northern Territory in the sense of having an ancestral association with a Northern Territory place or linguistic group, and whether they or their antecedents had been removed or fostered as children. The interviewees tended not to apply the urban/remote distinction to themselves, even though they often applied it to their policy and program subjects. The urban/remote distinction is used in the table to highlight an important finding: although most interviewees were now the residents of urban centres, many of them had originated in the kinds of remote places where their policy and program subjects still lived.

Table 3: Experience of fostering/child removal by place of origin

		Place of origin 50 self-identifying senior interviewees				
		Northern Territory (local)		Outside the NT		TOTAL
		Urban centre	Regional/ remote community	Urban centre	Regional/ remote community	
Experiences of fostering and/or child removal	Not fostered	8	10	4	6	28
	Fostered—self	0	5	0	0	5
	Fostered—family	2	7	3	3	15
	Origins not known	0	0	2	0	2
	TOTAL	10	22	9	9	50

Source: Author's research.

Thirty-two of the 50 self-identifying senior interviewees were Northern Territory locals. More than two-thirds (22) were the descendants of linguistic groups from remote communities or regional towns. These interviewees were descended from the Dogaman and Jawoyn people of the Katherine area, the Tiwi, Gurindji, Mudbura, Malak Malak,

Wadjygin, Kungarakany and other language groups to the north, south, east and west of Darwin, and the Anmatjere, Luritja, Western Arrernte, Warlipi and Warumungu language groups from the desert. These Northern Territory locals also had secondary connections across north Australia stretching from Torres Strait to Broome in Western Australia. Kahlin Compound and later the Retta Dixon Home in Darwin, The Bungalow in Alice Springs and the Croker Island Methodist Mission featured prominently at various points in their family histories, where many interviewees' grandparents or parents had been taken from remote communities or regional towns. Just under one-third (10) were descendants of the original inhabitants of the urban centres of Darwin and Alice Springs. Nine were descendants of Darwin's 'coloured mob' as the practice of polyethnic intermarriage had led Darwin's local language group, the Larrakia, and its extended families to call themselves in the 1950s and 1960s. These were part of strong urban-based networks. One of the 50 belonged to the Arrernte language group of the town of Alice Springs.

The other 18 were from outside the Territory: seven from Queensland, six from New South Wales and five from Western Australia. Unlike those of Northern Territory origins, those who came from elsewhere were evenly split across the urban/remote divides of their jurisdictions. None of these 18 interviewees had personally been fostered out of their families, but five had weathered the dislocations of such fostering in earlier generations. Only two of the 18 felt they lacked what one called the 'cultural aspects' of Indigeneity. The other 16 expressed a strong sense of attachment to their places of origin.

Whether interviewees came from the Northern Territory or elsewhere, most called on current experience of the connection with a place of origin that is characteristic of an Aboriginal or Torres Strait Islander identity. Their stories of origin highlighted multiple identities. Nobody spoke of being just Aboriginal or Torres Strait Islander or even just both. Personal histories, ancestries and places were all-important details in their accounts. Most interviewees wished for the opportunity to communicate their origins more precisely than the website allowed: 'I usually *say* Aboriginal and South Sea Islander, but they don't have the space', said Peggy. 'We're a mixture of Indigenous and European and the Asian side with their pearl divers and the fishermen', said Edith of how family members described their identity. Historian Regina Ganter has documented stories showing that 'the north is full of people who still remember its polyethnic past, for whom being coloured is the fabric of identity' (Ganter et al. 2006: 244) and who come to 'private, intimate' solutions for self identification (2006: 241). The same can be said of many of the Top End participants, particularly the Larrakia who had endless stories about the coloured families in old Darwin.

Wanda had ticked the box for Aboriginality, although she said this was not her usual practice. She usually ticked 'no', hoping for the chance to nuance this bland statement of a complex past. 'If it says: "Are you Aboriginal?" I tend to go, "No,"' Wanda said. 'But if it says, "Are you of descent?" I tick the box.'

Julia commented wryly that the identifier question did not allow her to refer both to her Indigenous descent and her 'white side'. As she asked rhetorically in her interview:

> Why can't you say I'm half white? Or I'm white? ... My father is a white Australian. Yeah but what makes you that other part of you?

'On the other hand,' Julia said in a later conversation, 'we're never black enough.'

Not only did the process of self-identification collapse multiple origins into the categories Aboriginal and/or Torres Strait Islander, it then aggregated these categories into the generic identifier 'Indigeneity'. The statistical reporting was interested in Indigeneity alone, which some interviewees felt glossed truer depicters of their identity.

Building quantity

Deborah self-identified so 'we're counted'. This was her antidote to the wiping out effects of colonial history. 'To show we're still *here*', she said. Another interviewee argued that ticking the box marked out the good intentions of Aboriginal Australians towards the government. Other interviewees identified to create a stronger voice for Aboriginal people and Aboriginal policy problems. Judy ticked the box as her 'contribution to Indigenous issues', which she saw as helping create 'a strong Indigenous collective voice in government'.

Carol had added herself to the Indigenous employment statistic because, she said, 'it translates into money', referring vaguely to population-based Australian Government funding distributions. Graeme explained: 'I'm in an area where I'm relying on that data. I mean, if anything's going to change or shift, we need baseline data to do it with.' These interviewees relied on Indigenous employee statistics in their work. Others working in Indigenous recruitment and workforce development self-identified for similar reasons. Self-identifying bolstered arguments for the distribution of resources within the public service, which very senior public servants were well-positioned to prosecute.

Sophie was referring to the Commonwealth Grants Commission formula for allocating public money to the States and Territories when she explained:

> Blackfellas are worth more money in revenue to the Territory than non-Aboriginal people.

Indigenous people draw a greater per capita income into the Northern Territory than non-Indigenous people. This calculation draws on information in the Australian Census. Sophie 'never had a second doubt that you fill that in. You *say* something.' Sophie's role in social policy had given her an intimate understanding of the potency of the Northern Territory's Indigenous statistic as a fiscal argument.

In these accounts, to self-identify was to enlarge the Indigenous statistics. Self-identifying enhanced the arguments of these senior public servants for improved social and economic programs for Aboriginal people. These interviewees drew actively on the Indigenous statistics they had helped create when they argued for resource distributions favouring Aboriginal interests. For many, this higher purpose eclipsed their objections to the generic Indigenous identifier.

Plunging in: Drawing on identity

Testing the water begins the process of acclimatising. Now there may be a forward plunge. How are the currents, the saltiness and floating seaweed? Work settings, opportunities and relationships combined to shape the progressive enactment of more substantive representation among the interviewees.

All who self-identified serviced the Northern Territory Aboriginal population in some way. Of the 50 self-identifying senior interviewees under discussion here, 40 were working in jobs specifically targeting Aboriginal policies and programs in 2007. Of the remaining 10, nine had managerial or executive responsibility for Aboriginal policies and programs as part of a wider role or had worked in an Aboriginal-specific job in the past. The only interviewee among the 50 who had not worked in an Aboriginal-specific area planned to do so, and had taken on a voluntary role representing Aboriginal and Torres Strait Islander staff interests.

Potent settings

The interviewees described hundreds of past and present public service jobs, but sifting through their talk drew out just four major work roles among the 50 self-identifying senior interviewees. These were building the Aboriginal presence, coordinating Aboriginal policy, facilitating partnerships with Aboriginal people and correcting Aboriginal behaviours that were seen as dysfunctional. Whether the interviewees who worked in these areas were most often in the field or deskbound, they were all engaged in intensive efforts to secure Aboriginal participation in the Northern Territory Government's social and economic vision.

The largest group of 16, or nearly one-third of the self-identifying senior cohort, had all worked on Indigenous employment policies; building the Aboriginal and Torres Strait Islander presence in government by advising on Aboriginal and Torres Strait Islander recruitment or supporting workforce development in health, education or other areas of service delivery. Few interviewees had *not* become involved in supporting Indigenous employment at some stage, but building the Aboriginal and Torres Strait Islander presence in government departments had been the mainstay of these 16 interviewees' careers.

The second largest group of 14 interviewees had largely formed their careers in policy coordination and advice, building their knowledge of social and economic policy and working across government or inter-governmentally. These were the more senior roles, in which some interviewees spoke of feeling strong personal accountability for the government's performance locally and nationally.

In the next group, 10 interviewees mediated relations between the Northern Territory Government and Aboriginal and Torres Strait Islander citizens by facilitating partnerships, governance arrangements and communications. These 10 interviewees drew on their connections to negotiate arrangements of various kinds between the government and Aboriginal communities.

Correcting Aboriginal behaviours was the fourth most populated field of work among the 50 self-identifying senior public servants. Under this theme, seven interviewees were primarily focused on bringing the most disaffected Aboriginal people into rehabilitative programs, whether that was in education, health, urban development, drug- or violence-related or prisoner services. These experienced operatives worked with local community organisations to bring Aboriginal constituents to the point of receiving services. Some were persuading others in government of the need for particular kinds of rehabilitative services and oversaw their delivery. Correcting Aboriginal behaviours—or corrective governing, as we shall later call it—was more significant in the larger group of 76 interviewees, given that a senior interviewee who did not self-identify, a number of non-senior interviewees and most of the Central Australian interviewees worked in this field.

The remainder of those who worked in Aboriginal-specific roles were involved in the direct delivery of health or education services or worked in cultural guidance as rangers or interpreters. I interviewed only a few of the many hundreds of teachers and assistant teachers, health workers, police aides and interpreters who lived and worked in remote communities, as these jobs tended to be non-senior.

Figure 1 shows the distribution of the major work themes identified by the 50 self-identifying senior interviewees, including the one senior self-identifying interviewee who was not working in an Aboriginal-specific role.

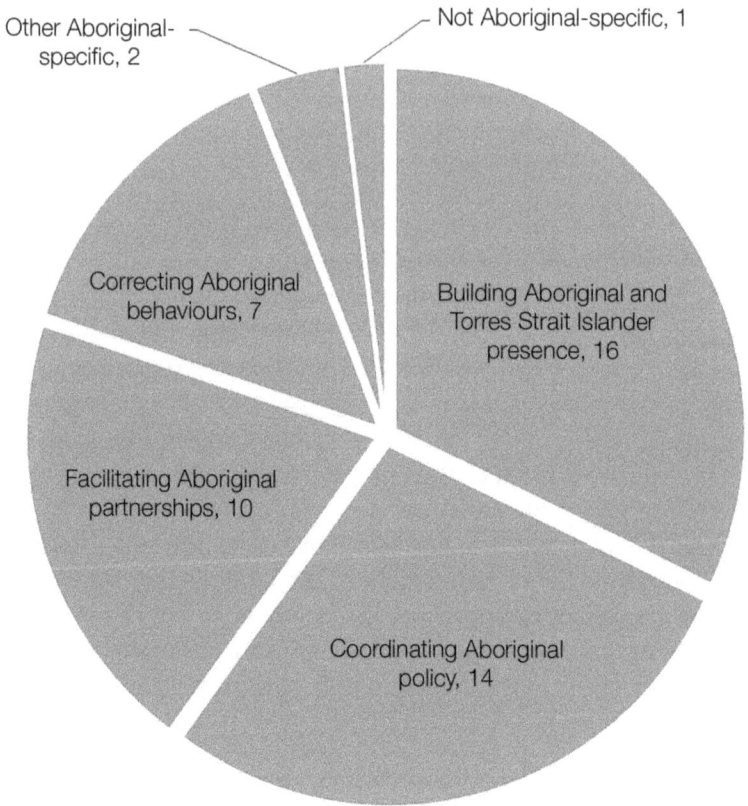

Figure 1. Work themes
Source: Author's research.

We will return to these themes in the discussions that follow.

Moments of representation: 'Sort of had to speak up'

Within these settings, Aboriginal senior public servants worked in relative isolation from each other. Those who were in the public service at the time of their interview were spread thinly across a dozen or so departments. A few worked together but many worked singly, mere specks in a vast sea in which a majority of non-Indigenous people were likewise representing their departments, divisions and branches as public servants do, marking out and targeting the unemployed, the disadvantaged, the remote-dwelling, the disengaged and/or unhealthy and/or uneducated.

The scarcity of Aboriginal people in public service divisions and branches intensified the opportunity for those present to do some kind of representing.

Lucy's public service career was nearly as long as self-government. In the following passages, Lucy describes the difference that 'being Aboriginal' made in her job encouraging her people to comply with programs supporting economic productivity. Lucy confirmed the importance of understanding her work role when she began by observing:

> People are restricted by their mandate for what they sort of *do*. Everything outside that might not be within scope.

Later in her interview, Lucy recalled occasions when she had advised non-Aboriginal colleagues on the conduct of dialogue with Aboriginal groups:

> ... when I've sort of had to sort of speak up and say well look, as an Aboriginal person you know this is what you need ... to approach a certain group. So it's knowing protocols and all of that sort of stuff that we've had, well you know, to be representative of.

If you were employed to do a job on the basis of your knowledge and connections as an Aboriginal person, it would not be considered unreasonable in the public service to draw on those credentials to offer advice on a matter pertaining to other Aboriginal people. This is especially so when your department has shown an interest in Aboriginal issues and has perhaps mentored you. But you would not have to 'speak up as an Aboriginal person.' Here is a moment of administrative discretion—Lucy's discretion. To speak, in these circumstances, 'might not be within scope' because public servants get their 'mandate' from the programs under which they are employed. Programs rarely spell out how to conduct dialogue with Aboriginal people and if they do, the rules of conduct would not cover all circumstances. Lucy was there, present and available. How should she respond? 'Sort of' suggests her hesitancy to speak up, 'had to' her sense of feeling duty-bound to do so. 'Had to sort of speak up' expresses well the kind of representation with which we are concerned, not the official representation that is prescribed by a job description but the unofficial, discretionary, partial, subjective kind.

Behind Lucy's sense of duty was all the weight of her kin-based, place-oriented and historically specific Aboriginality (she was working in her home town) and her identified presence in the public service. Perhaps she hesitated out of consideration of the ethics of public service. She may have asked herself if she was crossing a line by initiating this advice. Most likely, Lucy was hesitating over how 'speaking up' would commit her. She spoke, but perhaps wished herself free of the implicit expectation, brought on by her Aboriginal identity, that she do so. Perhaps it was her consciousness of an opportunity for some form of agency in the larger historic politics of Aboriginal affairs that lay behind her decision to speak, in spite of her diffidence.

Of the 50 self-identifying senior interviewees, it was only Harry who did not seek to represent Aboriginal interests in an active sense. Harry's responsibility was to convey Aboriginal cultural information, and he saw it as an asset that 'our family can't establish any real ties' to the Northern Territory region from which they knew they came. Harry could usefully 'distance' himself from his program clients, he said, in a way that 'real ties' would make difficult. Harry had made an asset of his lack of 'real ties', describing himself as self-identifying 'to do my bit'. Although it worried him that a 'white bureaucracy' was in charge of his program, a sense of propriety made him reticent. As he did not speak of any instances in which he would or could make substantive representations, he has the status of being the only purely descriptive representative among those who self-identified. The other 49 drew substantively on their identity. This placed them in a much more committed position than the purely descriptive representative of political theory. To the extent that they drew on their identity, these 49 had moved towards accepting the invitation to contribute to the public service *as Aboriginal people*. They had accepted that their Aboriginality was inescapable when the subject matter was Aboriginal people. And their subject matter was nearly always Aboriginal people.

Subject matter Aboriginal people: Empathy, knowledge and connection

Interviewees explained that it was difficult *not* to draw on their experiences as Aboriginal people in the performance of tasks that affected other Aboriginal people. To perform such tasks seemed to mobilise their Aboriginality in ways that seemed to be endemic to that identity, with some individual variations. The stories of three experienced senior public servants, Sarah, Sophie and Marcia, convey this point. These interviewees drew respectively on empathy for, knowledge of and connections to Aboriginal people in their work. Empathy, knowledge and connection characterised many other interviewees' accounts; but Sarah, Sophie and Marcia exemplified a particular quality of acceptance. These women were tolerant of the bureaucracy, but not uncritically so. Nevertheless, their critiques did not hold them back from contributing their identities to the public service.

Empathy

As a child, Sarah had experienced the profound loss of her family and identity. Born 'out bush' and 'sent, taken, I don't know' to a school just outside a regional town, she explained with great intensity the dilemmas of her legacy:

> Yes, I've got an education; yes, I have travelled; yes, I've been able to get employment but the flip side of that is I have lost my language, I have lost my culture, I have lost my family, I have lost my mother ... my own identity.

In middle age, Sarah was still 'learning the different ifs and whats' of her second language, English. In her lifetime of acculturation, she had made contact with her family and country and was confident of locating bush 'tucker' in her birthplace and mother's country.

Sarah's job was to communicate issues of importance to Aboriginal people that were part of a Northern Territory governance agenda. Her responsibility was:

> To make sure that people in bush areas really understand, so when they do get a choice to decide ... they've been well informed and they really understand the consequences.

Sarah evoked empathy as the basis of her contribution to government when she said:

> Put yourself for five minutes in their shoes and experience what they experience on a daily basis—then you can understand, then you can argue.

Was it to ameliorate the toughness in her life that Sarah had made it her mission to 'make sure' that bush-dwelling Aboriginal people were more visible and included in processes of government? Conversing on the smokers' balcony of the plush building, her humble desk bordered by partitioning plastered with posters designed for bush communities, Sarah described herself as a 'messenger between both worlds':

> I suppose I'm a bit of a messenger between both worlds to try and get people to understand which way, what Aboriginal people are *really* thinking.

Sarah's self-characterisation was reminiscent of the earlier days when Aboriginal locals were the 'eyes and ears' of self-government. But now, more confident of her benefit to her workplace, Sarah was prepared to be more direct in her advice, to lock horns with colleagues— the 'people' in the quotation below—over their assumptions about Aboriginal people. Here, Sarah outlines her position on Aboriginal communication:

> Too often, people think because there's a group of Aboriginal people sittin' there nodding their head, they understand. That's not what they say. 'We hear you', that's what they say. At the initial meeting, it's always, 'Yuwa. Yeah, we hear.' They need time to be able to discuss what they heard. Too often people take the nodding of their heads on their first meeting as if they fully understand it. *Which it isn't.*

Sarah was doing more than relaying messages. She was instructing colleagues on the conduct of dialogue with her people.

The American philosopher, Nancy Sherman, wrote an intriguing essay on the empathic imagination in which she concluded that 'it may just be that it is only when we concretely imagine … others as rational agents alongside ourselves that we are really disposed to take seriously their claim' (Sherman 1998: 114). Sarah drew on her empathy for those she perceived as left out in the cold, as she had been, from the decisions that affected their lives. Sarah was putting the case that bush-dwelling Aboriginal people, people whose rationality she could still imagine and took very seriously, were entitled to full information.

Knowledge

Sophie, a social policy executive, was born in a Top End regional town to a local Aboriginal mother and non-Aboriginal father. With her parents in low-paid jobs, Sophie had accepted a church scholarship to boarding school. Like some other interviewees, Sophie had risen to greater professional heights than her many siblings. She described herself as having come from a 'family of workers'. As for other interviewees whose families still resided in remoter places, relatives from out of town frequently stayed at her house. 'Like a bus load maybe sometimes', she good-humouredly explained.

Sophie negotiated with external organisations, Aboriginal and non-Aboriginal, from her social policy 'backroom' role. She described herself as having:

> … a good feel for what goes on, on the ground. I have enough networks on the ground, so that the advice I give is balanced with a view— several views, as well as the government's objective.

Sophie saw herself as bringing the views of Aboriginal people— her own views as an Aboriginal person, and the views of others— into policy. She suggested that she was able to be phlegmatic, though, when her advice did not prevail over other priorities:

> When you don't see that being implemented or taken up by government you think, 'Oh, I didn't achieve much there', but I think [my main achievement is] pursuing the line. I have a view that I'm achieving something by doing that, because you're constantly giving the line on something, even if it's rejected; you still give it because you think that it's a better line to give.

Understanding that other interests can prevail in the opinion-laden world of bureaucratic argument, Sophie judged herself on her consistency and the extent to which she drew on the views of other Aboriginal people. She asked herself often:

> Am I thinking adequately and laterally enough in order to improve the living standards, improve the social and economic outcomes for Indigenous Territorians? That is what really worries me.

For Sophie, the benefit of her presence was: 'to influence by way of conversation, by way of knowledge'. In saying this, Sophie was espousing Phillips' (1995) theory of the politics of presence, that to populate institutions with people from certain groups would influence those institutions through a kind of osmosis. Sophie shows us in her interview that she chooses her moments wisely, allowing us a richer understanding of her personal agency in that osmosis.

Sophie saw herself as a vessel for social improvement:

> It's a bit about being used and I don't mind being used in that way, if it's the right way to use it.

'It' was the colour of her skin. Sophie pinched the skin on her arm as she spoke these words in her corporate office, her secretary fielding visitors outside her semi-glass walls. Colleagues were waiting. Sophie allowed them to gain credit from her success and allowed her presence to authenticate the government to other Aboriginal people. Sophie was committed to a representative role on the condition that she was taken seriously and that her Aboriginality was used in the 'right way'. At Sophie's invitation, we met again in a more private setting. Concerned that she may have appeared too sanguine in her original interview, Sophie was concerned to place on the record:

> It's a *choice* thing that the NTPS [Northern Territory Public Service] is not culturally intolerable for me.

Sophie did not want me to downplay the tensions her Aboriginality brought to her work. It was not that she found the public service adequately embracing of cultural difference, she explained, but that she *chose* not to allow that lack of embrace to hinder her work.

Connection

Marcia 'looked after' the Aboriginal cadets and apprentices, building Aboriginal people's presence in a large service-oriented department:

> I've always worked in employment and training in all my career right through, to make sure people have an opportunity for their career in the government … [and] make sure people have the information so they can make an informed decision about what situations they get into sitting in their workplace, especially when strife hits.

Thus Marcia explained her advocacy for more junior recruits. In her own assessment, she had good networks within Aboriginal organisations and throughout the public service. Marcia's job involved 'a fair few calls from managers just asking for advice outside of the normal'. As she put this: 'They'll ask advice about issues they are having with Aboriginal staff. "Is this what's happening?", "What do you think we should be doing?", or "Am I on the right track?"'

Senior Aboriginal public servants were often asked to intercede on behalf of Aboriginal employees who had problems meeting the expectations of supervisors. Some resented that expectation by their department, whereas Marcia clearly welcomed the opportunity to troubleshoot staffing issues 'outside of the normal'. Marcia was unusually tolerant of the phenomenon that 'anything to do with Aboriginal' came her way:

> Our area is the first point of contact for a lot of people outside …
> I don't know why, but they see Aboriginal against our name, our section, and anything to do with Aboriginal … they'll come to us as the first point of contact and then we'll disseminate who they should be contacting.

Marcia volunteered the idea of her 'Indigenousness' to explain why she was so sought after by others, although she preferred to call herself Aboriginal. She saw value in 'having an Aboriginal point of view, an understanding, being available'. Like Sophie, Marcia espoused the politics of presence. Again like Sophie, she revealed that her presence was purposeful. Marcia had much to say about the public service managers, largely non-Aboriginal, with whom she worked. She described some as 'really good people in terms of showing you the ropes about office politics', but others:

> You can pick 'em straight away, those ones that don't want to shift from where they sit.

Marcia identified managers as immovable 'when they don't make things happen'. She expanded:

> … when they don't ask for certain advice or genuinely wanna do something. You can tell straight away, you know. There are some managers … they will say things with all the right words, but they don't follow up and you can see the lack of action behind it all.

Marcia had no intention of allowing those managers to dissuade her from her career:

> There's times when I think, 'Oh, yeah, there's lot of words and rhetoric and there's no real meaning or intent behind some of these [managers'] words', and you can walk out like that. But it doesn't achieve anything because they come and go.

She planned to outlast the intransigent managers: 'That's been my plan, is you focus on the ones that actually genuinely want to do things.'

How should we understand Marcia's mission? As she described herself: 'I'm not a traditional Aboriginal person, although I've got family who do that, they live traditional, or live out bush.' Marcia had been adopted young, after being neglected by alcohol-affected family members in a Top End remote community. She described herself as 'very lucky they [her adoptive family] came along'. Otherwise, she said, 'my life might've been totally different'. Marcia had transcended the socioeconomic disadvantage of her family of birth. 'I *choose* to live this way', she said with quiet seriousness about her urban lifestyle, 'I *like* where I live. It's less stressful.' In casting the social landscapes of remote/urban communities as traditional/non-traditional, Marcia was describing her personal experience of a huge cultural divide. Aboriginal people are needed in departments, Marcia said:

> ... for policy to kind of work right through ... to be getting feedback from those guys on the ground level working it, to those guys who are managing and making the changes to strategies and policies ... to the executive who is supposed to be pushing it right across.

'It's a start', Marcia said about just being present in the public service: 'If you're not there, then you got no basis to do anything.' So Marcia commended the presence of Aboriginal people, the Northern Territory's non-transient population, within the public service. By shoring up their presence and supporting them to sit out the managers who did not support Aboriginal people, Marcia was nurturing a channel for the kinds of connections and relationships that formed her own identity. 'Working in any department', she said, 'it's your Aboriginality comes forward.'

Deeper: Pinning down the absent

Representation has been described as 'a kind of political assistance' (Dovi 2006: 1) or 'mediation' (Williams 1998). Marcia and interviewees like her were representing in this sense when they assisted people who struggled to relate to government. The interviewees often said they worked for or on behalf of Aboriginal people—that their work as public servants was not 'about us', but about others.

Contextualised inquiry was needed to explore instances of representation through their workplace accounts. In answer to the direct question, 'Do you feel that you represent other Aboriginal people in your job?' only just over half the interviewees (28 of 50) responded in the positive. That nearly half responded in the negative suggests an uncomfortable association with representative advocacy or its less heroic underside, tokenism. The negative replies effectively circumvented any implication that an Aboriginal or Torres Strait Islander public servant acted inappropriately or was under external control. When interviewees spoke of relaying messages between the government and communities, they made it clear that they did not see themselves as under the complete control of either party, as they had to exercise considerable discretion at both ends. Some spoke of relaying messages on behalf of communities as a particular 'hat' they might wear transparently, as part of their work, but they emphatically did *not* see themselves as the delegates of communities.

Whether or not they were prepared to describe themselves as representatives, inviting interviewees to nominate the beneficiaries of their presence in the public service drew out highly nuanced answers about the ways in which some represented various intersecting categories of the absent: remote Aboriginal employees, proximate/ distant communities, Aboriginal Territorians and 'all Territorians'.

Remote Aboriginal employees: 'I take their viewpoints up'

A number of interviewees identified other Aboriginal employees as the beneficiaries of their work. These other employees were often situated elsewhere in the hierarchy, although some were directly supervised by an interviewee. Most often, the interviewees described themselves as supporting the remote community workers who were directly servicing the residents of remote Aboriginal communities— Aboriginal health workers, language interpreters, teaching assistants.

The manager of a field service with a widely scattered community-based workforce, Deborah identified the subjects of her representations as the field staff in her supervisory care, the community-based workforce and at times more generically as 'Indigenous Territorians'. Here Deborah discusses how she represented the viewpoints of her community-based workforce:

> Because I take their viewpoints up ... I certainly do [represent] and when I'm arguing and fighting for something for the service, it is on behalf of Aboriginal people in that role.

Describing herself as a 'front line person', Deborah reported having been counselled for protecting the viewpoints of her community-based workforce at the expense of other clients. In the case she was discussing, the clients were the agencies who contracted her services. She presented herself as an experienced and able defender of the service and its workers. That she had been entrusted with managerial responsibility suggests that she was known in public service terms to be good at her job. Feeling undervalued by superiors, Deborah explained that she kept at her job because of her identity. 'Because I'm Aboriginal', she said. 'It's the only thing. I can see the good that the service is doing.' Deborah had been told that superiors saw her as lacking objectivity towards the service for which she was responsible, and that this perceived lack of objectivity had jeopardised a proposed upgrade of her position. In Deborah's view, the government did not understand the extent and complexity of what made the service work. In this respect, Deborah was like a street-level bureaucrat, even though her management role meant she was not solely front line. She felt connected to clients, disconnected from the policy talk and not trusted for the grounded work it had taken to build the service:

> A lot of times we can't articulate what we want to say. And writing: I prefer to sit down and talk to a group of people than try and write a letter to them ... That thing, I think holds us back in our careers ... The other thing is it's like a lack of trust of Indigenous staff, that if we're going somewhere ... it didn't matter if we were working our butts off, it's a 'jaunt'.

Deborah had fully embraced the idea of representing her staff, but felt inadequate defending their needs in policy and preparing letters on behalf of the government. Deborah's self-styled 'arguing and fighting' might be attributed to the sense that her contributions to the service were being undervalued. Arguing and fighting ensured she was heard.

Carol understood herself to be representing other Aboriginal staff by 'running a job agency', by which she meant informally notifying her extensive network of Aboriginal employees informally of internal vacancies. Carol worked to build Aboriginal people's presence in her department, even though that was not in her formal job description.

Wanda was cautious about her representative claim:

> I probably represent their [Aboriginal people's] interests. I wouldn't go so far as to say that I represent them, but I'm sort of mindful of any evolving issues and I tend to let those people [Aboriginal field-based staff] know.

Thus, Wanda took care to explain that she saw herself as representing the 'interests' of remote Aboriginal employees, but not 'them'. Wanda felt strongly about the interests of Aboriginal field-based staff. She worked in environmental management, but she had just resigned, she said, because departmental priorities were constraining opportunities for local recruits.

Proximate and distant communities: 'It gives them a voice'

Kel was a public servant in the town where he was born and grew up. He had been educated in a southern city—his choice, he said. He had returned to work in Aboriginal organisations in his home town until, he said, 'blackfella politics' pushed him out. Kel managed an all-Aboriginal team in a government project aimed at securing the compliance of organisations and individuals in a service. Kel was one of few Aboriginal senior public servants who came from the town. He aimed 'to try and create pathways to get others through the system', to achieve 'a voice in [his work] at the higher level'. He identified the beneficiaries of his work as 'local Aboriginal people', a category he qualified as follows:

> ... which is mainly my family and friends, and then the remote community population who see me when I go out there, an Indigenous person with connections, kinships and strong connections to country and also to families in remote [communities].

He went on to explain:

> It gives them a voice and a level of understanding now. When I speak to them ... I sit out there and talk their language, I don't use the old government jargon.

Kel described himself as 'a link between the community and the agency' but 'even more so like a voice for them'. Kel saw himself as representing 'the Indigenous men' in particular:

> I represent the Indigenous men, the elders in the community—I'll just give you an example—in their decision making. I can go and sit down with them in the community. I can say, 'This is what the government's policy is' ... I talk through it, and then they tell me what they think of it but they tell me how *they'd* tell me; and I feed that back to my department. So I am representing my senior men, which are fathers and grandfathers, but also I'm representing young men who haven't got education.

Kel did this, he said:

> By being part of that group and male, to be there for them to question me, but also to give them information about policies.

Kel's account of representing specific subgroups was atypical. Mostly, interviewees described who they represented in ways that conformed more closely to public service norms; but Kel and his team had been encouraged by a manager, whom he described as having been unusually supportive, to have their 'fingers on the pulse' of the local community.

Leila had also spent her long public service career communicating with the residents of remote Aboriginal communities, primarily women in recent years. She had worked in many departments to build a solid reputation over decades in the public service and with communities. Leila had stood out for her preparedness to self-identify publicly, decades earlier:

I used to get a lot of criticism from the Aboriginal community because they said—whatever the government did and you were there, they felt that you should have changed the government's mind. I said, 'Yeah, but we're developing policies to *change their mind* in how to deal with it.'

When I asked Leila what difference it had made that she self-identified in the early 1980s, she said that 'they all knew', in government, and 'outside they knew', too, as she had been asked to promote the benefits of a public service career to other Aboriginal people. Here is how Leila described answering a group of Aboriginal students who asked her how hard it was to self-identify as a senior public servant:

It's hard, but if you *always know in your own mind* that *everything* you do is to benefit your own group and your own people, [this] is the thing that's always pushing you: to make sure you're part of that process.

Leila asked:

Because if nobody is there, who is going to be part of that process?

Leila's career had been propelled by the desire to benefit the Northern Territory Aboriginal community. She did this by looking out for those for whom she felt a particular responsibility, even, as we have seen, when they criticised her. As she recounted the way she had explained this to her people:

So no matter what we do and no matter what the government did, we'll be always there pushing. You mightn't see the changes but later on down the track you might … If nobody is there, it will never change. We'll still be the under, downtrodden people you know, but you have to be part of this process to be able to get above it.

'That's what I always told them', Leila concluded.

Kel and Leila had experienced different tensions in the representation of their communities. Kel described the tensions of proximity to his place of origin as being 'disowned' by both 'mobs', his department and community:

People like us, we get sort of like put out of place … we're not owned by this mob [his department], we're not owned by that mob [the Aboriginal community], we get disowned.

Kel felt he was the 'odd one out' as the 'only Indigenous one' in his senior management team. He would not draw on his identity as a 'pass to get to the next level', but the community did not reward his restraint:

> You're always called 'half-caste' ... what I'm saying is, if things don't happen quickly on the ground ... we'll get blamed by the community, for our Aboriginality.

He gave an example:

> People think that we in this department ... are driving [a particular decision]. Firstly they'll see you as a public servant and then ... I mean we get rubbished by our *own families!*

Kel was referring to a Commonwealth Government decision under the Northern Territory Intervention to make welfare payments conditional on participation in a government program. Facilitating a workshop between Aboriginal people and government to secure greater access to services in his town had exposed him to scapegoating by some of his extended family, similarly to the scapegoating of non-Aboriginal bureaucrats by Aboriginal community members to avoid blaming local leaders for 'unsatisfactory outcomes' that anthropologist Sarah Holcombe has described (Holcombe 2005: 224, 228). Although the analogy cannot be taken too far, feminist Anne Summers described similar terrain for 'femocrats' in senior public service positions in the 1980s, who felt distrusted by both the public service and their peers in the women's movement (Summers 1986).

Leila experienced different tensions working at a greater distance from her place of origin. She was explicit that as a long-term Northern Territory public servant, she drew her authority to generalise about communities from her continuing specific relationship with her community of origin. Leila recalled advising a colleague against the incautious amalgamation of Aboriginal local governing bodies into regional councils:

> This is wrong. You haven't really given the communities an opportunity to look at this properly.

Describing this conversation with her colleague, Leila sourced her authority to speak to her traditional association with country:

It's part of my country and so ... you could see the highs and lows, you could see the problems ... they'd ring me up: 'Leila, can you come and see us while you're there?'

Likewise, Leila drew on government knowledge to help her community come to terms with government decisions. In this case, she reported advising her community:

Government has done this now so you can't get out of it, but let's try and work out a best way ...

Summing up the ways in which she represented other Aboriginal people in her job, Leila saw herself as a 'community person first and foremost'. This did not mean she represented any particular community, as she saw herself working with 'most of the Territory':

I think because, I suppose, of the network and the way I've worked over 30-odd years, with communities. I feel part of those communities.

The limit on 'most' was the small number of communities she had never visited. Leila had had a long career in which she had represented 'those communities she had visited' by 'being Aboriginal and part of a group'. She had straddled her responsibilities comfortably by being transparent and diplomatic with non-Aboriginal colleagues. As Leila put this:

They'd say, 'Well, Leila, is that your view?' ... If it was my view, I'd state it but if it was the view of a group you know, a community or a group of people, I'd say, 'Well, this is what's come out of the community'.

Leila was clear and firm: 'So that's the way I've always worked.'

Distance had spared Leila the direct daily conflict that Kel was experiencing at the time of his interview, but that did not lessen other tensions for Leila. Her location in central headquarters meant proximity to advisers with whom she did not always agree. Here, Leila describes how she worked through those tensions:

There were times when I didn't agree with them ... Sometimes I'd get really angry and I'd just stay in my office and I'd think ... I'm putting in too much energy into anger. Let's look at the best way I can deal with this ... I talked myself through it and then worked out the best approach I could take. Instead of arguing with them, with the government ... I went back and thought about how I was going to do this without making it obvious to them that I was really in disagreement with them and even if the community said, 'Well, we don't like that Leila', I'd say, 'Why didn't you like it?' and we'd talk about that.

Distance from or proximity to their communities notwithstanding, Leila and Kel performed their public service duties on behalf of and with a sense of accountability towards their communities without ever, from their accounts, contravening public service ethics. Both interviewees had accepted the invitation to be representative, but their acceptance was not unconditional. These interviewees had earned their employer's respect—and in their eyes the respect of their communities—through long service, diplomacy and the effective navigation of the interests of their communities.

Aboriginal Territorians: 'What they tell me, I relay back'

Simon must have been referring to an older, paper-based system of self-identification when he claimed:

> I just put a square in and I ticked it and I said I'm an Aboriginal Territorian.

Simon's assertion of the pan-Territorian Aboriginal identity, 'Aboriginal Territorian', was based on a specific entitlement, which he expressed legalistically:

> I've got traditional entitlements to parcels of land in the Northern Territory.

These parcels of land were situated in the two linguistic regions of his paternal grandparents. Simon was scathing of the generic Indigenous brand, recounting his well-rehearsed position as follows:

> Don't refer to me as being Indigenous unless you know where I'm from.

For Simon, one could only be Indigenous to a locale. The public service self-identification options were too lumpish and inelegant for a specific and complex local identity and unacceptable to someone who was not 'non-Indigenous' but Aboriginal through a known language and place.

Simon's job was to communicate with many Aboriginal communities on behalf of the government. When asked how he handled the breadth of that role, Simon explained:

I'll take something, read it out, tell them where you're working, what you're doing, you need to talk to these people ... Yeah, go and talk to them. But what they tell me, I relay back ...

Simon did not want to interpret—'put my own spin' on—what other Aboriginal people told him or engage in banal comparison by claiming, 'Oh, this person's similar to that person or this community's similar to that community.' Simon's personal policy of not speaking on behalf of any other Aboriginal Territorian made it possible for him to declare: 'I'm an Aboriginal Territorian.'

Spike was equally unwilling to speak on behalf of any other Aboriginal Territorian, although he was less circumspect. Spike believed himself to 'speak on behalf of Aboriginal people, Indigenous people', he said, because:

When I'm asked a question ... the person who asked that question is asking me my opinion, which gives him a *broad* opinion of what Aboriginal people think.

Spike's Northern Territory connections were extensive, if more diffuse than Simon's. He had been brought up in a 'western type world', he said of his urban upbringing in Darwin. On the subject of feeling expected to represent other people in his work, Spike replied:

There is an expectation, but I can only speak for me. I can't speak for [my] mob ... I wouldn't speak for Larrakia [the local language group], I'll speak for me.

Like Simon but for different reasons, Spike could speak on behalf of Aboriginal people in general, but not for his 'mob'.

Both Simon and Spike preferred to fall back on a more general authority than to speak for their language group. Simon was even unwilling to contribute his personal opinion about a community visit, preferring to relay local views as a kind of emissary than be seen to interpret, generalise or compare. But many other interviewees similarly referred to a general, rather than specific, authority. Those who did so, whether or not they specified the identity 'Aboriginal Territorian', seemed to distance them from demands by individuals—demands made in the name of kinship or local association—while preserving their accounts of representation.

All Territorians: 'Building bridges'

'I'll be honest and straight up', said one interviewee:

> I would like to think my relationship with the Territory Government at the moment is ... building bridges in regards to better education, better health for all Territorians.

From this person's account, he was hoping to commend policy approaches that resolved emergent contradictions in Aboriginal lives. He illustrated his point by describing himself as 'more of a refugee' in the urban town where he worked. Because he owned property in the town, his community of origin would not allocate him a house; yet, the town was not his 'country or language'. His career in Aboriginal affairs, spanning various representative roles, had dislocated him. He thought it important that senior officials like him were able to return to their communities.

A number of interviewees said they worked to benefit all Territorians and not only Aboriginal Territorians, one of them reasoning that the wider Northern Territory public benefited when Aboriginal communities were well represented in policy. But identifying a sense of responsibility to this wider Northern Territory public was only ever in addition to, never instead of, Aboriginal subjects. For most, Aboriginal people *were* their Northern Territory public.

Trusteeship

By now, Aboriginal public servants have plunged into and are immersed in a representative role. Empathic, knowledgeable and connected, the interviewees produced nuanced analyses of their relationship to the represented. There was both connection and distance in this relationship. Connection validated the relationship, whereas distance was needed to make it representation. The interviewees' positioning as public servants not only gave them the chance to bring their communities into government, but to define, describe and talk about those communities in discretionary ways. Kel described Aboriginal and Torres Strait Islander employees as 'statespersons' with a dual role:

> We're not only seen as statespersons for government, we're also seen as statespersons for our people.

Along with this duality went a sense of being betwixt and between which Kel described as 'getting disowned'.

In the political theory, the unresolved tension between needs and wants has been one of the deep dilemmas of political representation. The needs/wants dilemma is the source of the distinction between the trustee and delegate styles of representation (see also Dovi 2006). Representatives who draw on their own judgement are exercising a form of trusteeship for the perceived *needs* of others ('statespersons for government'), whereas representatives who follow constituent preferences are doing what their constituents *want* them to do ('statespersons for our people'). The problem is that what people want is not always what other people think is good for them. Who should decide, and how does the decider know?

Put simply, trustees make independent decisions about others' needs and interests, whereas delegates act on instructions. When interviewees pointed to areas of discretion in the content and delivery of their advice to government, they invoked the trustee representative style. In their study of a representative bureaucracy in America, Karnig and McClain found that minority bureaucrats had a *'trustee relationship to minority communities'* in the sense that they 'personally felt a responsibility to make a difference by their presence' (1988: 143–4, italics in original). Peter must have done so, as he said he 'carried' the interests of Aboriginal people who could not be present in the bureaucracy. The represented cannot be 'really [be] present literally or fully in fact', theorised Pitkin (1967: 153)—but there was a catch. For a relationship to be one of representation, those being represented must have some kind of agency in the relationship. Guardianship is not representation, because a guardian protects rather than includes. The interviewees generally spoke of those they represented as having capacity and agency—they were not incapable, just absent. Some interviewees spoke as if they held trusteeship for the unmet interests of their communities of origin.

When Rehfeld made the observation referred to in Chapter One that the needs/wants, or the trustee/delegate, dilemma was present in any decision-making, he introduced some other distinctions as well. He pointed out that a trustee could aim for the good of the whole group or part of it, could rely on internal judgement or that of a third party, and could respond to disapproval or sanction to a greater or lesser extent (Rehfeld 2009: 215). The same could apply to a delegate—but we are only interested in trustees here. Our trustees invoked traces of these distinctions about aims (for example Kel, when he spoke for Indigenous men) and sources (see Sophie's reliance on evidence in the next section); and we will see later that their position on responsiveness depended on their proximity and connection to communities of origin. But Kel's eloquently described and *felt* distinction between statespersons for government and 'our people'—his sense of abandonment—was resonant of the trustee/delegate dilemma.

We have heard some interviewees speak of taking up the case of those they represented. In these cases, they were like representative agents. Sarah suggested this characterisation when she connected her empathy and understanding with her right to argue, a shift that political theorist Nadia Urbinati likens to advocacy or defence (Urbinati 2000). Sarah's was not advocacy in the sense of radicalism. It is within the bounds of public service ethics and indeed expected of a public servant to defend a portfolio interest or policy recommendation under challenge. In fact, all public servants working in Australian Indigenous affairs might be characterised as representative agents when they defend the interests of Aboriginal and Torres Strait Islander Australians as a portfolio responsibility.

To reiterate: the interviewees did not speak of themselves in the formal principal–agent sense. There was no unitary principal among their absent constituencies, rather a diversity of communities with whom their relationship was differentiated and complex. The interviewees were not instructed by any other authority than their work supervisors, nor formally accountable to any other entity than their employer. The interviewees were their own agents. They were autonomous individuals with a belief in their capacity to bring about real-world outcomes with intellect and discretion, people who chose when and how to agree or argue. But they did tussle with their

Aboriginal authorities. Although they felt more or less authorised by community connections, they were constantly checking those connections.

The styles of representation brought out in the interviews were flexible and not fixed dispositions. They were responsive to the job at hand. Sarah represented Aboriginal people, she said, by ensuring their access to the same information as the 'wider community':

> ... through my ensuring that what we ever get out or develop [for bush communities] is the same information that the wider community gets, so *by me being here.*

Sarah saw herself as making a difference to the information the government made available to Aboriginal communities. Through these lines, Sarah spoke as trustee and defender; perhaps also the self-appointed guardian of absent communities, albeit that this last characterisation was theoretically out of bounds. But Marcia, also deeply connected and committed, had another view.

> I can't say that, that's just not right. There's too many of us, it's too diverse, you know, and our good people out there that represent different groups of Aboriginal mob, different staff or professional areas of Indigenous people that know, experts, then they should be saying things on behalf of their mob.

Marcia was adamant that she did not represent others.

Why did some interviewees discount the idea of representing? Marcia drew a sharp line between the representational capacities of the Indigenous sector and the public service. She did not see herself as representing her people because she saw that as the role of Aboriginal organisations. As a public servant, she felt she had no mandate. Yet, as a public servant Marcia saw her beneficiaries as 'Indigenous people first off'. Nominating herself to make available 'an Aboriginal point of view, an understanding', Marcia both stood for and stood up for her people. Marcia satisfied the political theory's definition of a representative in both the passive/descriptive and active/substantive senses. She did not see herself as such because she was reluctant to supplant her colleagues in grassroots representative organisations, who had a clearer authority to speak on behalf of 'their mob'. But drawing on the theory, Marcia's sustained defence of Aboriginal people was a highly diligent form of self-authorised trusteeship.

Sophie spoke of portraying and relaying views that she knew she shared with other Aboriginal people or that were founded on 'evidence', rather than representing:

> I don't profess to represent other Aboriginal people, I profess to be able to portray and relay views and desires and needs that other Aboriginal people have, either through my knowledge and experience or my personal networks, all based on pure evidence that is so startling and stark in front of you, you can't not portray that.

Sophie distinguished carefully between speaking on behalf of other Aboriginal people and expressing views that she held and knew others shared:

> I don't speak on behalf of any Aboriginal person or group but I'm more than happy to be able to express the views that I know other Aboriginal people share.

Sophie was representing herself when putting forward her own perspective: she was merely present and being herself, not speaking for anyone else. But she was representing others when she put forward views that she knew other Aboriginal people (who were not there) shared. When she stated her reliance on 'pure evidence', Sophie attributed her actions to the indicators of Aboriginal disadvantage rather than her identity. When she drew on 'knowledge and experience or my personal networks', she edged closer to a more active kind of representation. All executives have knowledge and experience and personal networks, but Sophie's knowledge, experience and networks acquired a particular potency in the representational politics of Aboriginal affairs. Sophie had accepted representative bureaucracy's invitation, but like Marcia she was careful not to speak unduly for others.

Sarah, Marcia and Sophie drew on their empathy, knowledge and connections to speak for others, navigating their way carefully through decisions about the costs, benefits and timing of speaking. Those who specifically identified beneficiaries did the same. They took up their viewpoints, gave them a voice, relayed their messages and built bridges to the wider constituent community of all Territorians.

And so 49 of the 50 self-identifying senior public servants stood for Aboriginal people in the descriptive sense by self-identifying, and took representing further by standing up for them, or drawing on their own identity to speak for others. Their representations of, for and on behalf of absent Aboriginal people were invited by the general calls of representative bureaucracy and the conditions of their work. Trusteeship was the most acceptable strategy for Aboriginal public servants. The kind of representation they could most readily accept was that which allowed them to make autonomous judgements about the capacity of other Aboriginal people to represent themselves.

But let's look more closely at the hesitation that was expressed by some of the interviewees—most starkly by Lucy, Marcia and Sophie. Their hesitation suggests a double-edged problem. Assuming their community's authority to speak was not only problematic for them as public servants, but as Aboriginal people.

Political theorists have laid out the circumstances that justify speaking for others. Recall Alcoff's argument that the speaker is always situated somewhere in the social complex. Through speech and writing, he or she inevitably participates in the construction of 'others' (Alcoff 1995: 100–1). In speaking for or about others who are not present to speak for themselves, the speaker is 'participating in the construction of their subject positions' (as absent/excluded) and thereby representing them (Alcoff 1995). Alcoff suggested that it is only remiss to speak for others when the speaker has not paused to interrogate two issues: firstly, the situational advantage of speaking and secondly, whether absent 'subalterns' could speak for themselves. If after consideration the representative deems that the absent cannot be present and may be advantaged by being spoken for, Alcoff found it justified. Likewise, the postcolonial scholar Gayatri Spivak was critical of the 'intellectual retreat' when a representative who has the chance to speak 'essentialises' the disadvantaged by insisting on their direct voice—as though that gesture would negate their deeper exclusion (Spivak 1988).

Speaking for others was never straightforward.

Speaking *for* and speaking *as*: Trusteeship vs substitution

Hanna had previously worked in advocacy roles outside the public service, and had left the public service again at the time of her interview. Reflecting on her time in a senior policy role, she said that she saw her role as 'creating the space' for 'other voices to be heard'.

Hanna was emphatic on this point: her version of trusteeship reserved Aboriginal people's place at the table, without her presuming to speak for them. As Hanna recalled her position on representation:

> I certainly wasn't … ever presuming that what I had to say was being said for and on behalf of other people. That's not my role or place and I'm very clear about this too: it's very much about *creating the space* for those other voices to be heard.

So Hanna created space for other voices.

Sally saw things differently. For Sally, it was a sign of moral courage to step into the space of other voices and explain these absent voices. She acknowledged doing this at every opportunity she could, in her job mediating social justice issues between the Aboriginal community and government:

> I find myself as an ambassador for Aboriginal people, whether I'm at work or out in the street. I feel that I have to explain. If someone takes a bland view or a view that's one-sided or something, I feel it necessary that I explain to them, well hang on a minute, this is why we're like this. I do, I see myself as an ambassador, personally and professionally for Aboriginal people, to promote their interests and also to develop an understanding.

Sally shared a standing joke with colleagues about being the 'token black':

> I mean that's *part* of the reason that they employed me here … and that's what I played on at the interview, the fact that I am Indigenous, I have extensive networks in [this area of] services and they don't have any Indigenous staff here and … the majority of the service users are Aboriginal people … We've got a little joke here … when we have a meeting they'll say, 'Oh we'll ask Sally to come in and tell us about this.' I say, 'Oh, you want the token black do you?'

Sally's mother was a politically active Aboriginal woman from a local region and her father was a white man. She maintained her ties through both, but she would not accede to her father's request to call herself 'part-Aboriginal':

> It was my uncles and aunties that looked after me … It was my grandfathers that took me out doing things, hunting and all sorts of things, and that's why I identify with that.

Describing herself as 'grounded in her culture', Sally defended her people's ability to be 'flashy too if we want'. She said she was 'hard on her people' because she took them 'seriously'. She sometimes found herself in disagreement with Aboriginal colleagues:

> As an Aboriginal person working with Indigenous issues, working with government ... I feel like I have to follow everyone else and if I don't, I become unpopular or I'm a traitor ... *I've been viewed like that.* Even in this department, I've heard them whispering, 'I don't think you should speak to Sally, she doesn't actually agree with that sort of stuff' ... I just want to see our people and our kids happy and healthy, going to school and doing the cultural stuff but also being able to cope over here because ultimately, that's where we're *going to have to be.*

Critical when departments 'do everything for' Aboriginal people, Sally's view was that:

> They [departments] don't give any value to what Aboriginal people's own skills are, what their knowledge is or what they're capable of thinking about.

Where Hanna created space for other voices, Sally stepped in and spoke.

Hanna was politically careful, reserved and critical, whereas Sally's confident portrayal of the motives of others suggests her more enthusiastic adoption of the right to speak. Both of these interviewees made autonomous judgements about their role, thus fulfilling political theory's notion of trusteeship—but whereas Hanna used her judgement not to step into the space she felt the absent should occupy, Sally used her judgement another way and drew on her inner convictions to step into that space, *speaking as* absent Aboriginal people, as though taking their place.

We could interpret Hanna's reluctance to speak for others as abdicating a situational responsibility. But there is more to know about her constraints, and we will pick up her story in the next chapter. Other interviewees did subscribe to the idea of speaking for others, as we have seen, by taking up their viewpoints, giving them a voice and relaying their concerns. Most were more cautious than Sally. Most relied on external evidence and their knowledge of communities rather than so wholeheartedly on inner conviction. In her ambassadorial mode, Sally's references were internal, a representative style for which theorist Jane Mansbridge has suggested the metaphor of the gyroscope (Mansbridge 2003: 526). Having established her credentials, Sally sought no other permission to speak.

We have begun to explore a distinction between speaking *for* and speaking *as* the absent. In the terms of political theory, this is the distinction between *trusteeship*, which is to stand up for others by speaking for them if necessary; and *substitution*, which is to stand in for others and assume their voice. This is a fine distinction. The stances of trusteeship (speaking for, creating space) and substitution (speaking as, stepping in) can coexist in the same sentence—for example, 'Let's invest in a process of consultation [trusteeship], as the existing policy/program is already having adverse impacts for Aboriginal people in the region [substitution]'. But the distinction between trusteeship and substitution is important, and those who accepted the representative invitation had to navigate it whenever they made autonomous judgements about the capacity of the absent to speak for themselves.

Behind the representative role lay significant tensions for those public servants who accepted it. Trusteeship could be experienced as personal failure, if they could not find evidence that it had protected the beneficiaries from harm. What if they exercised the wrong discretion and inadvertently brought harm to people they meant to help? Substitution was no solution. Substituting yourself for absent 'remotes', where but for fortune you would be, only enhanced the sense of inauthenticity with which your peers would happily brand you. Sally didn't seem to mind this, but we shall see that many other interviewees minded it very much.

Swimming the currents, a self-identifying Aboriginal senior public servant could be swept into murky depths.

4

The limits of acceptance

Those who self-identify and who have not resisted the subsequent drawings on their Aboriginality will have stroked well out into the depths. They will have strategies to keep their heads above water in busy bureaucratic currents. It's not quite what they expected, but they have the skills to survive—until the tide turns. Who pulled out the plug? The water has become shallow and salty. Some swimmers are high and dry, shocked. Some still in the depths are pulled out to sea.

Some might enjoy this metaphor for the change of fortune that any bureaucrat could experience, from the buoyancy of success to feeling dumped, isolated or misunderstood. Others would distance themselves from the image of victimhood that the metaphor indulges, preferring to see themselves as wary and wise, deft at the bureaucratic game, cards yet to play. Most would fall somewhere in between—while they might acknowledge misreading the politics, they might not rule out the possibility that their representation of problematic others in their population could tarnish perceptions of their own performance. The signs were opaque, and some interviewees expressed deep existential uncertainty over their worth in what was always a localised experience in their own corner of the public service.

An ambivalent invitation is not easy to accept in any categorical way. There were limits to the interviewees' acceptance, which they marked out often as they recounted moments of moral anxiety, fallback, wry humour, cool observation and bittersweet retreat.

Their reluctance as representatives was often a kind of demurral, a matter of polite objection, avoidance or misgiving, rather than downright decline.

Creating space for others through trusteeship could feel futile if the policy failed or the proper consultation did not eventuate. Standing in for, or speaking as, others through substitution was ethically dangerous when it was transparently unauthorised. Interviewees were constantly shifting their stance between the two positions. Some blamed the state for their discomfort, whereas keener practitioners of the bureaucratic arts preferred to manage their discomfort through carefully timed speaking and constructive argument. As even the willing and enthusiastic ran the gauntlet of Indigenous politics to make something worthwhile of their public service opportunity, they always faced the prospect of policy inefficacy and/or feelings of illegitimacy. When those feelings ran high, some interviewees declined the invitation. But all who declined did not leave, or did not leave straight away. Some stayed, treading water in subtle withdrawal. But some who changed their position to decline left the public service for that reason.

Downsides of trusteeship: 'Is that what Aboriginal people think?'

The trustee is trusted to act opportunistically, to use his or her judgement to do what cannot be done or seen from the outside, and respond as circumstances allow. The interviewees were generally willing to contribute to government in this way, but for many there was a turning point when they experienced a downside.

We have seen that nearly all the interviewees had found themselves in Aboriginal-specific careers. Here, they soon became the repository for everything 'A-word' and a handy source of 'Indigenous spin'. Over one-third of the interviewee group found themselves the reference point for all things Aboriginal.

While some interviewees were philosophical about Aboriginal-specific careers, others questioned the expectation that they take on the burdens of other Aboriginal and Torres Strait Islander people. Even if they wanted to take on the burdens of their people at work, they questioned the assumption they would do so. Some saw self-identification as the problem. Among the 50 self-identifying senior interviewees, 35 also gave reasons why a person might choose not to self-identify. Self-identification came with conditions. Some called self-identification a 'tag' that allowed colleagues to infer that an employee had won a position on the basis of Indigeneity and not merit.

Recall there were 53 senior interviewees, including three who did not self-identify. From here, the three interviewees who did not self-identify are back in the story.

Ushered into Aboriginal-specific roles: 'You're always going to be looked at and labelled'

To be ushered into Aboriginal-specific roles signalled to some interviewees that they were viewed as not competent to tackle the problems of other citizens—that their value was only racial, and that they were not up to the opportunities afforded other public servants. When asked what if anything would make her leave the public service, one interviewee replied: 'You see some new person come in from down south and all of a sudden they're ... flying high.' Relatively inexperienced whitefellas from south were given the responsibility for Aboriginal programs, with no reciprocal responsibility for local Aboriginal employees in relation to the wider Northern Territory population. 'Everything is like a fight', she said.

Jay's effort to resist an Aboriginal-specific career was the dominant theme of his interview. Here is his caustic self-portrayal as he imagined how his department introduced him to newcomers:

This is Jay. He does all the Aboriginal stuff.

Jay self-identified without hesitation, as he wanted to acknowledge his race and to build the Indigenous employee statistics, but he explained that he had mounted a prolonged assault on the expectation that he would always manage his department's Indigenous issues:

I'd *love* to be in a job that isn't Indigenous-specific but the big problem with that is people know how well you can do your job with the Indigenous stuff. So you're always going to be looked at and labelled as that's what you'll be doing. I've got [two diplomas] and did the public sector management program and yet when I rang up about a job to do with a policy thing, the director for that nearly fell out of his chair saying, 'I didn't think you'd be interested in that, I thought you just liked doing the on the ground stuff.'

'*Perceptions* is probably the worst thing', Jay said.

Jay did not see himself as representing other Aboriginal people in any specific sense, yet he still felt that 'anything I do will be perceived as being an Aboriginal action'. He added:

> You're more or less just doing it to cover yourself in saying, 'I don't represent, my views don't represent the views of Aboriginal Territorians or Aboriginal Australia.' Now regardless whether you say that right up front, everybody listening to you as a black person talking about Aboriginal issues, they are going to see you and think, 'Is *that* what Aboriginal people think?'

Jay was haunted by the circularity of this phenomenon. His department had sponsored his attendance at the Kigaruk course in Aboriginal men's leadership that had received acclaim for its support of men like him—field-oriented, at the lower rungs of seniority and finding it difficult to win promotions. While Jay said he had gained from the camaraderie of the course, he felt it had not materially assisted his career.

Jean was one of the three senior-level interviewees who had not self-identified. This, she said, was because she preferred to 'fly low under the radar'. Not self-identifying was Jean's specific strategy to withdraw from the expectation that as an Aboriginal public servant she could only service her own population. Jean held a strong position on Aboriginal-specific roles. She had moved into a generalist job for this reason, but she was worried her occupation of the new job would trigger its reframing to an Aboriginal-specific job:

> If you just want to step back and do something that you can do quite easily and comfortably … I've actually fought hard to actually have that role seen as not based on anything to do with being Indigenous, it is just a role and that speaks volumes to other people.

Jean said that by working in a role in which Aboriginal and Torres Strait Islander people were not the primary or sole clients, she was making a stand for competency. She had led a high profile program in the past, in which she had worked to encourage her people's compliance with a major service in which her responsibilities were

Territory-wide. In 2007, her work was directed towards Aboriginal and Torres Strait Islander people, but only as one among the population sectors she served:

> In the government if you're an Aboriginal person who works on Aboriginal things, other people see you in a particular way … it's about sending messages.

Jean was sending messages to her detractors about the competency of Aboriginal and Torres Strait Islander employees, because:

> Sometimes it pops out of their mouth, you know, that they're *surprised* you write so well.

Working in a generalist position and not self-identifying were Jean's representational strategies. 'I do represent them [other Aboriginal people]', Jean said, 'by having made an unspoken comment about operating in a job that … doesn't deal with Aboriginal programs as such'.

Oversimplification: The 'A' word

> … anything that has got an 'A' or an 'I' in front of it comes your way all the time because nobody knows what to do with it.

With this comment, Sophie captured the view of many interviewees that their presence made them the reference point for all things Aboriginal. Aboriginal public servants were expected to take on issues that were in the 'too hard basket' for the relevant area of government.

Sophie's throwaway line, 'nobody knows what to do with it', is suggestive of the daunting complexity of remote servicing. Aboriginal-specific programming can seem to absolve other areas of government from the responsibility for services to Aboriginal communities. And some interviewees observed that the distinct issues of remote servicing, such as the size and dispersal of remote communities, were lost in the large amount of airplay given to the 'Aboriginal problem' in their department. An interviewee from the health portfolio questioned 'Aboriginal dementia services'. This interviewee, born in the bush, noted that treatments and support services for dementia experienced by Aboriginal people needed to be culturally attuned and suited to the context, but did not call for a different medical science.

Repeatedly, interviewees made the point that segregating Aboriginal services and programs led to the diagnosis of some problems as solely racial or cultural when they were symptomatic of other problems. In Sophie's judgement:

> It's about taking the word 'A' out of the front ... Anyone who sits at the management board of this agency and doesn't have Aboriginal issues as their key and core problem and concern to do, shouldn't be sitting in the job because I have to put 'A' in front of it for them to do it. They should be doing that based on the *need*.

Sophie was trying to persuade the executive management group of her social services department to focus on evidence of socioeconomic disadvantage, rather than take on Aboriginal issues merely in response to the presence of senior Aboriginal public servants. In a similar vein, another 'identifying senior officer', as Jade described herself, declared:

> If you do identify as Aboriginal, and you're the only person in a particular area, everything gets dumped on your plate.

But without Sophie's policy perspective, Jade blamed her extra duties on having self-identified. Whatever they saw as the reason, a number of interviewees felt they were asked to solve impossible problems by colleagues who underestimated what they were asking. Like a salve for the government's uncertainty, their presence seemed to distract the public service from Aboriginal people in need, fill gaps in programs and comfort those who questioned the policy settings. Some said they would prefer to hear admissions of defeat than encounter disingenuous confidence by government colleagues who did not have a deep understanding of the problems of their people.

Daniel was one of a rising generation of younger professionals who had been raised in remote communities through their parents' employment. Daniel's mother was originally from the region in which she had taken Daniel as a school-aged child. Daniel had been educated in a number of remote community schools, and had now returned to help improve services in his mother's region of origin. Daniel was working in the regional office of a large service delivery department, where he was managing a team of field staff who were developing an Aboriginal community workforce. Daniel felt he was considered fit for 'anything Aboriginal' and nothing else. Here, Daniel specifies his skills and capacities and tells how he felt about being allocated 'anything Aboriginal' in the distribution of responsibility in his workplace:

> A lot of them [his managers] don't know that I've had a fair bit of remote experience; I've been out bush all my life. I speak three languages ... I'm told I'm part of an exec [executive team], but I feel I'm shut out from a lot of things as well, you know that I could give valid input [to] in terms of operations out bush ... I do a lot of reading plus I've got the main clientele. I mean I grew up all my life around them, I mean I feel I've got things I can share there too, that could help with our operational aspects of service delivery, but I feel that I'm just 'anything Aboriginal'. Anything with 'Aboriginal' on it, I mean *I get the hint*.

In return for taking his responsibilities—'our' operations—seriously, Daniel was dismayed to have received race-privileging responses. These left him feeling that the skills and experience by which he assessed his self-worth were of little relevance to this workplace. Daniel felt token. His presence seemed to authenticate the work of his office, but his opinion was not respected. His use of the passive voice suggests that he saw this disrespect as a structural problem that was not specific to him:

> You at times you feel like you're a token. You know you bring along validation and not always is your opinion respected.

So Daniel found himself validating Aboriginal acquiescence in an already decided program of activity. He attributed his feeling token to his decision to self-identify, but felt he had no choice about that. For Daniel, working for the Northern Territory Government continued a family history of political commitment:

> I'm proud of my heritage ... I'm proud of my mother, she's my role model—a very strong woman. She's done a lot of great things for Aboriginal people over the years.

Daniel continued to self-identify, but he did not believe it was helping his career.

The compulsion of 'spin'

Many interviewees had responded to calls to Aboriginal and Torres Strait Islander employees to participate in voluntary activities that would build the presence of Aboriginal and Torres Strait Islander people in the public service. Daryl had established and chaired an Aboriginal employment reference group following the abolition of the position for an Aboriginal employment specialist in his large service delivery department. If the position was needed, then why had it been abolished, he asked, or why had not a human resources specialist been allocated the duties? When Daryl had dropped the extra responsibility for time with his family, he was disappointed it had not been picked up by another part of the department. He commented on the lack of a 'driving force' for the delivery of Aboriginal servicing needs.

Daryl felt that he was often expected to give the 'Indigenous spin'. He spoke of the potential for conflict of interest on interview panels, when Aboriginal and Torres Strait Islander people were invited to comment on the competence of others on the basis of racial likeness alone. Daryl preferred to assess job applicants against selection criteria. Daryl wondered why he worried about this issue more than he thought non-Aboriginal colleagues did. Some saw the ability to produce 'spin' as a rite of passage for seniority. In the following comment, Daryl presents 'spin' as advising on sound dealings with, and therefore 'sort of' representing, 'the broader remote or regional community':

> People put a lot of trust in you to put our spin on what's best on how things can be done in such a way, so you are sort of representing ... the broader remote or regional community.

Time after time, interviewees who were asked for an Aboriginal viewpoint rubbed up against the apparent inconsequentiality of the question to those asking. It seemed to matter little to those around them how or what they answered, yet how and what they answered were extremely important to the interviewees. This tension made the everyday workplace request for an on-the-spot, extracurricular viewpoint feel coercive. It was difficult to refuse. Asked whether they had ever felt they should represent other Aboriginal people to a greater extent than they did, interviewees tended to highlight that self-identifying and working for Aboriginal policies and programs had signed them up for more than they had intended. Even though self-identifying is a private act, ticking the box seemed to oblige Aboriginal and Torres Strait Islander employees to represent their population more actively than if they had not ticked it.

Could Aboriginal employees only ever contribute to the public service *as Aboriginal people*?

Substitutive moments: 'I'll ask Bertie, he's Indigenous!'

In work-based conversations around meeting tables and in corridors and tea rooms, many interviewees felt pressed by well-intentioned requests that they articulate 'the Aboriginal view'. 'You're *jumped* on straight away', said Lois, a non-senior interviewee in a regional office. Bertie caricatured non-Aboriginal colleagues as thinking to themselves: 'I can't pronounce this Indigenous word. I'll ask Bertie, he's Indigenous!' He continued the caricature by anticipating his response: 'Would Bertie know? What language is he?'

This simple, everyday occurrence contained the problematic expectation that Aboriginal people present in the public service would fill the place of absent others. This expectation was seen by many interviewees as callow and presumptuous, and it was roundly derided by all who discussed it.

'Behind all the applications of the descriptive view to political life', wrote Pitkin when introducing the idea of substitution, 'hovers the recurrent ideal of the perfect replica' (1967: 86). We shall see through the incidents below how substitution played into the idealisation of Aboriginal people. Plain-speaking Spike set out the key features of the substitutive moment graphically:

> You will sit in meetings and that and it'll be about an issue—I'm just trying to find an example—you'd be talking about a certain place and about issues in terms of Indigenous people and then they'll look at you and say what do you reckon? Now why? It's about everybody having input.

Q: You feel singled out then?

A: Yeah, because I'm the Aboriginal person in there and whether it's because they want the information from me or [want to know] how I feel about it—that shouldn't have any relevance. It should be because they're [his largely non-Aboriginal work team are] working as a group. It should be the group's input, not one person's. You feel that. I feel that sometimes. That they'll ask a question and then they'll flag it with you *because you're Aboriginal*.

Interviewees' objections centred on a series of assumptions they observed colleagues making: firstly, that Aboriginal public servants were objects of consultation; secondly, that they were repositories of a uniform, incontestable Aboriginal expertise; and thirdly, that they personified the problematic policy subject.

Substitutive moments were hard for senior public servants to refuse. Let us watch how these moments arose and how the Aboriginal senior public servants in this research responded.

Objects of consultation: 'Hear from [the communities] firsthand'

The following excerpts from Jay's interview outline the process by which a sense of trusteeship towards other Aboriginal people could entice an Aboriginal public servant into substitutive terrain. We have seen Jay struggling with the sense that his Aboriginality was career-limiting. Here, Jay imagines his colleagues' equivocation about trusting his advice, on the basis of his mixed descent origins:

Nobody looks at me as partly white. I'm seen as partly black. Until I start claiming to be Aboriginal and speaking for Aboriginal people, then they start saying, 'Well you're not really an Aboriginal.'

Jay went on to describe a typical expectation:

It's your usual classics, you know you can get asked what Aboriginal people want and you go back to your line of, 'You need to go out and ask Aboriginal people yourself.' I don't know what they want, so many people give you different answers ...

Jay's usual reply was to recommend consultation with Aboriginal people, and thus deflect the pressure to substitute himself for them. But, he continued:

And then when you're in a discussion about an issue and you put your point of view across, that's [seen as] an Indigenous perspective.

Substitution seemed inescapable. There was no deflecting it. Perceived as inauthentic one minute and as a provider of the highly prized 'Indigenous perspective' the next—then again as inauthentic, as we see from Jay's continuing account:

> … and if the person disagrees with it, that's where it comes out every time without a doubt. They will bring it up that, 'Ah okay, so that's your view but you're not really Aboriginal … I'd like to know what an Aboriginal person thinks, a real Aboriginal person.'

Jay was not describing a single incident but a condition of his job.

> You go to workshops, meetings here, senior officer meetings every Wednesday morning, this morning we had one. The discussion comes up and just the word Indigenous comes up and everybody looks straight at me and [he imagines saying]: 'You know I've got no idea what you're talking about!'
>
> Q: How *do* you respond?
>
> A: Oh, I'm at the stage now where I don't. So they'll look at me and I'll look back at them with a blank face …

Jay worked for a scientific research department. There was no overt conflict in his workplace. He spoke of warm relationships with managers and colleagues. But as the single Aboriginal person in his workplace, he had trouble finding a comfortable way to represent others. Jay could not avoid speaking as though he was 'Aboriginal people'. In the end, Jay could only resist the subtle pressure to substitute for the absent by arranging a 'blank face'.

Bob, a non-senior employee in Alice Springs, was concerned that if he allowed himself to be recruited to an internal Aboriginal staff forum, his department could claim to be consulting with the Aboriginal community:

> Q: Have you ever felt the government is expecting you to be a representative?
>
> A: Sometimes yeah, I've been put on some things.

Q: What's an example of that?

A: … Oh yeah, it was talking about communities and stuff like that, how they want to re-set 'em all up [speaking of the NT Intervention] and they [the department] asked us [Aboriginal staff] … I thought, well, that's strange, they never really asked us before … They wanted to get the Aboriginal staff on board and I was thinking, 'Well, they must be trying to sound like we consulted with Aboriginal people.'

Bob concluded:

Yeah, so I'm very wary about that sort of stuff, because I prefer them to actually go and talk to people out in the communities, hear from them firsthand.

Bob had participated, but had adopted a tactical reserve, and was uncommunicative when invited to substitute for those whom he felt should be heard 'firsthand'.

Some interviewees who discussed substitutive pressure referred to themselves as a 'sounding board'. Sarah referred to 'when people use me'. In such instances, she said:

I'll say, 'Well, let me think about it', and when I say that, then that gives me [time] to go back and talk to people *outside* so, and that's with anything I do … I always go back and get clarity from wherever, whoever—other Indigenous people, especially older people.

Sarah was buying the time to consult with Aboriginal communities herself.

The call of expertise: 'One … point of view and you've got it!'

Substitutive pressure arises from being connected and knowledgeable. Graeme observed:

You are considered the guru and nobody is an expert in our culture, nobody is.

Peggy too was cautious of the temptation to speak of the views of other Indigenous people. She said that she was willing to 'generalise to put a point across'. If she had specifically consulted with them, she 'might be able to represent *some* people', she said. But that was her limit. As she put this: 'I don't think you can represent *all* other Indigenous people.'

Daryl, on the other hand, was happy to provide an 'Indigenous perspective on policy' if there was a proper process for asking him:

> I think that it's a good thing. Sometimes it's a bad thing if it's not what they want to hear. Nobody wants to be a rubber stamp for anything but I think ... if there is a process for getting an Indigenous perspective on policy and I think it's probably important to try and sort of formalise it ...

For Daryl, it was good to contribute his perspective as long as he had consulted with Aboriginal and Torres Strait Islander and other colleagues about what was needed. He saw this as good government practice. He suggested that departments should adopt:

> ... a process of steering to a particular area of the department for a bit more in depth evaluation or what are the issues on a policy, rather than just give it to one person saying, 'What do you think?'

Daryl created the time to consult with colleagues by saying, 'I'd like to talk to people first about this. You've put me on the spot.'

Georgia tells us how she avoided certain aspects of the role of representative:

> There's some things that I will run a mile, run away from. If people expect me to get up and do these whole big PD [professional development] things on culture, that sort of stuff ... people do, they really, they just assume that we're kind of all the same.

Having come from a southern city, Georgia explains:

> I can talk about it generally, but I just didn't grow up in that situation, so that's where you've gotta call the right people in, and I understand and respect that.

Like Daryl, Georgia objected to being put 'on the spot'. She had observed many times the temptation to give offhand replies to critical issues, and had deflected such invitations in her major service delivery department:

Well, they might be just one-off things really, sort of, 'I want you to think about this.' Well, you haven't even given a person a chance to have a read ... if it's important, show a little bit of respect by giving someone a bit of a lead in. But they just think, 'Oh okay, that person will be able to think then and there on the spot.' If it's something that's really quite critical, often we'll just throw in a comment, but it's not always well considered.

Warming to her subject, Georgia exclaimed:

It's taken as truth! ... Just seek one Indigenous person's point of view and you've got it!

'We don't know every issue', she warned. Here Georgia sets out her criteria for a more rigorous approach to Aboriginal inclusion:

You've got to have *inclusive practice* to actually invite and open it up for input. It can be structured. It can be structured so that you're getting the right information, but there aren't the inclusive practices and the department suffers dreadfully from cronyism and that sort of thing, which is really sad, but no, the inclusive practices just aren't there.

She added: 'People can tell when they're not really being listened to.'

Deborah would have agreed. 'Just because people have got black skin, they don't *know* ...', she said. Deborah spoke wryly of the powerful temptation of speaking when one knew that one was going to be universally and uncritically believed:

Because I'm a black woman, they just agree with everything I say. I could tell them the sky is grey. But it's blue. How can it be?

How *can* it be? In substitutive moments, the public service was looking for the affirmation of a relationship, and not new knowledge.

Wrong gaze: Becoming the problematic policy subject

An interviewee who did not consent to being individually characterised or quoted made a uniquely astute observation: that differentiating oneself from other public servants enabled an Aboriginal public servant to be gazed upon as the problematic policy subject.

Here the substitutive moment takes an interesting twist. Self-identifying Aboriginal and Torres Strait Islander public servants are the subjects of Indigenous public sector employment policies. Recall that a representative must be like but not too like the represented—if a representative is too like the object of representation, then it is not representation. As the subjects of Indigenous public sector employment policies, Aboriginal and Torres Strait Islander public servants are simply themselves. It is only when they channel the absent that there is representation. But in the shifts and currents of everyday workplaces, the subjects of Aboriginal policies and programs—the homeless, the alcoholic, the unemployed jobseeker and even the self-identifying Aboriginal public servant—haphazardly roll into one. Aboriginal and Torres Strait Islander public servants might well be bewildered at the consequences. Offering to help government take care of Aboriginal people, the government *looked back at them*.

The obligations of trusteeship easily triggered the substitutive moments that so challenged interviewees' personal ethics and compromised their concern for communities. Paradoxically, accepting the representative role—self-identifying and drawing on identity in Aboriginal-specific programs—seemed to undermine their contribution. Yet accepting this role was the very reason many of the interviewees had joined the public service. Here were the limits of their acceptance.

To remain afloat, interviewees practised the bureaucratic arts with consummate skill. To make their presence tenable, they modulated it. They constantly judged whether the absent were competent or available to speak on an issue. Sometimes, it was worth going in to bat for a proper communication process between government and remote communities. Sometimes, they judged that it was better to anticipate the views of communities before someone else did. This way, they could stay representative without themselves becoming the problematic policy subject.

Declining the invitation: Stories of exit

Some interviewees felt so cornered by the obligation to act as Aboriginal people in the public service that despite having once accepted it, they came to decline the invitation altogether. This could happen at any time. It could be a privately held position without the employee leaving; we have seen many instances of embryonic argument that did not escalate to the point of resignation. But here, we will explore some instances of decline that led to exit from the public service. In each case, the exit signified a broken relationship from the interviewee's perspective.

These vignettes may be read as the exit interviews these interviewees were disappointed not to have been offered when they left.

Disagreements over Aboriginal employment policy

Forgotten walk-off

At one time, Julia had been the most senior Aboriginal public servant in the Northern Territory Government. Julia had participated in the 'staged departure' from the Public Service Commission in 1988. By 2007, a number of the interviewees did not know about this incident. Unlike the Gurindji people's famous walk-off from Wave Hill Station in 1966, in protest against working conditions and the occupation of Aboriginal land, Julia's administrative 'walk-off' barely raised an eyebrow after a brief airing in the parliament and local media. Reflecting on the incident and her subsequent Commonwealth career, this long-time public servant and activist spoke of Aboriginal and Torres Strait Islander employees just 'sitting there' in workplaces that did not accommodate their practical advice:

> They've got to do business different but the only thing that they're doing different is that they've got the person sitting there ... God knows don't bring your ideas and don't really try and change the way we actually approach our business and how we engage with the community.

In the Australian Public Service some time before, Julia said:

> I was never called on once to actually give an Aboriginal perspective ... It's like they want to increase Aboriginal people in their service because a lot of their clients are Aboriginal, so they're trying to bring some on with that perspective but ... [Aboriginal people are] the last person [people] that they'll actually ask ...

Julia was back in the Northern Territory Public Service in 2007, where she was finding no place for skills and knowledge she described as 'bi-cultural'. She had found a way to re-enter the public service of her place of origin by quietly assisting communications between the government and Aboriginal people in remote communities. She was to leave again soon for a position with an Aboriginal organisation.

A more modern exit

Since Northern Territory self-government, the Public Service Commissioner and later the Commissioner for Public Employment has assembled team after team to promote Indigenous employment. In 2007, the eventual dissipation of these teams had created a kind of diaspora of former Commission staff throughout the departments.

Yvonne was part of this diaspora. When she had been invited to review and develop an Indigenous employment policy, Yvonne described herself as having represented Indigenous people—her term— 'in a very broad sense':

> I certainly did it at [the agency] in that I was able to influence, policies and programs we developed for Indigenous people in my position as a senior officer, so this was expected of me as the senior Indigenous person in that organisation ... I would either agree, recommend or approve something or I would question it and say, 'No I don't think this is right for the betterment of this or for the general program.'

Yvonne distinguished between influence and advocacy by adding:

> ... but I always made it clear that I never advocated on behalf of Indigenous people ... and I never spoke on behalf of a family or group or clan; never.

But Yvonne's Indigenous audiences were relatively undemanding, as her traditional attachments lay outside the Northern Territory.

When asked to describe what she had found hardest in her time in the public service, Yvonne described agreeing to a text written by someone else that painted a rosy picture of Indigenous employment. She had felt that others would think the text represented her views. Yvonne 'just couldn't' agree, but she did not leave at that point. She took the advice of her boss, who counselled her to choose the battles she had a chance of winning, and found a way to disown the text. When Yvonne did eventually leave the public service it was for a different reason: the departure of this boss, who had been her mentor, and with him any chance that their program would be continued. Yvonne could face the unpalatable text but not the prospect of revisionism under a new chief. Representing 'in a very broad sense' had been workable for Yvonne, but she could not remain a senior public servant once she lost her influence.

'Walking the tightrope'

Bruce had left the Northern Territory. He was vexed at this outcome for a local Aboriginal man with professional qualifications, executive experience and a desire to contribute to the public service. His traditional connections extended from the north to the centre, but he was now residing interstate, 'living off my country' after a 20-year career in the Northern Territory Public Service. Starting as a trainee in the 1980s, Bruce had 'travelled the whole of the Territory' to rise through the clerical grades to become a senior project officer and an acting director—'although in areas involving Indigenous', he added. Earlier he had been a field officer in community development, one of the government's 'eyes and ears'. Bruce had been a casualty of the Aboriginal Liaison Officer upgrading and had self-funded his professional study to change his prospects. Offered a cadetship in the final stages of his degree, Bruce was disappointed:

> No one [in my workplace] wanted to see my marks or anything. I was taking the money, but I could have been failing.

His worst fears had been realised when he was 'shafted in a sense', as he put it, when he was not given the chance to use his new credentials on return to the public service.

Bruce was then elected to a representative position as the chair of an Aboriginal council, an opportunity he described as 'awesome'. In this role, he was proud of having obtained a large amount of funding for social compliance programs by persuading his colleagues in the council to sign off on an agreement with the Northern Territory Government. He recalled assuring these colleagues, who were wary of the government:

> It's not just about words, you know. It's about government functioning better.

'We showed good faith in getting this money', Bruce said. According to the agreement, the money was handed over to the government in return for an in-kind contribution to the same value. But 'they never ever came to the party', Bruce said. His next move was purposeful. He re-entered the Northern Territory Public Service, he said, 'to know exactly what sort of in kind they were giving'. Bruce accepted a newly created position in which he had carriage of the government's side of the agreement and the charter of 'looking at new ways of doing things'. He recalled saying to the official who recruited him:

> I'm not sure how serious you are about this ... I'm going to give you my full honesty.

Once in the job, Bruce realised that 'the money was gone'. He stayed in the public service for a time, but:

> In the end, people were just going around me because I wouldn't agree to some of the stuff they were putting up ... After a while, they were not hearing me.

Bringing the trust of Aboriginal organisations into the public service, Bruce had felt that his contribution was priceless. However, he had been questioned by superiors about his continuing membership of a number of boards, and eventually decided that he was 'more needed on those boards' than he was in the public service. He:

> ... just left after [20 years] with the government and didn't have an exit interview, nothing ...

Bruce saw himself as more principled than some:

> I could have sat there and collected my $92,000, my phone, travelled around the Territory and do whatever I liked and drove a car too and had a free car park, but hey, you know, are they for real or just using me as a picture, just sponsoring me how they want to?

His conclusion?

> You can't go to work *really wanting* to help blackfellas ... If you get into the government, it's all about give them what they want and maybe have a few of the things that come.

It was not unusual for interviewees to be headhunted—indeed, Bruce was soon to be enticed back into a much more senior role. Nine interviewees had been encouraged into seniority by being headhunted. Attracted by the prospect of being 'agents of change', some had been left to fight losing battles with immediate supervisors lower down in the system when their senior executive mentors moved on. Bruce said that the government expected Aboriginal employees to represent Aboriginal interests, but that:

> They [departments] just don't take it seriously, you know.

Finding the government's invitation shallow was not in itself a reason to leave. What made Bruce leave the public service was feeling dispossessed of a role he could have played. His ties and credentials as a local Aboriginal person went far and deep, but at that point in his career he had concluded they were of no consequence in the Northern Territory Public Service. As he put this thought:

> We're buried to whitefellas.

Bruce's program concerned matters of the most problematic and violent kind for Aboriginal communities, but he was unable to protect the resources that had been earmarked to help. Bruce had remained firmly grounded in the community relationships that past workplaces had encouraged him to build, but the department that had triggered his resignation was uncomfortable with these relationships. As Bruce summed up what had happened:

> If you try and walk the tightrope, one group's going to have a go at you. The Indigenous mob just criticise you. The other group [the bureaucracy] will go around you.

He concluded: 'So it's really difficult.'

Bruce would have endured the tensions in his role if departmental colleagues had been sensitive to them. But from Bruce's perspective, departmental colleagues had discouraged the balancing act that sustained his community relationships and benefited the public service. Bruce's resignation reflects too taut a rope. At the moment when Bruce needed to show the Aboriginal community that the government trusted him, he encountered collegiate anxiety. He refused to be trivialised, at least in full view of his Aboriginal public.

'Better outside': The state effect

Hanna had been a social policy executive in a central agency. She had been irritated by the assumptions of non-Indigenous senior colleagues that she might misuse her family connections with local Aboriginal parliamentarians:

> I could have very easily picked up the phone and rung any one …
> But I never did.

Hanna had not drawn on her relationships with local Aboriginal parliamentarians, nor indeed her relationships with national Indigenous leaders, but she did not believe her restraint had been noticed: 'I don't think it's recognised. I don't think it's respected or acknowledged'. Referring to her knowledge and understanding of the ethics and ways of the public service, Hanna mused, 'Maybe we've been conditioned and trained too well'.

Here is Hanna's perspective on the family connections with Aboriginal parliamentarians that had concerned her colleagues:

> [Aboriginal] Members of Parliament are incredibly aware of it and very conscious of it in terms of where the boundaries are, what you can and cannot do, and likewise I think it's absolutely well understood by the Aboriginal members of the public sector. I think people are very careful about it …

Many interviewees spoke of managing connections to Aboriginal parliamentarians. Such connections were common in the tightly knit Northern Territory polity. Like many Aboriginal public servants, Hanna was always managing her local connections. The misplaced wariness she experienced from colleagues was a source of frustration:

> I've been offended actually by being reminded by people of what my role was, and to have been … let known … that I needed to be careful about my relationships.

Hanna had come to the public service as a senior person with a public profile from years as a respected Aboriginal advocate:

> I've always worked in the area of, well, policy, advocacy, that kind of work, and I guess there was a certain expectation on my part that there would be an opportunity to really engage and to make a contribution.

But the message she had received, on arrival in the Northern Territory Public Service, was 'tone it down, tone it down', she said. Hanna had found this difficult because 'the fact is, I know my stuff'. She noted with disappointment: 'I thought that it would have been seen as a resource.'

Hanna saw herself as drawing 'practical knowledge' into government, and she explained that her skill base:

> ... comes from drawing from practical knowledge and experience of what works and what doesn't on the ground ... You know, if it's not grounded in people's practical realities, then the chances are it's not going to work.

Hanna explained her position on representing:

> I didn't actually feel that I was there representing other Aboriginal people per se. I think I saw my role [in the Northern Territory Public Service] as presenting relevant information and insights and understandings that perhaps may not have otherwise been considered.

With this mild agenda of public service contribution, Hanna had met 'absolute and utter frustration in my inability to actually get Cabinet submissions to Cabinet'. An instance involving a remote community employment program had triggered her resignation. 'I recoiled at the lack of critical thinking,' she said, 'the bureaucracy itself ... [is] almost wilfully obstructing any kind of reform'. What had driven this seasoned advocate to depict an inanimate object as wilful? Here is Hanna's crystal clear articulation of her reception as a senior Aboriginal public servant:

> It's like you're meant to be there as this *process worker* ... rather than this real appreciation of ... particular skills or abilities or networks or whatever it is you have.

Hanna had decided she was 'better outside of government'. From the outside, she felt she could do what she had thought she would be able to do on the inside. 'I can go and meet with the senior bureaucrats and with departmental heads and so on', she said. 'I have that flexibility to cover the field in a much more strategic kind of way, and a *constructive* way.'

Reviewing the reasons for her departure from the Northern Territory Public Service, Hanna concluded that the idea of contributing to public service policy and decision-making was 'a really unrealistic assumption and expectation':

> If you think that one or two or a handful of Aboriginal people are going to make one iota of difference ... We're working within the dominant paradigm ... There's a whole culture here that's been built up in the NT Public Service over the last 30 years. The capacity to change the way in which that culture operates, I think, is a big ask.

Public service senior executives are encouraged to challenge the status quo, take risks and innovate to solve intractable Aboriginal policy problems. Hanna left for two reasons. One was that she could see no prospect of the public service trusting her enough that she could be influential over Aboriginal policy—the reason she had entered. The other was the state effect. Hanna had encountered a bureaucracy that contained and limited those whom it marked as representative, just as it would contain and limit those who argued with that representation of them. Unwilling to be so contained, there was simply no reason to stay.

The exits described here were all triggered by intellectual disagreement, on top of a sense of inefficacy and rising dissatisfaction at feeling like the convenient Aboriginal policy subject. These interviewees had insisted on being heard on Aboriginal issues, and that insistence had led them out of the public service and into the Indigenous sector.

The Indigenous sector orbit: Resolving ethical ambivalence?

Of these four former public servants, two went straight into senior roles in the Indigenous sector, where they quickly became public interlocutors with the government. The other two tried employment in other governments before making similar moves. Each had been encouraged to make special contributions to the government, particularly those who had been personally approached to take up senior and influential positions. Each had ended up in conflictual relationships with less amenable colleagues. Some had found their knowledge snubbed and their loyalty tested.

Are we any clearer what part, if any, ethical ambivalence played in the extent of mobility that the research process revealed between the public service and the Indigenous sector? HC Coombs, CD Rowley and other public intellectuals of the self-determination era saw Aboriginal public sector employment as a training ground for the 'black bureaucracy', or Aboriginal representative organisations, where they proposed that Aboriginal people would build and could sustain an external political identity. CD Rowley proposed that the supported growth of Aboriginal representative organisations would help build a 'legal carapace' to protect the vulnerable from the whims of policy (1980: 241). In their own organisations, Aboriginal people could be consulted without the conflicts of identity—Rowley called it 'de-Aboriginalisation'—that came with government employment (Rowley 1976: 361). Rowley's argument was not that the public service should not be representative of Aboriginal people, but that once they were in the public service it was too hard for Aboriginal people to retain their identity sufficiently to represent their communities.

The mobility between the spheres suggests that the public service has, if unintentionally, provided the anticipated training ground for more clearly representative Aboriginal organisations. This seemingly forgotten purpose of public sector employment, to improve the administration and governance of the Indigenous sector, is important. Political scientist Will Sanders has drawn attention to the potential of the Indigenous sector as an order of government (Sanders 2002; see also Rowse 2002). Anthropologist David Martin has written of the role of Indigenous sector organisations in facilitating 'strategic engagement' between Aboriginal and Torres Strait Islander people and the formal institutions of government (Martin 2003). Despite reduced public funding over the following decade, anthropologist Patrick Sullivan has argued more recently that the Indigenous sector continues to warrant recognition as a distinct sphere of governance— distinct from other non-government organisations as well as from government—by being a source of political and social identity for Aboriginal and Torres Strait Islander people (Sullivan 2010: 1). There are also important continuities between the spheres, as I have argued, when we recognise that 'government at a distance'—the term coined by liberal theorist Nikolas Rose (Rose & Miller 1992: 180–1)—*is still government* (Ganter 2011: 391).

In support of this view, the interviewees did not describe a purely external political identity, but an orbital one in which Aboriginal and Torres Strait Islander participants were courted by both sectors as an asset in the government's engagement with their people. As long as Aboriginal and Torres Strait Islander participants were respectful of the concerns and priorities of their employers, they could move easily across sectors, and through this mobility forge an identity that was relatively autonomous of both.

Conditionality and grounding

Fifty of 76 interviewees, two-thirds of the entire cohort of senior and non-senior public servants, spoke of having placed some personal condition on their employment in the public service. They had done this by articulating a personal principle or standard of contribution for deciding whether they would stay in the public service—for example that they had achieved a particular level of influence by a specific time, or a promotion or development opportunity. They watched the public service closely, shared information about opportunities and considered their options carefully. Nearly everyone set limits to their acceptance of the government's invitation to be representative, so voicing limits was not in itself a reason for moving to the Indigenous sector. We have seen that some of those who did move, came back. No position was fixed. Some who were disgruntled or destabilised by events in their public sector career only left to retire. For example, Matthew, one of the fall-outs from the Aboriginal Liaison Officer upgrading, did not ever become senior. He was still in the Northern Territory Public Service in 2007, where he was supporting youth programs in his town. Matthew said during his interview that at one point in his long career as a field officer in various welfare-oriented departments:

> I got the wrong end of the stick because I stood up for my communities.

Matthew expressed enduring pride at the action that precipitated his 'shafting', and viewed it as a personal victory that he had outlasted those who had given him the 'wrong end of the stick'.

Some interviewees spoke of finding work more 'grounded' in the Indigenous sector. Some found the Indigenous sector a safe place for identity-building when the bureaucracy ceased to feel real.

Leena, whose story we shall hear in the next chapter, said that Aboriginal public servants should be able to 'step into community organisations' for 'time out'. Local Aboriginal organisations were places 'where you like the frameworks around you', places that 'strengthen that sense of who you are'. Wanda had resigned to establish an Indigenous sector organisation. Louis, of whom we will hear more later, had already done both. While some saw the Indigenous sector as desirably 'grassroots' and more authentically representative of Aboriginal and Torres Strait Islander people, others found it the poorer employer for being under-resourced and less orderly than government. Wherever their views rested on this continuum, the interviewees did not romanticise the Indigenous sector. While many questioned their efficacy in the public service, they also acknowledged that sometimes in the public service their formal duties were clearer, their career opportunities were better and the processes more transparent. It was all a matter of timing and circumstance.

Simon had been an Indigenous sector leader and political advocate, and was a trusted government adviser when he was interviewed. Simon saw no solid boundaries between Indigenous sector organisations and the public service, only permeability. He saw this permeability between the two contexts as facilitating Aboriginal representative accountability:

> I think they need to be here [in government] and some people need to be out, keeping others accountable … people out there and people on the inside.

Some interviewees saw the Indigenous sector as the place where they could come to terms with a difficult career history or gain the seniority they had not achieved in the public service. One of the former field officers, Davey, had joined the revamped Aboriginal Liaison Officer service in the mid-1980s. But moving into one of the senior positions had made Davey feel foolish. Here, he laments his sense of futility as the 'eyes and ears of government or something':

> Really you just walked around and had a look and went back to the office … You feel stupid.

Returning to the office after such community visits, Davey had been unable to implement what he had learned and felt that his field knowledge was inconsequential. 'You'd be pulled back, pushed back' for presenting alternative viewpoints from the bush, he said. Davey was the energetic Chief Executive of an Aboriginal organisation at the time of our interview. He was one of the 10 non-senior interviewees who had become successful in the Indigenous sector. Seven of 23 non-senior interviewees said they had left the public service expressly because they had felt unable to achieve a position of influence. Six of these seven were among the 10 who were in the Indigenous sector in 2007; only one had moved elsewhere.

Another former field officer, Nick, had broken through the 'glass ceiling' to achieve a senior administrative position in the regional office of a public service department, but said that once there, he had not been offered higher management opportunities. He was granted leave to take on the leadership of a local Aboriginal service delivery organisation. After a successful term, his request to extend these arrangements would be approved, he had been advised, if he 'didn't do anything that would embarrass the minister'. Nick had 'flatly refused', he said—not because he had intended to abandon his political judgement but because, like Hanna, he had felt underestimated by the insinuation.

Overnight, like Davey and indeed Bruce, Nick had acquired a new level of influence when he joined the Aboriginal service delivery organisation. In this passage, Nick contrasts being 'CEO of an NGO [non-government organisation]' with being a bureaucrat:

> There's a whole heap of different things, as a CEO of an NGO, you wouldn't do as a bureaucrat, so having that knowledge and experience I should be able to come back and make a greater contribution ... I'm more wary now about joining the public service and just being a foot-slogger.

Nick was clearly in orbit between the Northern Territory Public Service and the Indigenous sector. He was honing his bureaucratic skills through the Indigenous sector posting to do what Bruce had done: return as a more senior public servant.

The orbit in Aboriginal and Torres Strait Islander careers suggests that the boundaries between the government and the organisations delivering services on its behalf are more permeable than each sector would claim. To speak from the Indigenous sector was one way to enact a representative identity, but to speak from a senior position in the public service was more highly prized. There was a ricochet effect as the inadequacies in one sector propelled Aboriginal and Torres Strait

Islander career-seekers into the other. Generally, the Indigenous sector was not the interviewees' preferred employer. Even if they craved the raw energy of the Indigenous sector's political independence, they appreciated the greater orderliness and better working conditions of public service departments. Once there, we now know that they tussled endlessly with the tensions of representing and struggled to feel accountable to their people.

Ethical ambivalence may well have swung interviewees between the public sector and the Indigenous sector. If so, it kept them swinging in what political scientist Jonathon Malloy called 'colliding worlds' in his examination of the relationship between identity groups and government in Canada. Malloy found a 'permanent identity of ambivalence and ambiguity' among aboriginal participants in government policy agencies, and noted that these participants did not necessarily accept the Canadian Government's sovereignty over them (Malloy 2003: 111).

While some of the interviewees in this research likewise questioned the government's sovereignty, they did not always find the moral high ground outside government. The search for representative accountability and social meaning was a constant in the interviewees' careers, whichever sector was employing them. Their mobility was strategic, a way of positioning themselves for the greatest efficacy and policy influence.

Entitlement

Meet Edith again. She had been referred by another interviewee because she was known to be dissatisfied after a series of temporary, senior-level contracts with the Northern Territory Public Service. Working in the Indigenous sector in 2007, Edith had an intense desire to join the public service on a permanent basis. In this marvellous rhetoric, considerably abbreviated, Edith compares the public service she desired with the Indigenous sector where she was located in 2007:

> I would love to get a position in the NTPS [Northern Territory Public Service] and have my five weeks' leave a year and take them without worry that I can't take them ... the government outsources this tender ... [and] expects NGOs to do it with half the resources and stands over the top of them and when they get criticism, they blame the NGO, they say, 'Listen, we've outsourced that service...'

As Edith then portrayed the dilemma of 'sitting pretty':

> ... I would have to compromise the thoughts of people like me saying: 'What are you mob doing in there? How are you helping your people? Are you there to help your people?'

Edith was emphatic that working conditions were secondary to something more important. She was asking to contribute to the government of her place:

> I am entitled to contribute at a senior level in the town that we grew up in.

However, in an eloquent reminder of the feelings of many interviewees about the sense of being ushered too quickly and too finally into Aboriginal-specific roles, she requested in her imaginary conversation with the Northern Territory Public Service:

> Don't sit me in Indigenous sections.

So Edith laid out her condition for accepting the role of public service representative—hypothetically, since she had not been made an offer. She wanted to be a self-identifying representative Aboriginal *permanent* senior public servant. Were she to be invited, she did not want her contributions pre-judged. Edith's eloquent plea was for something we have seen was almost impossible for an Aboriginal or Torres Strait Islander public servant: not to be 'sat in Indigenous sections'. With her comment that 'we're all married to each other now', Edith expressed her wish for the public service to acknowledge the Northern Territory's complex demography. After a long history of mixed Aboriginal and Torres Strait Islander and settler descent, she was asking: why not embrace that history, rather than singling out Aboriginal people as the chief policy problem?

Here is the argument so far. Those who effectively navigated their acceptance were not naïve or unaware and hapless tokens but mindful professionals who were alert to the fine line between contribution and argument. They trod it carefully, motivated by a sense that this was the effort needed if they were to be influential. In so doing, what made the public service workable as a source of employment for many interviewees was the prospect of keeping space for the absent. The problem was that being public servants often took them into that uncomfortable space. Trusteeship worked until the desire to defend

Aboriginal people tipped into substitution and Aboriginal public servants found themselves speaking as though the absent would never be present, indeed speaking over their silent voices. Trusteeship worked until liberties were taken and Aboriginal public servants felt they had become the problematic policy subject. Disaffected employees reduced their presence, blanked their features. Few declined the invitation outright, although over time many moved quietly into the Indigenous sector, awaiting a good opportunity to return.

This chapter opened with the comment that the interviewees sometimes found it difficult to know their worth in workplaces. The signs were opaque to them. Some were genuinely perplexed as to how seriously to take the invitation to be representative. Listening as their interviewer, and replaying their accounts later, it occurred to me that some were taking the representative invitation more seriously than it was meant. The invitation was superficial and callow, even if the invitees wanted it to mean something.

But regardless of the expectations of the participants in a representative bureaucracy, blithe calls to representation are unacceptable if they cannot in all practicality be met.

Where were the limits of acceptance? For the interviewees, the limits of acceptance were at any point where acceptance trifled with their Aboriginal relationships. These limits were reached, indeed breached, in ordinary public service workplaces, when the interviewees found their history too forgotten or the absence of vast numbers of their people too unseen.

5

Sustainable selves: Recognition and role modelling

The ideas of acceptance and limits of acceptance capture the interviewees' dispositions towards what was appealing and/or awkward in the everyday invitation for Aboriginal and Torres Strait Islander public servants to represent others in the corridors of power. In the shifts between trusteeship and substitution, the interviewees were frustrated by colleagues' obliviousness to the effects of policy change on their communities. On the other hand, they could be disappointed by collegiate over-compensation and naïve requests for their superficial or last-minute involvement. An ambivalent invitation is not easily answered.

Is it just too hard for Aboriginal and Torres Strait Islander public servants to contribute meaningfully to the work of public service departments?

In the protocol of hospitality, there is a response that is not acceptance and not decline. An unacceptable invitation may be deferred or put off until the answer is clear. In the space thus created, the unacceptable invitation may be reframed to make it more sustainable to the self. 'Sorry not to get back to you sooner but we can't make your party tonight. Come for dinner at our place next week?' preserves social protocol by making a counteroffer, avoiding the original invitation without awkwardness. If the invitation is made on an incorrect or outdated assumption about the invitee's identity and can't simply be ignored, it must be reframed. 'I have a new partner/I've changed my name/I've had a serious illness. [*I am not who I was to you.*] Come around [*my ground*] and we'll catch up.' This metaphor has a theoretical underpinning in Iris Marion Young's famous 'deferral' of the dilemmas of group representation in public institutions, on the basis that it was less contentious and more politically inclusive to allow that perspectives derived from 'socially specific and politically relevant' experiences have their own legitimacy and need no other authorisation (Young 1997: 365–7).

Generally, the interviewees in this study wanted more than the opportunity to contribute their perspectives to the public service. They did want this, and they believed in the legitimacy of their contributions, but they did not want the voices of their people who were absent from the public service to be lost in the noise. Their 'deferral' was a counteroffer for their people to be heard, and to be taken into account.

Reframing acts on, and ideally improves, the terms of recognition. This is important, because as we have seen, self-identification can be experienced as misrecognition. Identifying one's race acknowledges the preceding generations who have suffered Australia's colonial past, but it also demands that a choice be made between limited options. They do not even form a logical set—Aboriginal and/or Torres Strait Islander or non-Indigenous? If you can't tick the box for Aboriginal or Torres Strait Islander as your primary identity and you're not both, are you necessarily the alternative: non-Indigenous? For some, self-identification was Hobson's choice—take it or leave it, declare membership of Indigenous policy's problem population or disavow your race. We saw the tensions of social recognition when the interviewees discussed their dilemmas with self-identification in Chapter Three. The eminent political philosopher, Charles Taylor, tells us that by singling out some people for inclusion and not others, 'the supposedly fair and difference-blind society' can be 'in a subtle and unconscious way, itself highly discriminatory' (Taylor 1992: 43). As Taylor so eloquently describes the problem experienced by those prepared to swim the administrative depths as self-identifying senior Aboriginal public servants: 'only the minority or suppressed cultures are being forced to take alien form' (Taylor 1992: 43).

In response to a question about the extent to which they saw themselves representing Aboriginal people in their job, around half the total group of 76 interviewees described themselves as role models. The interviewees described themselves as role models to local youth, family, remote communities, lower-ranking Aboriginal and Torres Strait Islander employees and Aboriginal community workers. The role modelling self-account was pervasive, although those who described themselves this way were divided as to whether they thought of role modelling as representation. Some said role modelling was the way in which they chose to represent others; others who called themselves role models were less comfortable claiming representation. The differences on this question were partly semantic and partly due to disquiet with the idea of representing at all. Interestingly, the interviewees' ambivalence mirrored an ambivalence in political theory on the relationship between role modelling and representation, as we will see in the final chapter. Regardless of their views on representation, role modelling moved those interviewees who spoke of it from a passive position as the recipients of an unacceptable invitation to a position of greater self-agency. History was beyond their control, but as role models they could at least improve the terms of recognition.

A word about the impact of the Northern Territory Intervention. There can be no doubt that the Northern Territory Intervention heightened the sensitivity of Aboriginal public servants to demeaning depictions of their communities. These images were everywhere in 2007. Politicians building a sense of emergency fed on the public outcry. As one analyst later described this time, the implication was that 'Aboriginal communities are themselves the problem' (Manderson 2008: 249, italics in original). Indigenous leader Marcia Langton summed up the situation with the observation that 'the crisis in Aboriginal society is now a public spectacle, played out in a vast "reality show" through the media, parliaments, public service and the Aboriginal world' (Langton 2008).

It is possible that the Intervention's demeaning imagery of remote Aboriginal communities focused some interviewees on image-making to a greater extent than might have been the case without the unfolding drama. Some interviewees did discuss the ways in which the Intervention's powerful representations of dysfunctionality was affecting their image as public servants, but it is unlikely the Intervention generated the high incidence of the role modelling self-account in this research. Representations of remote Aboriginal dysfunctionality were not new in themselves, and aside from the fact that most interviewees resisted the Intervention's approach, many of the events they recounted predated it. Role modelling was their account, and it reflected longer term issues than the 2007 whirlwind.

Despite the Intervention's whipped up panic, most interviewees held onto nuanced personal stances they had refined and nurtured through practice. Few were fully invested in the rushed package of emergency measures they watched overrun the fragile local services they had been helping to make work from the bottom up. But to try and temper the Intervention narrative was seen as condoning child abuse. The interviewees were only too aware of profound disadvantage and social disturbance in their communities, but they were suspicious of the methods and promises of political newcomers who would leave fresh damage in their wake. Despite these misgivings, few denied hoping that newfound political attention would help alleviate suffering in their communities.

Some interviewees who were working in Northern Territory Government departments in 2007 were vocal in their support for the local employees of community schools and health clinics whose image was being shattered in the tabloids. Many presented themselves as guardians of these voiceless and defenceless hardworking local employees against the representations of dire social emergency. Some were advising the Northern Territory Government. Some were working in service delivery organisations. Some were helping mobilise new services, at the same time as trying to defend the worthy elements in services that were suddenly being ceased. Some were finding grim satisfaction at seeing their own previously ignored advice about under-serviced Aboriginal communities vindicated in the tabloids. Without exception, the interviewees shared abiding concern for the good people they knew in communities, knowing that some were grateful for the Intervention. Some interviewees were even prepared to examine their own responsibility for poor community outcomes. But as seasoned public servants they were generally sceptical, and saw the Intervention as a transient, if exploitable, peak of policy attention in a larger history of government neglect.

Because the Intervention closely followed the dismantling of the regional representative structures of the Aboriginal and Torres Strait Islander Commission in 2005, some interviewees might have been left feeling that their internal representative voices in the administration of Australian Indigenous affairs were as good as any. But the interviewees were certainly reframing their invitation to participate in the government of the Northern Territory when they described themselves as role models. Through their accounts, senior or non-senior, self-identifying or not, we will see that role modelling was not only a way to represent Aboriginal people to government but also, for some, a way to represent government to Aboriginal people. Examining these two representational directions—Aboriginal people to government and government to Aboriginal people—we shall see that for those who subscribed to it, role modelling improved the terms of recognition and sustained a more workable sense of self.

We shall also see that role modelling was highly instrumentalist for those who were prepared to draw on their position in government to *speak to*—even, stand up to—errant community members.

Representing Aboriginal people to government: Improving the terms of recognition

Louis, a non-senior interviewee in Alice Springs, spoke of 'the visual judgement of people'. Louis was resigned to feeling overlooked as a mixed race descendant of the original owners of his town. 'If they're looking for an Indigenous person,' he said of senior colleagues, 'they won't actually look *for* me, they'll actually look for a black face.'

It was a recurring theme of the interviews that regardless of whether or how they self-identified, Aboriginal employees felt exposed and misrecognised by judgements about the phenotypic characteristics of their race. One interviewee wore a uniform, but it was not this he thought that non-Aboriginal colleagues noticed first. 'They see your features straight away', this interviewee explained. He could tell by how 'some of them talk to you'. Another interviewee commented that 'the presence of an Aboriginal person makes other people be careful what they say'. Intuiting that they were seen as Aboriginal people first and public servants second, many interviewees concluded that their contributions were filtered through visual judgement.

Deborah discussed how unspoken judgements about her being a 'black woman' diminished her sense of contribution. She could tell how she was perceived by 'gut feeling':

> I can walk into a meeting and I'm a manager, but they don't see that.

But she did recall a telling piece of evidence:

> I've been in some meetings where … a white man … will go, and they'll give him hell; and I'll go and because I'm a black woman, they just agree with everything I say.

This was when Deborah observed that no matter what she said, the sky was always grey. Deborah felt misrecognised by invitations for the look and feel of Aboriginal involvement without the content. Deborah operated according to a different personal standard, when she differentiated 'doers' like herself, who were prepared to work with Aboriginal people, from the 'rule-makers' or 'talkers' who were the 'gammon people … getting Aboriginal people together on the policy thing'. In Aboriginal English, 'gammon' means 'pretend' or 'false'. For Deborah, what was misrecognised was a professional standard that was equally critical of Aboriginal colleagues and non-Aboriginal colleagues. Aboriginal people were not virtuous, Deborah said, as they could just as easily be drawn into meaningless 'talking' as anyone. Deborah disparaged obsequious racial respect, and also any Aboriginal colleagues who went along with it. Deborah did not garner Aboriginal opinion for the sake of it, nor offer herself as a substitute for consultation with absent communities. She applied fine judgements in her daily work, battling the saccharine responses of colleagues who, 'because I'm a black woman … just agree'.

Those whose features could not be 'seen straight away' also encountered visual judgement about the phenotypic characteristics of race. If Aboriginal public servants did not 'look Aboriginal' but wanted to speak and could speak and felt they should, some thought that what they said was not recognised anyway. Nine senior public servants spoke of 'not looking Aboriginal'. Intriguingly, this cohort overlapped significantly with the group of nine that was less directly involved in Aboriginal-specific programs. Not looking Aboriginal seemed to give some Aboriginal public servants access to wider career choices—even if they wanted to specialise in Aboriginal areas.

Wanda had identified as Aboriginal in her research-focused department but she was not recognised as such by colleagues. Here, she provides rare proof of the subtle visual process at play in her workplace:

> I was at a senior meeting about five years ago now and [the Chief Executive] came in and basically gave us the big drum about recruiting and mentoring Aboriginal people and he basically said, 'Well look around the table, we don't have any Aboriginal people sitting here'. And I'm goin', 'Okay, obviously he doesn't read his stats'.

Wanda described herself as white. Her mother had been the last full speaker of an Aboriginal language in her home state, but Wanda said, 'most white people don't know'. The assumption made by her boss was familiar and understandable to Wanda, but she had found it distressing nonetheless. Self-identification had been 'very complex' in her family. Her mother had not told Wanda until very late about her own early life in an Aboriginal camp in a segregated town, nor of her language. 'They've been flogging it out of us for 50 years', her mother had explained to Wanda. Wanda had not corrected her boss because she thought her colleagues would interpret this as a bid for special treatment:

> If you do stake your claim, they see that as then here comes the race flag: 'Poor blackfellas, we're gonna have to look after her because she claims it' ... So I left it.

To secure a role in which she could better serve the interests of Aboriginal employees, Wanda was about to establish her own Aboriginal employment agency and had already resigned from the public service.

Ron, an executive in another department, was raised in a southern city. His mother had been institutionalised as a child, but his family had not been forced to disavow its racial origins. Not only did Ron self-identify, he had openly declared his Aboriginality to staff and colleagues. Despite his willingness to contribute vast experience and a commitment that he attributed to his Aboriginality, he observed that he was often passed over when comments on Aboriginal issues were being sought. Ron reflected:

> It's quite hard being a fair skinned Indigenous person in a place where you're not from … I find it very hard to be taken seriously as an *Indigenous* person.

Ron felt refused. The invitation to contribute to the public service seemed to exclude Ron and the eight other senior public servants who spoke of 'not looking Aboriginal'. Each made observations of this nature, and each attributed their subtle exclusion to their unclear racial status. Some had conducted private tests to confirm their observation. The research data supported it. Visual judgement was at play independently of the private act of self-identification, at least in their eyes.

The 'visual judgement of people' introduced by Louis was a social fact for the interviewees, and while they found it understandable, it was also unacceptable. This was not how they wanted to be recognised. Those whose phenotypic characteristics distinguished them as Aboriginal people did not like to have their representation assumed. Those whose Aboriginality was less recognisable were sometimes more keen to represent others than was subtly allowed them. To be courted and not heard properly was as much of an impost as it was to be overlooked and not heard at all. Whichever way interviewees experienced the effects of visual judgement, they looked for a more instrumental and efficacious stance.

Regardless of the observable characteristics of Aboriginality, interviewees often reported the difficulty of building careers that were independent of Aboriginal policies and programs. *Most interviewees made reference to this issue.* Recall that Jean's move into a generalist role and her non-self-identification had been intentional representational strategies. Jean regarded herself as a role model by having reduced her institutional obligations to other Aboriginal people, along with the associated typecasting. This was how she wanted to represent Aboriginal people to government—by fighting to 'have that role seen as not based on anything to do with being Indigenous' because 'that speaks volumes to other people'. She represented Aboriginal people by modelling competency, and thus upgrading their image.

True merits: Grounded, local, Aboriginal Territorian

The interviewees expressed faith in the merit principle, but they did not always see it working. Stuart had been an executive in the field of Aboriginal employment in the 1980s. In 2007, he ran a successful local business, employing and training Aboriginal and Torres Strait Islander staff as his personal mission. Stuart had been diagnosed with a terminal illness at the time of the interview. With the permission of Stuart's family, who told me this later and asked that his name be revealed, Stuart's eloquent plea for the recognition of Aboriginal skills is reproduced here:

> Few people want to get anywhere just [because they're Aboriginal] and are regarded less than the real thing ... This 'less than' issue is big, because if you're Aboriginal are you 'less than'? I think you're 'more than'.

The 'real thing', 'less than' or 'more than': comparative measures were on Stuart's mind. Many stories were littered with the language of competitive hierarchy—winning positions, higher duties and professional development opportunities. Interviewees were resistant to the inference that they themselves were in need of special representation. Aboriginal senior public servants saw themselves as highly ethical. They were sharp observers of the fairness of decisions. But many entering seniority expressed an enduring anxiety about the reasons for their employment through comments like, 'Hoping that I did win it on merit rather than being Indigenous', and wondering if peers thought, 'Has this person been recruited because they are Aboriginal or do they have the goods?' Regardless of rank, interviewees tended to frame their goods as more delivery- than policy-related. While acknowledging that policy was not their strong point, some found policy skills overrated.

A deep and recurring theme of the interviews was that these senior public servants were finding the public service generally oblivious to their true merits. Distilled down from all the anecdotal evidence and reflective self-accounting, the image of the truly meritorious Aboriginal public servant was one who was grounded, local and Aboriginal Territorian.

Merit 1: Grounded

Marcia spoke of policy 'hitting' the ground. She described the ground as the place where policy is 'implemented' and people are 'affected'. Sophie had a good feel for 'what goes on' through her 'networks on the ground', referring to her connections with Aboriginal organisations. Sally was 'grounded in her culture'. Sarah wanted to empower people 'on the ground', by which she meant 'in the bush'. She contrasted 'the ground' with 'government departments' that had *their* values' and *their* views' on what should be done for Aboriginal communities:

> It's not about that [the values and views of departments], it's about how do the people on the ground access that?

For Leila, 'the ground' was the community in general. She spoke of a senior executive who would 'really need her comments' because he wanted 'the view from the ground, from the community'. Kel's 'ground' was the place where the community saw him as responsible for policy decisions—the regional office where he worked remotely from Darwin.

'The ground' was a very common idiom. The word was mentioned at least once by nearly half the senior interviewees, irrespective of their job and their place of origin. If 'the ground' had a vernacular meaning, it was the distinction between the concrete specificity of places where Aboriginal people lived and the disembodied policy words directed towards the improvement of their lives. We see this in Lucy's contrast between policy work and where the 'outcomes' were:

> You're writing things and you're having the meetings with other groups, which I guess is for outcomes for Aboriginal people on the ground.

The meaning of 'ground' shifted with context, but it was always associated with the absent policy subject and juxtaposed with what seemed to some interviewees to be superfluous, rhetorical, not evident and ground*less* policy. 'The ground' was the point of differentiation between Aboriginal contributions and the contributions of others. Julia said she knew 'exactly what's needed'.

The interviewees saw themselves as the all-important and underestimated deliverers of government programs. Interviewees often claimed that in working through the people and the politics to make Aboriginal communities reachable and serviceable, Aboriginal public servants had skills and capacities that non-Aboriginal public servants did not. Being grounded gave Aboriginal public servants the unique ability to implement the programs of government.

To be grounded came from connection with Aboriginal lives— preferably, local connection in the Northern Territory.

Merit 2: Local

You did not have to have come from the Northern Territory to recognise the value of localness and work respectfully with locals. You could be locality-oriented. But interviewees who had not come from the Northern Territory, even if they had married into the local Aboriginal community, spoke of a lack of standing compared with those who were locally born. Furthermore, interviewees with local parentage pointed to something obligatory and fundamentally authenticating about having Northern Territory origins, even if they had been born and raised interstate and were still tracing local connections.

Three locally born interviewees who had become public voices in Australian Indigenous affairs had more demanding views of localness. Hanna suggested that Indigenous public sector employment 'ought to be targeted to Territory Aboriginal people'. She specified further, that priority should be given to those working in 'Aboriginal-specific areas'. Hanna's argument was that 'Territory Aboriginal people' had 'knowledge of Aboriginal issues in the Territory' that 'those people that come from interstate' did not have. Jade was more inclusive of non-locals, preferring to see Aboriginal public servants 'either from that area [in which they worked] or those that are trained to work within that area. Aboriginal people in other countries—that's okay.' Simon's theory was more demanding still:

> The government has a responsibility for delivery of its programs, to have the best person to deliver the program or to become the public service for that region, the designated area that requires servicing.

'That's fine', Simon said. 'They can become public servants, as long as they're *local people.*'

These were proposals for geographic representation by Aboriginal people in the public service. Each actively promoted the idea that Aboriginal public sector staff should be local to the Northern Territory. While Hanna's view was that local people should be supported to do local work if they came from the Territory, Simon and Jade were stronger on more localised geographic representation. Simon took the selection criteria, 'understanding contemporary Aboriginal society' and 'communicating with Aboriginal people', very seriously. He had found it hard to 'get a response' to questions designed to elicit these criteria from job applicants 'when they don't belong to the group'.

In defending specific and localised understandings against an abstract pan-Indigeneity, these interviewees might have been expounding Iris Marion Young's theory of 'situated knowledges'. Or were they Dovi's 'unjust excluders', whom good representatives should keep at arm's length? Aboriginal identity is a situated identity that draws on connection to country and language. When we understand this, we can see that although Hanna, Simon and Jade's assertions of the primacy of localism were exclusionary, they were not necessarily unjust.

If you did not have local connections in the Northern Territory, you could still contribute situated knowledge as an Aboriginal Territorian.

Merit 3: Aboriginal Territorian

We have seen that the interviewees who saw themselves as representing Aboriginal Territorians identified a spectrum of meaning for this identity. Simon was chief proponent of the view that to be Aboriginal Territorian was to come from an identifiable place in the Northern Territory. Others allowed that Aboriginal Territorians might include members of the Northern Territory's Aboriginal and/or Torres Strait Islander constituency who came from other parts of Australia.

Nineteen of 76, or 25 per cent of the total interviewee group, had places of origin outside the Northern Territory (although five had been locally born and raised). These 19 interstate interviewees, as we shall call them, were more likely to have finished school and tertiary education than locals. All but one (18) had been senior in the Northern Territory Public Service and more than half (11) were senior public servants in 2007.

The interstate interviewees were less likely to leave the public service than locals, but they often felt like outsiders and navigated local relationships with care. Georgia, who came from a southern state, explained:

This just, you're not, this isn't your place.

This was said without rancour or question. Georgia said she had felt like an outsider for the entire 22 years she had been employed by the Northern Territory Public Service. In her reckoning, she had worked productively with local Aboriginal groups while employed at senior levels over this time. Paradoxically, it was Georgia's acceptance of her outsider status that seemed to give her the credibility and relationships to do grounded work.

On the other hand, Margie, who was a relative newcomer, was confident that although she had 'only gone out to a couple of communities', she would be able to understand the needs of 'Aboriginal Territorians' when shown around by a local person. Margie was struggling with her role and finding it 'hard to get a sponsor', as she put it. Her assumption of inclusion had not endeared her to local residents. When Margie said, 'Anything I'm doing here is on behalf of Aboriginal Territorians', she seemed to be excluding herself from that category.

Those from interstate were keen to produce evidence of connection through long residence or local marriage. All Trevor knew of his ancestry was that he was born in the Northern Territory. The urban Aboriginal family who raised him had come from elsewhere. Trevor's 'working class, urban background' had given him 'no amazing insight into Aboriginal culture', although he thought the 'competitive advantage' of his birthplace 'sort of cut through' the questions: 'Who is this bloke? Who is this bureaucrat? What does he want?' Rose, married to a prominent local Aboriginal person, believed she had missed out on a job to a local applicant from 'a remote background' because she was seen as an 'urban Aboriginal person'. She did not even entertain the possibility that she had missed out because her traditional connections were elsewhere, because she saw herself as a local through her marriage to a local person. Likewise, recall that Ron and Wanda felt sidelined for their less recognisable Aboriginality, not for their interstate origins. But the nuances of long-term residence and marriage were lost in the limited choices of self-identification.

Observing the interviewees from interstate straddling identities, outsiders by birth and insiders by race, the term Aboriginal Territorian emerged as a loosely inclusive identity. At its core were those who could name a Northern Territory origin. At its periphery were those whose connections were more attenuated. The rules of membership were not clear or agreed upon. It hardly mattered. A member of the Northern Territory's Aboriginal and Torres Strait Islander constituency who was anywhere on the spectrum of the identity 'Aboriginal Territorian' could role model the skills and capacities of Aboriginal and Torres Strait Islander people to the Northern Territory Government in a general sense.

But there were some kinds of role modelling only locals could do. Only local Aboriginal public servants could show government that some descendants of the Northern Territory's original inhabitants were now willing participants in the wider social world, and only locals could draw on the authority of public employment to speak to their people.

Representing government to Aboriginal people: Speaking to others

To see yourself as a role model is to imagine that others hold you in their esteem. When role models offered positive representations of Aboriginal people to government, they imagined that the government would esteem Aboriginal people more highly.

Here we will explore the relationship between differently situated Aboriginal people: between professional public servants who overtly represented government, and their less privileged communities.

Self-discipline: 'What kind's this woman?'

Mary explained that Aboriginal audiences expected Aboriginal employees to exercise public sobriety and behavioural self-discipline when they were in senior positions:

> A lot of our mob, we want to be seen as a good role model—like you can't be out drunk and misbehaving otherwise [they will say], *'What kind's this woman?* She's supposed to be there representing us and ... look at her behaviour!' With blackfellas, because people really look at you, you know, because there is only so many people in key positions that are having an influence ... you really are being watched a lot ... if you stuff up, well everyone is going to hear about it. So it's that sort of a thing, a close network.

Mary did not work alone. She was the member of a group. This was the 'close network' of her extended family, community, peers and colleagues in Aboriginal affairs. Her representations were on display.

Mary's career spanned representative roles in the Indigenous sector and the Commonwealth and Northern Territory Governments. To explain role modelling, Mary detailed the hazards of 'demand sharing' in Aboriginal relationships. In traditional Aboriginal society, demand sharing redistributes material goods by transfers among kin (Peterson 1993). To make a demand is to confirm a relationship, as Austin-Broos discussed more recently in her ethnography of a desert community's encounter with the welfare economy and the idea of work (Austin-Broos 2003: 128). Mary described having experienced this demand as a public servant using the metaphor of 'my auntie's car':

> It's like, 'Oh yeah, you broke my auntie's car', you know, a long time ago. You'd better look after it or the people will, you know, then people will just carry on about that for years and years.

'You get blamed for a lot of things', Mary said, referring to problems in government service delivery. We saw the same with Kel, who felt 'rubbished' by his community. Note the indirectness of the passive voice in these descriptions of relationships with other Aboriginal people: to '*get* blamed' or to *be* 'rubbished'. Unlike in their workplace, there was little personal agency here, just the felt consequence of being in a group that embraced its members in that way.

To think of yourself as a role model was to expose yourself to blame. In Aboriginal kin relationships, this blame could be indirect and oblique. As urban people, many interviewees were immersed in complex kin relationships that placed subtle demands and expectations upon them. Mary did not speak of being better than others, but she spoke of *being expected* to pitch herself that way within her group. Role modelling was a phenomenon of Aboriginal relationships—albeit that it was empowered by officialdom. Mary had ways to measure the esteem in which she was held by keeping close to her networks.

Others were less sure. For example, Ben's engagement with the Aboriginal community was tentative. He had only recently returned to the Territory after years away. Less well known, he could not so easily be blamed, but Ben still called himself a role model to others by having had a truncated secondary education. Ben worked in a major infrastructure department. He too used the passive voice when he explained that role modelling was to 'be looked up to':

> I would like to think that as an Aboriginal person you may be a role model or be looked up to. Maybe people would come to you, to me eventually for advice or for direction, you know, but I don't think I represent Aboriginal people. No. I think I can show the way, be a role model … This is all possible and if you want to get up the top I think the opportunity is there. And as I said, I had one year of high school.

'To represent people they'd have to ask you to', Ben added, espousing the delegate theory of representation. Ben saw himself as a role model, but not as representing others. In Ben's view, if others saw him as a role model for getting to a senior position with only one year of high school, this did not give him permission to speak for them. Ben left it to his beholders, in this case the more junior Aboriginal staff in his department, to respond to his success however they saw fit. Although he was not closely connected to the local Aboriginal community, Ben's achievement of public service seniority with a vastly incomplete education gave him the chance to assist others.

Randall was 'looking after' activities on Aboriginal land by encouraging traditional owners to take up economically viable behaviours and activities. Randall spoke of 'representing the Northern Territory Government and plus like even my own people, *my* people'. He went on to explain, 'They see me working and they like what I do for a living'. Randall was gratified that a community member on the street had recently said to him of his work: 'That's good.' Randall likened himself to 'a role model to younger people that's trying to have a go'. As he explained:

> Indigenous people see an Indigenous man coming from the Northern Territory Government coming to help. They sort of accepted me in there, coming into their land and showing them what to do … that's a really good feeling. I suppose I've been around town, that I've been working with the Northern Territory Government and some people know me really well … that I've got a bit of Indigenous blood in me.

Thus, Randall professed himself a broad-ranging representative of government and his people.

Randall introduced a more substantive purpose to his role modelling when he explained that he was a role model by 'Indigenous people seeing an Indigenous man' from the government who was 'showing them [Indigenous people] what to do'. While acknowledging his racial heritage, Randall did not cast himself as Aboriginal. Randall is the second of the three interviewees who did not self-identify. He set out his position in these terms:

> In the old days, the old full blood man said that the yellow fella was a mongrel … You know when one of the big old TOs [traditional owners], the black man, said that the half-caste man is a mongrel breed bastard … I've got a white father and black mother; I reckon it's pretty clear. You can go either way. With that Aboriginal side, if you're a man you follow your father's way.

Randall was expressing a patrilineal principle of Aboriginal descent, although he had inherited 'that Aboriginal side' through his mother. Randall also disqualified himself because 'I sort of haven't been brought up on the community or in the camp'. Yet, working in an Aboriginal-specific program, a skilling program for Aboriginal people living on their traditional country, Randall described a profound commitment to 'our clients out there':

> It's just not the four men and the six ladies that you deal with when you're having a meeting, it's the whole clan, so you're looking at thousands of people that you're giving to, to the elders that are taking the advice and what's behind them old people is their tribe and then the kids coming up … if you get them thinking now, this is what your country needs and this is the best scenario or way to go about it to make it viable and having an income for your people and getting that information out there, that's a bonus … *I'm going to hear a tear drop in a minute.*

Randall's aside about the tear drop was all the more theatrical for its near-inaudibility. His muttered self-deprecation was only discernible later, playing his recording at high volume. Through it, Randall caricatured those who wore their heart on their sleeve.

Randall's personal policy not to self-identify was not due to qualms about working in the Aboriginal interest or being known as Indigenous. He saw himself representing Aboriginal people to government and government to Aboriginal people. He was a role model in both ways. Randall elected not to self-identify because, in the judgement he imagined his own role models would make about him, he hadn't earned the identity.

Notes of didacticism: 'How the government operates'

Notes of didacticism crept into the meaning of role model as differently positioned interviewees told how they had taken opportunities to exhibit and explain self-discipline to their people. Carol represented Aboriginal people in her work by 'trying to teach people things'. Simon, too, 'wherever you're working and your mob is proud of you', said that they—'mainly family'—often told him 'you need to be this, you need to do that'. In return, he said, 'You get an opportunity virtually to explain to them how the government operates'.

In the relationship between Aboriginal public servants and their clients in the Aboriginal community, role modelling could be moralising. But role modelling was not just about the government's benevolent hand meting out lessons to the citizenry. Partly governmental in its bid for social order and partly designed for wider audiences, the role modelling espoused by the interviewees was Aboriginal business. Some role models were comfortable exuding knowingness and seeming better off than other Aboriginal people. These interviewees were deeply embedded in Aboriginal relationships. Confident of their kin relationships and sure of being heard within their community, these individuals did not shrink from being seen as 'better than'. They strutted their positional authority with pride, without pandering to political correctness. When viewed in the context of Aboriginal relationships, the role modelling described in some accounts was the expression and realisation of a familial right to comment.

Some interviewees took role modelling to another level when they drew on their government authority to correct problematic behaviours. They did this through jobs involving correcting governing. Those who worked in corrective governing roles did not all characterise themselves as role models, but nevertheless discussed doing work that acted directly and explicitly on the deportments of others in their community.

In these jobs, interviewees were speaking to other Aboriginal people—their policy or program subjects—*as Aboriginal people in government*. When they role modelled the socially desirable deportments of self-discipline, they *were* government in the Foucauldian sense of the 'theories, proposals, strategies and technologies' for guiding conduct; or famously, the 'conduct of conduct' (Rose 1999: 3; Foucault 1988; see also Foucault 1991). Michel Foucault's concept of 'governmentality' goes beyond the institutions and strategies of government to take in the governing 'know-how' and historical process of bureaucratisation—the broader rationality of government (Foucault 1991: 102–3). As Nikolas Rose explained, Foucault's governmentality 'embraces the ways in which one might be urged and educated to bridle one's own passions, to control one's own instincts, to govern oneself' (Rose 1999: 3). However much role modelling suited the government's 'normalisation' program, what was important to the interviewees was the representation of small 'g' government within Aboriginal relationships.

Corrective governing: 'We were senior Aboriginal people in our town'

> I wouldn't come to your country drunk. How dare you come into my office drunk?

So Deborah recounted her spontaneous admonishment of an Aboriginal man who had entered her office under the influence of alcohol. The inebriated man had first wandered off the street into another section of her department. Deborah surmised that 'fear of not being seen to be politically correct' had motivated non-Aboriginal colleagues in that other section to send him to her. Deborah was renowned for her directness with Aboriginal people who sought to abuse the resources of the office, a shop front on the main street of the town.

Thus some interviewees used their positional authority to go beyond speaking *for* others as trustees, or *as* others as substitutes, to speak *to* other Aboriginal people to reprimand antisocial behaviours. When she did so, Deborah drew a parallel between this man's 'country' and her 'office'. This was more than just witty story-telling, although it was indeed that. Deborah's equation of 'country' and 'office' suggests pride in her positional authority. It also suggests protectiveness towards those Aboriginal and Torres Strait Islander staff who were 'good' citizens by maintaining traditional lives while earning livelihoods. Deborah was prepared not just to stand for and stand up for, but to *stand up to* Aboriginal people when antisocial behaviour threatened her carefully built program. The drunk's behaviour trampled on the right of her staff to work for their people in peace. Deborah came from interstate, so her country was elsewhere. Her office was her domain in a way in which the town was not, although she had settled in the Northern Territory many years earlier.

Corrective governing took many forms. Six senior and three non-senior interviewees had been involved in a project we will call the Social Discipline Project. The Social Discipline Project involved locally recruited Aboriginal and Torres Strait Islander employees in governmental efforts to manage the antisocial behaviours of swelling numbers of Aboriginal itinerants in Northern Territory towns. All who had been involved in the Social Discipline Project referred to it when asked what they found hardest about working for the government. They were invited to reflect on what they had found difficult and why they had worked in it nonetheless. These questions drew out some interesting aspects of role modelling.

The Social Discipline Project was 'something that we didn't want', said Sophie. But Sophie had persuaded herself to participate in it, because, she explained, the project was 'an opportunity to provide intervention services to a group of people who didn't know how to access them'. Within government, she explained further, the project aimed to encourage 'agencies who had primary responsibility to take those primary responsibilities'. But working on the project had placed a number of Aboriginal and Torres Strait Islander public servants in the public spotlight. Sometimes, these public servants were in the line of fire of disgruntled local Aboriginal organisations, local businesses and community groups. As Lucy described it, the Social Discipline Project was:

> Targeted towards the remote community people that were coming into town ... and got stuck here—we'd encourage them to go back home or do something more productive with their lives.

A former manager of the project, Lucy, had left the project 'because of the social issues that we were confronted with all the time'.

Other past employees of the Social Discipline Project had been more willing to embrace the role modelling opportunity it presented, though their involvement had challenged them. Sandy, who had also managed the project for a time, said that it 'tested us tremendously':

> You get tested to every aspect of your moral fibre from both sides of the agenda, both the black and the white ... I'd get NGOs [non-government organisations] beating up on my staff verbally ... You found yourself walking this line on behalf of the NT Government. 'Who made the decision?' I said well this is the decision; it was made by the government. 'Who specifically?' They wanted names and numbers and the time the decision was made ... That was really hard but—good—at the same time, because it really tested me as an individual, tested what I was about.

For Sandy, the 'hard stuff' had been acknowledging antisocial behaviour by community members:

> That's the hard stuff that some Aboriginal people don't acknowledge that there is bad behaviour there in the streets ... those were the moral issues and the tough issues that we had to sort of come to grips with and deal with and face head on.

Explaining why she had taken on the Social Discipline Project, Sandy downplayed her Aboriginality and emphasised her empathy:

> I'd like to think it's because I'm a caring person. Maybe it was a little bit easier because I'd got the networks and you have that empathy and understanding and you're prepared to work in that environment ...
>
> I don't want to sound as though, yeah, because I was Aboriginal, I made it work. I don't know if I did. But I'm just letting you know that I think my heart was in the right place.

Entreating acceptable behaviours from Aboriginal townspeople had made Sandy examine her relationship with the Aboriginal community more generally:

> At times I would go home, look at myself and think, 'Am I betraying Aboriginal people by being like this and saying these things, that it [antisocial behaviour] is not acceptable?'

Sandy had faced the possibility she could be viewed by her family and community as siding with racist ill-feeling, but she saw herself as standing up for women's rights:

> You'd get up and have to talk about antisocial behaviour and how
> wrong it is and not condoning Aboriginal men bashing women in
> public … I don't condone that. Any sort of violence against women
> is terrible.

Indeed, Sandy saw herself as standing up for human rights when
she said that such violence was 'not acceptable at a *human* level'.

Sandy was a long-serving public servant with traditional connections
to places near the town. Her own people were subjects of the project.
For Sandy, being on view as a government representative was a small
price to pay for a sense of efficacy in dealing with these tough problems.
Role modelling had substantive content, as Sandy deliberately stood
up for the humane treatment of Aboriginal women and children
by facing confronting issues even when doing so was bristling and
uncomfortable.

Edith, another self-described role model in the Social Discipline
Project, had resolved the discomfort she felt at calling out the
behaviour of relatives and townspeople by taking the responsibilities
of public service seniority very seriously:

> I started to get uncomfortable but we were really, we were *senior*
> *Indigenous people in our town* and if we didn't stand up and …
> do something about it or educate the uneducated about it, what's
> the point?

Edith's 'educating the uneducated' meant explaining the reasons for
Aboriginal itinerancy to local businesses, the police and other town-
based services. Edith represented government to Aboriginal people
through her stance on antisocial behaviour, and she represented
Aboriginal people to government when she explained their behaviour.

Edith's kind of role modelling was highly instrumental. In her view,
corrective governing was her responsibility as a public servant and
her entitlement, recalling her earlier words, as a local Aboriginal
person with the connections and the capacity to help.

Recall that one of Dovi's criteria for good descriptive representatives is
that they have relationships of mutual recognition with dispossessed
subgroups. In this part of her argument, Dovi drew on Cohen's critique
of the 'ethnic model of inclusion' or *'advanced marginalization'*,
as Cohen called the 'uses of power and privilege *within* oppressed

communities' (Cohen 1997: 574–5, italics in original). In advanced marginalisation, some group members 'police' others in the interests of their own inclusion, and thus abuse their privilege in the representative relationship. 'As groups vie for the label as legitimate, normal, and citizen', Cohen told us, 'they confront the requirement that they regulate and control the public behavior and image of all group members' (Cohen 1997: 575–6). In other words, the relationship between representatives and dispossessed subgroups needs to be robust enough to mitigate the risk of abuse.

Was Edith's relationship with her community robust enough to mitigate the theorists' charge of abuse? We need to understand her better.

Entitlement and connection: 'It's my home town'

Edith did not come from a family of itinerants. She was local to the town, and she had very extensive, multi-linguistic connections. A 'coloured mob' descendant, Edith was proud that her grandfather 'came to Australia and married an Indigenous woman and then fought, all his life, for the rights of coloured kids'. Speaking up for racial justice was her calling. Edith had felt 'entitled to contribute at a senior level in the town that we grew up in'. She was adamant that being a local person with the requisite administrative experience entitled her to a permanent appointment to the public service. Edith had worked on the Social Discipline Project on extended temporary contracts. Although she had made her desire for permanency known, her position had never been secure:

> I was going home at night saying, '… They're entrusting me to go out and do all this stuff … but they're not rewarding me by giving me security of tenure.'

'This is what I needed', Edith said. '[Security of tenure] would have made me do it even better.'

Edith's connections had enabled her to moderate between transient populations and the wider community. In return, she had sought a particular kind of recognition from the government: to fulfil her destiny as a racial descendant of the town environs, by becoming a senior public servant as of right. After all, this was *her* 'home town':

> It's my home town and this is the structure that's going to be there for my kids when they come up. I want them to pick up Hansard and see their mother's name in it. I want them to see that their mother contributed to these things, just like I see in my grandfather, who got locked up for a bottle of beer because his father was white and his mother was black. So the history goes on and we've got a vested interest in all of this ...

Edith was firm and eloquent: 'I believe that *I* should be and my *kids*, *we* should be the ones [in the public service].'

Edith was speaking of her right to take on the responsibilities of government, and to model that responsibility to her community. Through Edith, we see that role modelling could enact a political conscience. Edith did not see herself as abusing community relationships, but as defending and strengthening them. Role models like Edith wanted to tackle the Northern Territory's deep historical problems because they had been affected by them and emerged relatively unscathed. This role model made demands of the public service *in her place of origin*. This role model brought her privileged social position to bear on the fates of less advantaged members of her community. Here was the path to honour and achievement. This was her political action.

Recall Sally's comment, 'We can be flashy too if we want'. Sally went on to say, 'We can achieve really, really well but still be grounded in our culture.' As they argued their relevance to absent families and communities, some interviewees were proud to be 'flash'—like, but not too like, those they represented.

A regionalised representative bureaucracy

A truly representative bureaucracy might strive to maximise situated knowledge by positioning locals close to their communities. It was an intriguing finding of this research that Aboriginal public servants were working *as closely as possible to their region of origin*. A regionalised representative bureaucracy was already in place. This was without any organised striving or acknowledgement by the Northern Territory Government, as the aim of matching Indigenous employment rates to local demographics was announced later in 2007.

Table 4 shows how a (descriptive) representative bureaucracy had already been regionalised in the Northern Territory. The table sets out the relationship between the interviewees' work locations and regions of origin. This is best demonstrated by looking at the entire cohort of 76 interviewees, because the small number of senior public servants interviewed in Central Australia (6) obscures the relationship. The framed area of Table 4 shows that of 57 interviewees who came from the Northern Territory (40 from the Top End and 17 from Central Australia), 50 were working in their region of origin (37 in the Top End and 13 in Central Australia, the darker shaded boxes). Only seven (4 in the Top End and 3 in Central Australia, the lighter shaded boxes) came from the other region.

Table 4: A regionalised representative bureaucracy: Northern Territory Public Service (NTPS) work location by region of origin

| | | Region of Origin 76 interviewees (53 senior) | | | |
		Top End	Central Australia	Outside NT	Total
Last NTPS work location	Darwin/ Katherine/ Nhulunbuy	37 (27)	4 (4)	17 (16)	58 (47)
	Alice Springs/ Tennant Creek	3 (1)	13 (3)	2 (2)	18 (6)
	Total	40 (28)	17 (7)	19 (18)	76 (53)

Source: Author's research.

We have seen that the interviewees who came from Darwin and Alice Springs often worked in those towns. Interestingly, most interviewees of mixed Larrakia/Arrernte descent had worked in both towns at some stage in their careers. But those whose places of origin were in surrounding remote areas also worked in those towns—we may assume—because of the lack of senior positions in their places of origin. To add to the picture of regional fealty, the higher availability of senior positions in Darwin had not generally enticed Central Australian Aboriginal public servants north, but had opened the field to recruits from outside the Northern Territory.

Aboriginal public servants who came from the Northern Territory were embracing the problems of their region of origin in their work, even if that embrace was disembodied or attenuated. As it was not always possible for Aboriginal public servants to work locally, those who came from the Northern Territory worked as locally as possible by staying in their region of origin.

This important finding suggests that the relationship between Aboriginal senior public servants and those they represented included some sense of loose accountability to their communities of origin. Indeed, through their shared history and continued proximity to those they represented, the relationship must have included mutual recognition.

The exception proves the rule: The Top Ender in Alice Springs

There was one Alice Springs–based senior public servant from the Top End (see Table 4). This was Jerome. Although he did not call himself an Aboriginal Territorian, his mix of remote, urban, local and interstate associations is suggestive of that archetypal pan-identity.

Jerome was born in Darwin after his grandmother and great-grandmother were taken to the Kahlin Compound from a Top End remote community. After an interstate education arranged by Jerome's non-Aboriginal father, Jerome returned and rose through the ranks of a Northern Territory department. In Alice Springs in 2007, Jerome had responsibility for a set of mainly Aboriginal clients and was presiding over their rehabilitation and return to communities in a corrective governing program. His goal was to convey a positive image of his clients to other Aboriginal people and to the town. On arriving to take up his posting, Jerome had announced his Aboriginality and had encouraged other Aboriginal and Torres Strait Islander staff to do the same. Jerome said that he was:

> Probably looked upon as something like a bit of a role model, to get me to where I am at the moment.

Jerome had wanted to show those below him in the hierarchy that it was possible for Aboriginal people to 'beat the system'. He had started out as one of two local Aboriginal recruits in Darwin. In that role, he described himself as 'looking after your countrymen Aboriginal way'. If he found it difficult to continue doing this when he moved to Alice Springs, he did not say so. He said he was constantly explaining his origins to Aboriginal locals who could not place him among kin. He was employing local Aboriginal staff. Local Aboriginal people, he believed, 'know the problems in those communities, and ... they've got more of an idea how to fix it'. Jerome said he represented them 'in how I moved my way up through the ranks'. Jerome wore the mantle of Aboriginal senior official with unassuming pride. He never once returned an email; his secretary managed our research relationship, then and later, but his interview was memorably warm and engaging. His minders had his trust and he had theirs as they opened his institution to this study.

Jerome was one of the 11 senior executive-level interviewees employed by the Northern Territory Public Service in 2007. Seven were from the Northern Territory. Six had major responsibility for services in their region of origin. One worked in her home town. None presented his or her race as a substitute for the relevant public service capability. Their normative theories were individualised and related to their different work responsibilities, but each defended groundedness, localness and being Aboriginal Territorian as the qualities Aboriginal senior public servants should have. Not all of them worked in disciplinary roles like Jerome, but each, like Jerome, drew on Aboriginal connections to be authoritative as public servants.

If the exception proves the rule, what does Jerome's exceptional willingness to take on a disciplinary role in another region tell us? Jerome has given us an alternative social imaginary: competent, empathic and determined Aboriginal officialdom in the government, not only of Aboriginal Territorians, but of non-Indigenous people too.

The present–absent relationship

Wherever role models were positioned on the continuum between communities and government, their role modelling came through the interviews as a kind of argument, or claim. The claim being made was that Aboriginal public servants were not merely the symbols of functional, self-disciplined Aboriginality and not necessarily liked or popular, but socially and politically effective.

Role modelling is a complex idea. Through role modelling, the interviewees could convey something not just symbolic but substantive to their government and to other Aboriginal people. The self-styled role models among the interviewees modelled comportments and behaviours, learned from their forebears, and derived—if we go back far enough—from the educational efforts of the Northern Territory Administration. Noting that the audience for representation may not only take in the represented but a 'third party' as well, Pitkin described 'symbolic representation' as 'standing for' others 'in the mind of the governed' (Pitkin 1967: 104–6). For some interviewees, the third party might have included non-Indigenous audiences. Nick Theobald and Donald Haider-Markel found that citizens' attitudes were highly sensitive to the racial background of police officers (Theobald & Haider-Markel 2009: 410). 'Symbolic representation', observed these researchers, 'works cognitively on the audience of those who belong to a group that is to be represented' (Theobald & Haider-Markel 2009: 410).

Mansbridge (1999) argued that descriptive representation should not only convey 'social meaning' to the disadvantaged, but also impose 'substantive consequences' on the advantaged. In the interviews for this research, role models conveyed social meaning to the disadvantaged when they exhorted them to more functional behaviours. On top of this, role models imposed substantive consequences on the advantaged. This occurred when the role models' portrayals of socially and politically effective Aboriginal people confronted longstanding public service views about the Northern Territory's problem populations. The government needed these public servants. In fulfilling that need, role models took the opportunity to generate a different possibility for their people—an alternative 'social imaginary', to draw on Charles Taylor's evocative term (Taylor 2004). Role models posited a social imaginary in which Aboriginal people are not mere policy subjects or the passive recipients of welfare. In the social imaginary that inspired them to be role models, the Northern Territory's disadvantaged Aboriginal and Torres Strait Islander population had choices and capacities.

The problem in the relationship between the present and the absent is this: because those present have invariably transcended their original disadvantage, the absent have no sanction over any representing done by those present. But in the politics of presence, recalling Phillips (1995: 25), members of historically disadvantaged groups who cannot participate in public institutions feel better when they see other members positioned there.

Do the absent gain self-esteem from the success of elite members? *Do* they feel better, and is feeling better enough of a benefit? The study did not set out to test this question, but some interviewees who were former public servants, lower ranking or working in remoter locations, volunteered relevant views. In short: the success of elite members did not make them feel better, and feeling better was not what they were looking for. Some Central Australian interviewees aimed stinging rebukes at their more senior counterparts in Darwin. They too had to take public stances towards antisocial behaviour in their town—only they were much closer to the ground, and they had less support from their departments. The Central Australian interviewees painted a distinct social world, two days' drive south from the capital. They may have been located at the periphery of the Northern Territory Government, but they were at the front line of corrective governing (see also Ganter 2011). And they felt forgotten. They did not seem to gain self-esteem from the success of their more privileged counterparts in the Top End.

As the Central Australian interviewees narrated their conflicts with head office, it became clear that they too saw themselves as role models. Indeed, in their self-assessment, they made better role models than those they observed in the north.

Those 'untouchables' and their 'high-level writing': Views from the periphery

Gabby had spent her childhood in a town camp in a desert town. Her mother was 'always down the street, she was literally belly up'. She had left Gabby and her siblings to bring up other babies, 'kids raising kids' as Gabby put it. Gabby remembered 'doing all my times tables in a house full of drunks'. She hadn't finished Year 12, but 'the teachers didn't really mind because you're an Aboriginal'. In Gabby's reckoning, her childhood experiences gave her insights she did not see in those at senior levels of the public service:

> Indigenous people, through no fault of their own, that are at those levels, well they have never had an Indigenous lifestyle, so they can't relate to the Indigenous person walking down that street ... They're like the untouchables, and then they're put in there and they're making policies that—[we] may as well not even have them there as far as representation [goes]—it might as well be a non-Indigenous person ...

To make it to the upper levels was the converse of having lived an 'Indigenous lifestyle'. By Gabby's measure, this meant having had personal experience of grinding disadvantage. Of course, Gabby's suspicion of Aboriginal senior public servants had been fanned by her desert town's historic distrust of the priorities of Darwin. Top End Aboriginal people residing in the more populous northern electorates were seen to reap benefits not available to desert people. Gabby called them 'untouchables', which I understood to mean beyond criticism, and from that, less accountable. Gabby saw herself as a better kind of role model by being more grounded in her place:

> That's what I'd like people to think—'Well, if she can do it', because I've just normal schooling like everyone else, 'We can do it too' ... My thing is whole of picture, and that's what I mentor kids on.

For Gabby, being a public servant was all about role modelling: 'It's about the way you behave.'

Louis described having been 'handed around', as a child, among unfamiliar Aboriginal groups:

> I came from a very bad background. There was a lot of violence, there was a lot of alcohol, there was a lot of sexual and mental abuse.

Louis had lived on the streets of a southern city before returning to a Northern Territory desert town to find his family. They had turned out to be alcoholics living in a dry creek bed. So intense was his need to know his family that Louis had joined them there for a while. Then he cleaned up his life and joined the public service. Now running his own local business, he concluded:

So—and now I work with … people who've got a violent history I understand where the violence comes from. If I work with people who've got no education, I'm a person with no education. So I can empathise really well and I think that this got me to where I am.

Despite the shocking circumstances of his earlier life, Louis described his fall from grace in the public service as more shattering than anything he had experienced. Louis had been encouraged and supported to complete a qualification, but taking up the opportunity had initiated the problems that had broken his career. Louis had questioned the authority of his Darwin-based senior Aboriginal manager to give advice about remote issues, asking if this manager had travelled in remote areas. The manager had come from interstate. 'We had people writing policy in Darwin that had never worked on the ground', Louis explained. His sense of injustice at what he saw as inauthentic, disconnected Aboriginal representation was stark and revealing of the standard he set for himself.

Two people who preferred to be interviewed together, Lois and Nolan, spoke candidly of mounting proud challenges to government from their outback desert town. Lois was still in the public service. Nolan had left to pursue an activist career. Lois said that Nolan had been an 'outcast' when he was in the public service because he 'always shot from the hip'. But Lois was outspoken too, as she described having insisted that superiors 'tell it straight' to her Aboriginal clients. Lois and Nolan contrasted their representations with those of a more compromised senior Aboriginal colleague who '… wouldn't be there if he/she didn't know how to say, "Yes sir, how high do you want me to jump?"'

Carly's family had settled in Central Australia. Her mother had been taken from a Top End remote community. Checking whether she could be 'honest' with me, she commented of her department that it's 'their way or the highway'. This was an apt metaphor, as Carly went on to describe how Aboriginal people in her region perceived Darwin-based public servants at the north end of the Stuart Highway:

We all say, 'The Top End mob'. We see that Top End mob are more exposed to information than the Centre. The Centre from probably other side of Katherine down, Central people … we take a bit more time. I don't know whether it's because of law and culture or just because of the exposure to information, exposure to the bigger picture stuff … [but] you hear that now and again, just in conversation, 'Oh, *them* mob get *more* than us.'

Thus, Carly contemplated whether the uneven resource distributions she had observed between Top End and Central Australian communities came from Aboriginal rivalries.

With a similar perspective, Gerry, a man of stature in local politics, described Aboriginal senior public servants in Darwin benefiting Top End communities by their greater ability to participate in government structures that favoured the more populous northern electorates:

> I still live in the hope that the Northern Territory Government actually listens to the aspirations of people south of Katherine [three hours' drive south of Darwin] and actually don't just continue to consider just because the numbers are all in Darwin and the northern suburbs that's who they need to cater for … *and that includes the public service.*

A feeling of missing out typically characterises the relationship between those at the centre and periphery of government. But Gerry and Carly's critiques were important. From positions both inside and outside the public service, they saw their public service as neither trustworthy nor impartial, and not made any more so by the presence of Aboriginal senior public servants. Their departments felt to them to be places in which Aboriginal rivalries could be transformed into bureaucratic power. But hear Carly's wistful, hesitantly confidential tone as she revealed her desire to unlearn how to 'write like I talk' so she could do 'high-level writing':

> I wanna learn about all that sort of stuff too. I write like I talk and I think I need to—I don't wanna be—you know, that *high-level* writing: I probably wanna tap into that at some stage …

Seniority invoked complex yearnings, especially when it seemed unattainable.

While these non-senior interviewees critiqued their senior counterparts, they still aspired to have what their senior counterparts had. There was authenticity in proximity to clients, but there was respectability—professionalism, influence and external reward—in distance. As representatives, those in the desert, and perhaps those in any regional office, sought to locate themselves somewhere on a continuum where they could be role models, but not too flash.

Vicarious authorities and accountabilities: 'Eyes are watching'

Even though, according to the interviewees, most Aboriginal and Torres Strait Islander public servants self-identify, Jean and Randall's accounts effectively untie that private act from any assumption that it is a necessary condition of the representative relationship. Recall Jean's stance on competence (representing Aboriginal people to government) and Randall's scenario for a viable livelihood for clients living on their country (representing government to Aboriginal people). Neither self-identified, yet both took their relationship with the Aboriginal community extremely seriously, crafting their accountability to other Aboriginal people carefully and self-critically.

The third interviewee who did not self-identify was Leena. She said she could not take the pressure. Although also from a local family in a remote region, Leena found it neither 'comfortable' nor 'safe' to 'tick anything anymore'. She told her story in elided, ill-fitting pieces. Leena had supported and recommended a community's employment and training proposal. Her office had not acted on her recommendation. She spoke of 'community pressures' inside and outside the public service. Her loyalties were split between 'the strategy on the one side' and 'Aboriginal people on the other'. 'Eyes are watching', she said:

> This is what you carry with you, you carry it with you from the time that you're born, you know your values, your world view and I also think that the community actually reminds you of it too … negatively, positively they remind me of it. You know, *eyes are watching*.

Leena felt her responsibility to other Aboriginal people all too keenly. She had felt them watching, and had ceased self-identifying out of a sense of accountability to the Aboriginal community that was so strong she could not reconcile it with being a public servant in an Aboriginal servicing role. Refusing to self-identify had been a private act. By changing her career path altogether, Leena had effectively made her representative identity fade away. Leena acknowledged that her withdrawal had been made possible by the fact that she was not widely recognised as Aboriginal. This meant that she was not the subject of visual judgement, and the absence of this element had effectively freed her from any representational role. She had broken out of her Aboriginal-specific career and at the same time, placed her relationships with Aboriginal colleagues and community out of reach of interference from the public service.

Leena's bitterness about her need to do this was palpable, as she satirised her previous department's interest in the contributions of Aboriginal and Torres Strait Islander employees:

> Oh *right*, Aboriginal people, important viewpoint.

Leena told of dislocated, ever-present authorities and accountabilities that she respected, but needed to resist. She had taken the option of vanishing into thin air, for the purposes of the Indigenous statistic, to find a role where neither the public service nor her community could find her.

Mary, whose deep traditional connections spanned northern Australia, was more comfortable straddling community relationships. She too spoke of vicarious authorities in her advice that Aboriginal public servants 'respect elders, even though they might not be your elders—because they're *someone's* elders'. Marcia too explained that no matter what you look like, if you are known in the Aboriginal community as someone's descendant, that makes you Aboriginal to other Aboriginal people.

Some interviewees pointed to more direct and demanding authorities and accountabilities. Recall Sally saying she was 'hard on her people'. She had to answer to the community:

> They don't consider me as Indigenous in some areas ... because I've got an education, I'm white-skinned ... and I don't live on an Aboriginal community anymore, I live in a house.

Sally recalled justifying her relevance to detractors with the argument that she had been 'brought up around Aboriginal people, by an Aboriginal woman'. For Sally, it was a necessary condition of authenticity as a public servant that someone had 'grown up Aboriginal', even if this criterion was not quite sufficient for everyone. Some, like Gabby, insisted that senior officials should also have experienced disadvantage.

Ted said, 'A lot of people look to me that way', when asked if he saw himself as representing other Aboriginal people in his work:

> Most of the old people, I ask, talk to them about their options. That's outside of work. They ring me at home … I'm there for Indigenous [service deliverers] 24/7, 365 days a year.

Agnes, too, was comfortable being available on demand to her local community while on short-term employment with a cultural institution to develop a project in a Top End town. Agnes's honest explication of working with and for her 'family' reflects the open connectivity made possible by the nature of this project, in which she held a non-senior role:

> … my aunties, they've known us since we were small. They had no problem with me and if there are problems, like 'Get Agnes, get Agnes', I [would say]: 'Come on Aunty, I had enough of that!' [laughing] … I think my knowledge and my experience and that gave me a better look-in for the project they've got here … I meet with the [local language group] people next week. I don't do anything without consultation with my family.

Most interviewees were more circumspect about their accountability to the represented. 'People may not even realise', said Peter, the interviewee who 'carried' Aboriginal interests, the interests of youth in his region. He had framed his metaphor carefully:

> How do you put it? I think I carry—and people may not even realise— but I feel that I'm carrying their interests, you know—for those kids to get a better education and have more options in their lives in the future. I really strive for that.

Old people, kids, family, 'the remotes'—interviewees conjured many imaginings of their absent, which as we have seen ranged from the specific to the generic Indigenous. Their diverse and scattered connections, always imagined, never forgotten, legitimised their presence, in the absence of direct evidence of the views and opinions of the represented. 'How's it helping the oldfella or the youngfella sitting under the tree or on the beach?' Jay asked himself all the time. Pending a plausible answer, he kept up the pace of community visits, working hard to get confirmation that his presence in government was helping.

Perhaps it was to compensate for the lack of direct checks and balances in their relations with absent Aboriginal constituents that the interviewees closely watched each other's performance. 'We are hard on one another,' said Simon, 'but that's *just us*'. Aboriginal senior public servants measured themselves against each other. Remember that Simon spoke of the public service/Indigenous sector orbit as facilitating Aboriginal representative accountability. When Simon spoke of 'people out there and people on the inside', he said that he meant some kind of 'cultural' accountability:

> I just see it from a *cultural* perspective that you've got to have that balance.

Simon's account suggests that Aboriginal officials watched each other's performance as the differently positioned caretakers, inside and outside government, of some mutually understood absent constituency.

Speaking of forthcoming negotiations between his organisation and the government, another interviewee, Nick, expanded on this theme of watching each other's performance inside and outside the government. Nick was requesting the attendance of a particular Aboriginal senior public servant who had 'cultural connection' to his region. When asked to elaborate on what this person was expected to do, Nick explained:

> I want X *in the room*, simply because X has a cultural connection [here]. We fully understand X's position … It would still be an advantage … so I've asked X to be involved in our negotiation … just to have that *senior bureaucratic representation*.

What did Nick mean by 'senior bureaucratic representation'? Representation of whom, by whom, through what means and why? We could fill in the missing words: senior bureaucratic representation of local interests by someone who shared those interests, through taking care of those interests to the extent possible—because without that close-in effort, those interests might be forgotten.

It was similar for any bureaucrat with deep knowledge and commitment to a portfolio. The Aboriginal senior public servants who gave the interviews for this research had no formal constituency in, authorisation from or accountability to any other group than their employer. Nevertheless, they were members of the Northern Territory's Aboriginal and Torres Strait Islander population, their loose authority to act in the interests of that population was up for all to see, and their accountability to that population was keenly felt. They acted within the rules, but their sense of accountability to Aboriginal and Torres Strait Islander people could often be greater than their sense of accountability to government.

Is representation a choice?

Can an Aboriginal senior public servant choose not to represent others? Recall that Harry was the only purely descriptive representative out of the 50 senior interviewees who self-identified. We now know that three senior interviewees did not want to be descriptive representatives at all. We also know that two of them, Jean and Randall, chose active/substantive modes of representation anyway. Only Leena refused to do *any* kind of representation in the Northern Territory Public Service. But we have seen that this was only possible because her Indigeneity was not widely known. So now we can answer the question. An Aboriginal senior public servant *can* choose not to represent others, both descriptively and substantively—as long as his or her Indigeneity is completely private. At one out of 53 senior interviewees, this was rare.

If representation is a choice, it is a choice from which it is difficult to extricate oneself. We are now in a position to understand the reluctance of Aboriginal and Torres Strait Islander bureaucrats to represent their people. They are reluctant because they know they have to do it anyway.

A political claim: Fit to govern

Frustrated, offended and sometimes rejected as representatives of their people, the senior public servants in this study drew on a social imaginary to refashion the ambivalent invitation to represent the Aboriginal community in the Northern Territory bureaucracy. In this imaginary, they were competent, indeed exemplary, Aboriginal Territorians, who did not ever forget their people and did not ever forget their past. They worked for a more socially inclusive future. Role modelling sustained this work, and sustained the self. Role modelling offered an alternative to the descriptive symbolism of 'bums on seats' that seemed to satisfy government, by giving effect to a relationship of political substance.

To be a role model is an inter-subjective process. But to call oneself a role model, all one has to do is imagine the esteem of others—in the case of the interviewees, youth, the unemployed, the residents of remoter communities. When the absent matter and they cannot be asked, their views must be imagined. It makes sense to imagine their esteem, because doing so builds self-esteem. To have been excluded from voting at some point in a population's history, Mansbridge argued, conveys the message: 'Persons with these characteristics do not rule.' Descriptive representatives convey the opposite: 'fitness to rule' (Mansbridge 1999: 648–50). Here, Mansbridge drew on Cole's finding from a study comparing the experiences of black and white elected officials in America. Cole found that among the ways in which black officials could 'make a difference' were linking with black citizens, role modelling to black youth, reversing stereotypes of white superiority and demonstrating their fitness to rule (Cole 1976: 221–3). Mansbridge concluded that descriptive representatives brought 'de facto legitimacy' to a polity, even if those they represented occupied that polity painfully (Mansbridge 1999: 650–2). If Mansbridge was right, we may see the role models in this research as fulfilling a lifetime opportunity to demonstrate that Aboriginal people are ready for the responsibilities of government.

Role modelling was a relationship. Was it a representative relationship? Some called it that. Role modelling looked and sounded like representation, and it echoed representation's dilemmas. Was it good representation? It was the best representation under the circumstances—the representation that it was possible for 76 Aboriginal and Torres Strait Islander public servants to achieve with the opportunity they had. And they did what representatives do. They argued *for,* and to the greatest extent possible *with,* their beleaguered communities, even if the pressure of circumstances demanded that they sometimes had to construct their communities imaginatively. If the quality of their representation can be measured by their sensitivity to Aboriginal relationships, it was good quality representation. Role models were making a substantive proposal when they claimed for themselves and for others: Aboriginal people are fit to govern. This role modelling was not merely symbolic representation, but raw politics.

6

Speaking truth to theory

... the road to justice must be found, often by desk-bound, prosaic and repetitive routines, through those bureaucratic tangles which increasingly restrict and frustrate the rest of us and the world at large. The same tangles and routines will continue to be used by those who oppose change, inside the bureaucracy and outside it (Rowley 1978: 207).

Research can surprise you. But the findings of this research would not have surprised CD Rowley, who wrote his prescient words about bureaucratic and political entanglement nearly 40 years ago. Exploring the experiences of Aboriginal and Torres Strait Islander Australians who became senior public servants in the Northern Territory in the years to follow, I found representative agents with expectations of influencing their people's future. These agents moved easily and often between government and the Aboriginal and Torres Strait Islander organisations funded by government to deliver services to their people. Inside and outside the bureaucracy, these representative agents, both desk-bound and field-based, participated in the prosaic and repetitive when they stood for, stood up for, and spoke for others. They spoke to the government as Aboriginal and Torres Strait Islander people when they felt they had to, and they spoke to their people as the government when they thought they should. I found them fundamentally reluctant to represent their people under all the terms on offer, but prepared to represent their people nevertheless. They were connected to each other and to their communities as well as they could be.

I found theories that made sense of their dilemmas and theories that did not. Least helpful was the theory of representative bureaucracy that sits behind Indigenous employment policies, because it has never explained how the presence of minority groups makes a difference to government. Although the interviewees sometimes felt they were 'just bums on seats' to the government, they presented themselves as the active agents of others. Most helpful were theories of the political representation of historically dispossessed groups, which acknowledge the centrality of the relationship between representatives and the absent, or the people they represent.

No doubt the intensity and flavour of the representations discussed in this research were shaped by the representational options available to the interviewees as Aboriginal and Torres Strait Islander Australians in 2007. We do not know the counterfactual case in which Aboriginal and Torres Strait Islander people are able to run their own affairs with full electoral representation, but we could predict that this opportunity would engender other, more clearly accountable representational styles. As it is, some of the interviewees found themselves doing what political representatives do when they make present those who cannot be present themselves. They constructed the absent as constituencies, while managing their speaking with the ethical restraint that is expected of public servants.

I had a second round of conversations with some interviewees in 2010, and some are still in touch at the time of writing. In 2010, Edith was still hoping for the permanent public service role to which she felt entitled. Jay was still doing 'the Aboriginal stuff' in his department, although I have heard that he ended up leaving for a more influential position on the outside. Deborah said she challenged her superiors more than she used to, and felt more appreciated. She is still there, a mature and well-respected professional insider. Carly told me she still wrote like she talked, but she did not mind as much. What bothered her more was being advised not to 'let passion get in the way'. 'I'm still trying to understand that', Carly said. 'If we don't have passion, we're just doing it any old how.' I have since heard of her career success in her regional town. Sophie indicated she was comfortable with my use of her interview, although she was waiting with interest for the final product. She read the thesis, and I look forward to discussing her reaction to the book. Since then, some interviewees' careers have skyrocketed. From the anecdotal evidence, many are still in orbit between government and the Indigenous sector.

The ambivalent invitation

The invitation to Aboriginal and Torres Strait Islander people to join the Northern Territory Public Service has felt profoundly ambivalent to many of its recipients. Indigenous employment policies have invited Aboriginal and Torres Strait Islander employees to represent their communities. Bureaucratic discretion permits this kind of representation, whereas public service norms weigh against it. The interviewees recounted inner conversations in which they grappled with the tensions of their role, knowing that without their presence, absent communities would have no voice in the administration of government.

The public service has both welcomed and denied Aboriginal and Torres Strait Islander people. It has welcomed them by inviting them to confirm their Indigeneity and contribute to policy and decision-making throughout its ranks. It has denied them when it has left them to flounder in unenlightened workplaces. The problem of representative bureaucracy is not that it is improper for public servants from identified populations to represent others, but that *all public servants represent others*. This happens daily, in meetings, in emails, at desks. The invitation rings hollow when people from identified populations have to tough it out at the discretion of managers who are uncritical of their own norms. The Aboriginal and Torres Strait Islander public servants who participated in this research preferred colleagues who could look beyond their own backgrounds and *see them*.

We have seen deep history in the relationship between Aboriginal people and government in the Northern Territory. Some interviewees attributed their work ethic to earlier generations of government workers. The terms of the invitation were very different back in 1911 when the Commonwealth used Aboriginal labour to help in the control and protection of the Northern Territory's Aboriginal population, but that history was very much on the interviewees' minds. Many of their parents and grandparents had emerged from the protectionist and assimilationist eras as 'released half-castes' when Aboriginal people of mixed descent were given access to public housing in Darwin and Alice Springs in the 1950s. Some interviewees *were* the steady trickle of domestics, labourers and mission workers who had aided the Northern Territory Administration during the early years of Commonwealth control. The idea of representative bureaucracy coincided with the policy era of Aboriginal self-determination and the language of Aboriginal empowerment in the 1970s. The Northern Territory was granted an inheritance on self government in 1978— an incidental, embryonic representative bureaucracy of some 1,100 Aboriginal employees, many of them temporary or community-based. In seeking to mirror the Northern Territory's social composition over the next 30 years, the Northern Territory Public Service encountered repeated instances of personal agency. We heard the stories of Matthew and the other Aboriginal Liaison Officers who were squeezed out of their positions; Julia and the trainers who together abandoned a project for a principle; Yvonne, Bruce and Hanna whose decisive departures left them smarting; and many others besides.

Many thousands of Aboriginal people living in remote communities in the Northern Territory exercised another kind of agency by not replying, perhaps not even hearing, the invitation to join government. In 2015, Aboriginal and Torres Strait Islander employee numbers were only a little over their level of more than 30 years ago. Disappointing as this sounds, we have no way of knowing what their numbers would have been without the invitations of representative bureaucracy. It is possible that without any targets, policies or strategies, the Indigenous employee statistic might have disappeared altogether.

The statistic is a measuring tool, nothing more—and an inaccurate one at that. An employee who is seen to display the phenotypic characteristics of Indigeneity adds to the perception of a representative public service regardless of whether or not he or she self-identifies. Same Indigenous face, different impersonal brochure, it doesn't matter if you don't know the person and don't notice the repetition. We have seen that the presence of a person who is known to be Aboriginal or Torres Strait Islander has an effect whether or not he or she self-identifies, and even if he or she is silent and opaque. And that an Aboriginal or Torres Strait Islander employee who isn't seen to display the phenotypic characteristics of race struggles to add to perceptions of the representativeness of the public service or even be heard. Pitkin was right when she said that in its purely passive form, descriptive representation only depicts and informs but does not act, and may equally be achieved by an inanimate object (Pitkin 1967: 80).

So in striving to be representative, why does a bureaucracy invite Aboriginal and Torres Strait Islander employees to self-identify? The answer is that the representation that is invited in strategies and brochures and counted in the statistics is fundamentally about bums on seats. If the other kinds of representation that are implied by the call for Aboriginal and Torres Strait Islander contributions are not measured, we are left to assume they are not materially important to government.

The reply

The 64 Aboriginal senior public servants whose statistic inspired this study really had formed 2.2 per cent of the senior public service by 2006, and an intriguing, inexorable consequence of their seniority, as we know from interviews with some of them in 2007, is that these public servants saw themselves as role models to others. They managed growing Aboriginal workforces, not only health workers, teachers and police aides but new brokers in communications and local economies, interpreters, community rangers and others who looked to them for a voice. They tuned in to each other at work, returned to the familiar domesticity of longstanding interracial families every evening, played sport, went camping on weekends and returned to their communities of origin when they could.

The organic interviewee recruitment process revealed Aboriginal and Torres Strait Islander public servants' occupation of a relational space that was both collegiate and combative. The 76 interviewees were located in schools, clinics, prisons, rehabilitation services and policy units where they dealt with education, health, housing, local government and essential services, business services and the problems of Indigenous public sector employment. Interviewees who had left government were in land councils, academic faculties, community-controlled health services, representative bodies and the private sector. In government, their commonest role was to build their own employment numbers. They were also key hands at helping make Aboriginal people more serviceable, and helping government feel it was reaching their communities.

This book has situated Aboriginal senior public servants as both the agents of government and the obligated members of communities. To accept the invitation to represent their people in government was to navigate an identity that was governmental and relational. They willingly contributed their empathy, knowledge and connections to improve Aboriginal policies and programs. They faced the continuous flow of discursive pressures this brought. They were protective when they believed that Aboriginal people who were absent from government could not exercise their own agency. They exercised the options of political representatives. They were trustees for those who looked to them for assistance in navigating government. Some were ambassadorial when they explained the behaviours and motives of other Aboriginal people. Trustees spoke for others, creating the space for communities who could and should be there and suggesting how the government could relate to them more directly.

Their trusteeship felt ineffective to some interviewees, when their department ignored their advice. Sometimes they found it felt more legitimate to speak *as others*. But substituting for others also seemed to collude in their absence. Substitution could feel disingenuous, if Aboriginal voices on the inside took the place of outside voices who could have contributed if asked properly. Whatever Aboriginal or Torres Strait Islander public servants said, the interviewees found it received as the 'Aboriginal viewpoint'. Mostly, they found ways to moderate the expectations of colleagues and client communities within the general limits of acceptance. Sometimes, swimming the currents of trusteeship and substitution moved them to argument. Some felt marginalised, distrusted and ineffectual, and left for more clearly representative positions in the Indigenous sector.

Many shifted the terms of recognition to role modelling. In this disposition, we heard interviewees imagine the regard of absent communities. We heard them acknowledge that being in the government of their place sometimes gave them authority over their people. We heard some decide to accept this authority, knowing that if they didn't accept it then someone else would—someone who might not understand their communities so well.

Although the interviewees differed in the intensity, volume and style of their reluctance to *speak for* or *as* others, they had all felt compelled at some stage to do something meaningful with the opportunity. They had vernacular terms for the problems of political representation. The dilemmas of speaking were well-trodden ground. Role modelling enabled some to *speak to* the represented. Role models proposed themselves as grounded, locally oriented and politically committed Aboriginal Territorians. Some fulfilled their political conscience by guiding Aboriginal communities towards social compliance. The interviewees were generally uncomfortable with the public service patronising their distinctly Aboriginal contributions by calling their contributions cultural—but only the culturally empathetic could do what they did. If we see Aboriginal senior public servants as citizens and not just bureaucrats, as hard-headed criterion-seeking self-critics and not unthinking recruits to a government agenda, we see the political dimension in their role modelling. Here was an alternative to the merely symbolic and rhetorical, and a significant counterproposal: to be included in the government of their place, as a matter of entitlement and birthright. Role modelling was the active assertion of their modern selves.

The interviewees' authority to be so engaged with their people came from tied-in lives. Their authority was not absolute or uncontested, and nor was their modelling. People questioned them. They explained, discussed, justified, withdrew or pushed on, in engagements that were not always consensual but were at least dynamic and grounded. The interviewees showed that the guiding authority for some Aboriginal and Torres Strait Islander public servants is knowing that they, as those present in government, could still have been absent if it were not for fortune. The Aboriginal public servants in this research were willing to be the voices and agents of social discipline as long as they could draw on their reserves of empathy, knowledge and connections and do it properly.

The interviewees would acknowledge the dilemmas of group or 'self-representation'—that promoting social identity over contribution can encourage competitive claims to identity (Williams 1998: 11–14; see also Kymlicka 1993), and can reduce accountability through the assumption that all those who claim a particular identity think the same way. Defining a representative by the duty to serve a bounded category can inhibit the search for common ground and the public good (Phillips 1995: 22–4; Williams 1998: 4–8). The interviewees articulated these problems and more besides. They found self-identification creating ambiguous distinctions between them, they felt compromised by speaking for others who should be present and found their contributions inhibited by their social identity. Hence their reluctance as representatives—not that this stopped them.

The representatives in this study had to participate in government if they were to improve the construction of others. Their reluctance does not disprove Saward's point about the representative claim constituting the community (Saward 2006, 2009), but supports that point by showing how it was done.

When Phillips acknowledged that 'who the bureaucrats are (their gender or ethnicity or race) can have a decisive impact on what they propose' (Phillips 1995: 185), she was conceding that her politics of presence could be extended into the context of representative bureaucracy. But this throwaway line was as far as she went in applying her important theoretical insights beyond the electoral sphere. The interviewees knew the politics of their presence in the bureaucracy only too well, and some would argue that it was not necessarily better to be present.

Phillips defended the presence of descriptive representatives in democratic institutions on four grounds. First, it raises esteem for members of historically disadvantaged groups to see others in influential positions (role modelling). Second, it is not fair for advantaged groups to monopolise public institutions, when others might make better trustees of the interests of historically disadvantaged groups. Third, descriptive representatives can contribute 'overlooked' perspectives. Fourth, institutions can show legitimacy if they include the members of groups with different orientations (Phillips 1995: 167–8). The interviewees echoed Phillips' arguments: it was important for other Aboriginal people to see them in positions of influence (they could be role models); it was unfair for non-Aboriginal views to prevail (Aboriginal people made better trustees); their perspectives were not already in evidence in the public service (their presence was a daily reminder of overlooked perspectives); and they were fundamentally different from the dominant public service staffing population (they couldn't contribute if they weren't there).

Role modelling was the interviewees' primary self-account. So why did Anne Phillips see role modelling as the 'least interesting' reason for descriptive representation (1995: 63)? Phillips' offhand dismissal was that role modelling has 'no particular purchase on politics per se' (1995: 63)—but perhaps she underestimated its political purchase. Mansbridge followed Phillips, leaving role models to their 'usual treatment' as matters of 'individual psychology' and showing doubters that descriptive representation's 'social meaning exists outside the heads of the members of the descriptive group' (Mansbridge 1999: 651).

I argue that role modelling is more significant and interesting than this.

Why role models are interesting

These theorists were arguing with other theorists who dismiss descriptive representation as de facto, lightweight and undemocratic. Role modelling was the least persuasive reason for having descriptive representatives, to Phillips and others, because they were trying to influence those who had no faith in the competence of descriptive representatives. Phillips and others were theorising fairness and justice, not describing a real world struggle by a set of descriptive representatives who were trying to be heard, as we have in this book.

In reply to Phillips, our real world descriptive representatives have spoken. Their mere presence in government is not enough. It's only a start. Recalling Sarah's opening words: they also need to be heard. Otherwise, they really are just bums on seats—and that is unacceptable.

Virginia Sapiro is known in some circles for the observation that interests become interesting only when they are politically relevant and therefore 'representable' (Sapiro 1981: 703). But to whom do interests need to be relevant, to make them interesting to political theorists? Can the test of 'interesting' be that interests are politically relevant to marginalised people? It is of great political relevance to Aboriginal and Torres Strait Islander itinerants when their people in government move them on from sleeping outside suburban grocery stores and hairdressing salons. And it is surely of great political relevance to government when its own public servants tell it they are entitled to their place in government and are fit to govern. In the politics of recognition, colonised peoples seek liberation from a 'demeaning picture of themselves' by demanding explicit recognition of their cultural difference through claims that are political (Taylor 1992: 36–7; 65). Role modelling is a claim for that liberation. And this claim has consequences for those trying to build a workforce of Aboriginal and Torres Strait Islander public servants, because role models bring access to others.

The problem for political theorists is that 'the word "symbol" often bears the unspoken modifier "mere"' (Mansbridge 1999: 652). Those who believe symbolism is 'mere' might find otherwise if they search harder in the nexus between democratic institutions, the people who inhabit them and the people with whom they cohabit in their lives outside work. Social anthropology excels in this terrain. Applying the postcolonial theory of social anthropologist Michael Taussig, we might see that at the same time as appropriating the aims of government, role modelling caricatures the imperfections in the norms of settler Australians. Role models who exhorted compliant behaviours from their communities established likeness by being local, and established distance by being didactic. These role models cooperated with the liberal vision, but they were not mindless simulators. Some critiqued the government mercilessly. Role modelling simultaneously fulfilled role models' sense of connection with others, and confirmed their standing in government. Role modelling is suggestive of the mutually reinforcing sameness and difference—'mimesis and alterity'—Taussig described as the 'magic of the state', in which colonised peoples parody colonial behaviours at the same time as adopting them (Taussig 1993).

As anthropologist Francesca Merlan noted in her sensitive ethnography of Aboriginal–state relations in Katherine: 'representations of Aboriginality ... come to affect who and what Aborigines consider themselves to be' (Merlan 1998: 150). The role models in this research participated in the making of representations about Aboriginality. Role modelling gave the government efficacy. These employees helped authenticate the government's 'normalising' vision for Indigenous Australians, and thus helped reproduce the government's account. But this is not all. At the same time, role modelling confirmed for all to see that the government needed public servants with connection to the Northern Territory's Aboriginal and Torres Strait Islander constituency that the government lacked.

When role models defended an upgraded image for Aboriginal people, their role modelling was substantive political representation. This is what makes role modelling interesting.

It remains to consider the interviewees' position on another question— whether and if so how, role modelling *compromised* or *realised* their understandings with other Aboriginal people. The assumption that institutions reflect the people they serve merely by having people from those populations present, is as flawed as the theory of representative bureaucracy. It just doesn't happen that way in circumstances in which populations have experienced colonisation and historic dispossession, and in which racial identity is at stake. Mere presence works for the middle-class professional person who competes on a level playing field with other middle-class professional people from similar backgrounds. Phillips acknowledged this reality, although she still urged women to participate in institutions as professional people and not as women. Special privileging was undermining, she argued, and not being present meant trusting women's representation to men (1991: 90). Phillips concluded that descriptive representatives who can, should press their ideas, even if this meant being elitist (1995: 176–8). But we have seen that doing this was not so easy for Aboriginal public servants.

Recall that good descriptive representatives gain authority not just by being present but by having strong mutual relations with the dispossessed—relations in which they strive to impart what needs to be known, interact fulsomely, explain themselves and hear from others.

Let's hear from the interviewees on elitism and on the mutuality of their relations with the dispossessed.

Compromised elites? 'We need you in government!'

> With management comes responsibility, comes a whole package of behaviours in the way you operate. You get into a—paradigm, I guess, in the way you see things …

Sandy was an executive. Her eyes were wide open. She acknowledged the trappings of seniority and her embeddedness in the bureaucratic culture that bestowed them. Neither Sandy nor most other executive-level bureaucrats would have completely dismissed the twin charges of compromise and elitism. They advocated, with care, and accepted that a level of tokenism was inevitable when working for government. Aboriginal senior public servants are irredeemably elite to those below them, and by inference also to those outside the public service. They cannot become senior public servants without accepting government. But to speak of compromised elites is to judge a complex political identity on a single dimension.

Normative theorists tell us when it is legitimate to speak for others. This is when it would be remiss not to do so, and when the speaker cannot arrange the presence of others. Aboriginal and Torres Strait Islander public servants encounter these circumstances often. Legitimate speaking resists the impulse to know for others. Legitimate speakers interrogate their advantage and take into account the likely effect of speaking. It is too easy to call 'sellout' when office-bound Aboriginal senior public servants, distanced from their communities, are on the spot to have the last word in policy discussions. Senior administrative positions are not readily available in the government's service outlets close to the ground and significant local projects are outsourced to external providers. Sure, Aboriginal senior public servants incidentally endorse and legitimise the work of departments when they participate in the diagnosis, management and evaluation of Aboriginal problems. They do acquire powers of definition that are not available to those who are absent and have no voice in the bureaucracy. But the interviewees articulated deeper struggles: should they leave that defining to their colleagues, or might other Aboriginal people benefit from their contribution? Often, after thinking it through, they relished interceding.

Some outside government would begrudgingly admire Aboriginal senior public servants for their ability to do what one interviewee called 'unpalatable' things. It is plausible to see them as exemplars of self-discipline and morality when they are prepared to stand out from the crowd. We have seen that they could not rely on the esteem of peers. Many believed the public service did not recognise what was salient about their identity, or their commitment to public service ethics. They received few meaningful accolades and had no direct evidence that they were held in anyone's high esteem, since those they represented could not readily acknowledge their commitment. They had accommodated government, and they knew their numbers were not shifting. But by striving to channel others by being grounded, localised and part of a Territorian Aboriginality, Aboriginal senior public servants could judge themselves meritorious.

There was no unanimity over the criteria for judgement, and there was no single Aboriginal authority. However, some saw their self-discipline and tutelage as connection with the absent. It would not be difficult to imagine community members finding relief in hearing Sandy's protectiveness for those suffering from neglect and violence, or urban itinerants appreciating Edith pointing out to the police that their women and children needed a place to stay. Family members must have heard Simon on the way government works. Aboriginal public service recruits and remote community workers must have benefited indirectly from those who defended and explained them to the public service, who showed them how best to receive its services. Jerome's rehabilitative programs could not have alienated already-alienated lives any further. Even Deborah's inebriated office intruder now knew what to do, from someone who understood how to tell him: leave and sober up. Aboriginal people could be frank with each other. There was little romance or idealisation in this relationship. These interviewees were neither the 'bleeding hearts' of Lea's ethnography nor black facsimiles of Kowal's 'White antiracists'. These interviewees stepped in where the politically correct feared to tread, drawing on their relationships to aid the government of their towns. Exemplifying self-discipline, they would reason that Aboriginal people had to speak this way to be heard within Aboriginal relationships.

Corrective governing was one way in which a succession of committed Aboriginal senior public servants could ensure that policing was not only *done to* their people. Should they have recoiled from policing roles, allowing others to prosecute their people for public drunkenness or violence, or tackled such behaviours themselves, working with local organisations on solutions to the rampant homelessness that lay behind? These interviewees chose the latter. They got their hands dirty. As they articulated the costs and benefits of participating in the administration of policies affecting Aboriginal Territorians, their deliberations were not false consciousness, but reflective of the sensitivity and inner knowledge an effective operative brings to difficult work. Recounting conversations with hard-living relations, interviewees spoke of negotiating their authorities carefully and not lording it over people by elitist tactics. When they spoke of engaging their families and communities in conversations about these authorities they evoked a sense of mutuality and respect, albeit that they often felt these values went unseen by their employer.

Two interviewees, young men who had both lived rough lives, had had their aspirations to seniority foiled. One was in Alice Springs, one was in Darwin. Both had family in town. Hear their hopes of government and their interactions with their communities in these passages from their intense, searching interviews.

Vincent arrived at his interview hot, dusty and late, having had to change a tyre on his four-wheel drive in the long journey from the homeland he had established to start a new life for his family. In the public service, Vincent had come to feel ostracised for his personal politics, so he had left. His job had been to open communication channels between the local Aboriginal community and the government. As colleagues from a former office, we had some shared understanding of working in government. Here, Vincent describes his moral courage and a deep commitment to service.

> So you have to be like a man of your own words I guess and you have to like tread a fine line ... because you get dragged into domestic violence, or disputes with other families or things like that. You've got to be able to stand above them and say, 'Look, I know these families are fighting but I've still got to conduct my job and I've got to get on with these [families] too.' At the end of the day, I've got to be able to sort of move between these groups, so I can't afford to sorta like take sides. I can say, 'Hey look, I'll sympathise with you but I can't fight your battles for you because I need to be able to make a living and *conduct* myself and I need to work with the other group that you're fighting with.' Otherwise I become *inefficient*.

Vincent's high personal standards included that his efficiency as a public servant, of which he was immensely proud, was never at the expense of community relationships.

Jett had been seconded to a non-government organisation to cool his heels following angry outbursts at work. In Jett's view, years of substance abuse and alienation qualified him to a place at the top of decision-making:

> It's put me two feet in front of a lot of other people in regards to what I know [about] ... how to go about fixing the social problems. That ain't just done at grassroots level ... *That's why I need to keep going up* because for me to make real effective change in regards to Aboriginal people, I've got to be up there, at the table with them when they make the decisions ...

'*You blackfella*,' Jett told me Aboriginal people where he came from had said to him, 'We need you in government!' That, Jett said, made him want to 'do the right thing by Aboriginal people'. A year after the interview, Jett had finished cooling his heels and was 'back at the table'. He emailed me another recounted conversation in 2008, in which it seems his hard-won knowledge of the correctives for Aboriginal self-abuse had both horrified and impressed non-Aboriginal colleagues:

> I sit in amazement at people who sit in a meeting—say nothing, agree ... then after I have said something that goes against the grain ... say 'that's good what you said, you are right' ...

Jett continued to wonder what his colleagues' ambivalence suggested about the point of his contributions, and left again. I have heard he is now back.

Vincent and Jett both wanted seniority, but both encountered resistance from other colleagues when their mentors moved on. From different geographies and personal stories, their commitment to Indigenous improvement was as clear as their belief that public service seniority would be worth the compromise—if only they could achieve it.

Some interviewees found some of their colleagues less grounded than themselves. But there was no arbitration on this point nor systemic responsiveness to levels of grounding, in the public service around them. There was only the understanding and connection each brought to jobs they felt privileged to have. Unlike the political theorists, Aboriginal senior public servants in the Northern Territory didn't have the luxury of avoiding intimate associations with government policies and programs. Being seen as elitist came with the job, even though they were themselves subject to the representational powers of those above and around them in the public service hierarchy. They could choose to help on the terms available, or alternatively do nothing. To the charge of compromised elitism, they might look back over the history of their people and answer that their people had known far worse things than compromise. These were indeed mutual relations, in which the interviewees strove to impart what needed to be known, to interact fulsomely, to explain themselves and to seek out opportunities to listen to others.

There is a final criterion. Recall that a good representative relationship must contain mutual recognition. The parties must respect each other's membership in the group, even if they are situated differently within it. Representatives and the represented must recognise one another. This may be through historical connection and the sharing of fates.

As a final step, we need to consider how these may be present in the bureaucracy today, where the government self-account has been determinedly ahistorical.

Sharing fates in the bureaucracy today: 'We're what's on the ground'

Representative bureaucracy came to the fore in Australia in the 1970s, at a time when the discretionary/deliberative view was prevalent and values-based public service openly acknowledged. During the 1980s and 1990s, the New Public Management style of government reinvigorated the rational/technical view of bureaucracy—but in a new form, as departments served economic-rationalist priorities by contracting services to external providers. After decades of outsourcing, New Public Management (see Hood & Peters 2004) is still the guiding account in many parts of the public service in Australia. But past accounts never completely fade away. In 2010, more than 30 years after Coombs first promoted the idea of a socially diverse public service, the Australian Government was still proposing that 'the APS should mirror the diversity of the broader population' (Moran 2010), regardless that the government no longer offered the direct delivery work that had attracted some in the broader population. And New Public Management is under review as scholars like Charles Sabel argue that governments are, or should be, decentralising through 'experimentalist' approaches that acknowledge local discretion and support ground-up learning (Sabel & Simon 2011). These approaches are reviving the discretionary/deliberative account.

The discretionary/deliberative and rational/technical views of the public service are both still true, and still in tension. Descriptive representatives might blend in well in the flatter, more flexible structures of today, but find their ground-level and issue-specific contributions undervalued in parts of the public service that reify the holistic, the short-term and the generic. In support of this hypothesis, Julia made a telling comment on public service managerialism:

> A bureaucrat working in ... [any] public service now, in Indigenous Affairs, they almost want you to be content free.

Recall that Julia and her colleagues had protested at the separation of policy from its underpinnings in practical implementation. This long-term activist described Aboriginal employees as just 'sitting there' in workplaces that did not value pragmatism.

Sharing fates conjures something inescapable, enduring and historical. This seems at odds with Julia's image of under-utilised Aboriginal people in 'content free' bureaucracies. But it is the case that the interviewees had long memories, and they spoke of families with even longer memories. Their families had endured relations with government that contained profound and prolonged distrust, and the interviewees were mindful of this history. In their minds, their fates and the fates of the Northern Territory's remote population were profoundly linked. They felt needed. There is support for their intuition in political theory. According to Mansbridge, the need for descriptive representatives is strongest when historic distrust calls for repairs to communication and disadvantaged groups have 'uncrystallised interests' (Mansbridge 1999: 636–8). We have seen prolonged distrust in the Northern Territory Government's relationship with the Northern Territory's original inhabitants. Aboriginal Liaison Officers, the government's 'eyes and ears', were asked to facilitate communications between the government and their people from the first moments of Northern Territory self-government. The Northern Territory's remote Aboriginal communities have evidently not crystallised their interests, as they are still the objects of policy's soul-searching. Under Mansbridge's criteria, the interviewees were indeed needed. Northern Territory Aboriginal constituents do qualify for the special justice of having descriptive representatives among the bureaucrats who serve them—regardless of the tensions involved in their work.

Vulnerable populations are entitled to representation by the best in the business. Just being a group member might not qualify someone for the responsibility of representing the unarticulated interests of the dispossessed. Asking provocatively, 'Will Just Any Woman, Black, or Latino Do?' Dovi argued that the represented should be able to judge representatives on the content of their work (2002: 738). Dovi advises us that how descriptive representatives represent is more important than why they do it.

It is rarely possible for the represented, so deserving of descriptive representation yet so distant from government, to see the content of the policy work that is about them. Some interviewees were sensitive to this void, saying they had no authority to speak for other Aboriginal people in government. When they did venture to contribute their voice, they felt their lack of accountability to the absent keenly. When considering how representation's key requirements of authority and accountability were met in the circumstances of this study, it helps to think of representation as Iris Marion Young came to understand it, as a relationship that 'moves between moments of authorisation and accountability' (Young 2000: 129). Authorisation and accountability do not need to be synchronous or even current, but they do need to have a source. The idea of diverse and scattered connections, supporting diffuse and indirect authority and accountability, resonates well with the lived reality of bureaucratic representing that was articulated by the interviewees. Their representations were not based on clear instructions and immediate sanctions, but on the sum of their knowledge and connections. Were there any sanctions over these representatives? If they paid no heed to their people or their history, they risked mutual recognition in the relationship with their people.

A sense of sharing fates may provide the authority for the kinds of representation enacted and discussed by the interviewees, including the corrective governing of others. The interviewees knew that absent policy subjects could not know or judge them to the same extent that they could know and judge their absent policy subjects. But the interviews show us senior Aboriginal public servants tussling with their political conscience and trying to achieve a sense of reciprocity in their impossibly non-reciprocal relationship with their absent policy subjects. Behind their use of standard public service expressions like beneficiary, client and program recipient, their stories and descriptions invoked enduring interactions. Role modelling was their way of connecting with their policy subjects. Role modelling confirmed their worth in a public service that did not seem to recognise them as other than *different*. When role models modelled particular comportments in their corrective governing, they could have been trying to create the conditions for mutual relations with the dispossessed. If they judged themselves the poorer when they were not in a relationship of mutual

recognition—when their represented absent did not know them—
we see that Aboriginal senior public servants were accountable to
a sense of shared fates.

In good enough representation in a bureaucracy, those present
would share aims and fates with the absent and feel accountable for
the quality of the present–absent relationship. There is nothing in
the present-day bureaucracy that would prevent this being true for
Aboriginal and Torres Strait Islander public servants, either in theory
or in practice. Indeed, their orbit between government and the non-
government authorities that do government at a distance suggests it.
Those in orbit were making strategic use of the relationship between
the government and its service providers. Here, emerging from the
tightening belt of government contracting, was an enthusiastic and
committed cohort of professional managers who looked for the chance
to work more seamlessly than government itself could, by influencing
policy and implementing it as well.

History provides the evidence that structures of discrimination have
been reproduced over time, Melissa Williams tells us, whereas memory
'highlights the subjective side' as marginalised groups come to terms
with that history in their present (Williams 1998: 177, 181–7). While
the sense of past wrongs among the interviewees was profound, they
were prepared to look at pragmatic present solutions as long as the
government was connecting with their people. A common history
made the interviewees part of a collective local Aboriginal identity,
indeed a political community. Their career stories were like the
scattered pieces of a puzzle—which makes the patterns that emerged
from them all the more profound. The political theory helps us again
here. Williams describes 'communities of shared fate' in which the
relationships that are 'ethically significant' may not be consciously
chosen but are understood by those who are in them (Williams
2009: 43, italics in original). A community of shared fate arises from
'imagining a set of human beings as socially related to one another in
the past and the future' (Williams 2009: 45). If legitimacy is not agreed
in this community, it is at least contested. If people even agree there is a
'story to be told about this relationship', that is a start (Williams 2009:
45). If stories compete, there is no neutral position and no arbiter, only
'imaginative judgement' from the community (Williams 2009: 51).

Williams was speaking of global citizenship and we are considering a prosaic circumstance in Australia's far north and desert heart. Nevertheless, the interviewees evinced theories of identity and action that suggest the sharing of fates. They felt part of a collective history in which their commitment had a place. In keeping with Dawson's theory, the difference in education levels between the present and absent in this study had indeed intensified rather than diminished the interviewees' sense of sharing fates with a community in which so many were absent from the public service.

So the public servants in this study remembered, respected and fulfilled mutual relations with their people by seeking to influence the process and content of policymaking. Many interviewees were the single exception in remote-living families. Some worried that their adolescent children were being attracted back out into youth gangs. The fact that their efforts were not always recognised or successful adds weight to their legitimacy as the representatives of their people. We have seen that they judged themselves the poorer if their relationships were not grounded. Localness was a virtue, but groundedness was a necessity. Proximity to the ground and exposure to the inner workings of government positioned them uniquely. In government, they watched one another with unsentimental camaraderie. They saw themselves sharing fates with the absent. They evinced a collective historical memory and an ethic of practice both imaginative and concrete enough to qualify them, at least in theory, as participants in a community of shared fate. At its highest level of abstraction, this community of shared fate was not the community of Indigenous Australians but the community of Aboriginal Territorians.

In working to build Aboriginal people's institutional presence, coordinate their policies, facilitate their partnership, secure their compliance and deliver their services, Aboriginal senior public servants were clearly agents of the postcolonial enterprise. But being blackfellas in the bureaucracy had not silenced them. Absent before, present now, Aboriginal public servants are, in the well-chosen words of Rowley, the 'twice involved' (1978: 206).

Perhaps this is what Matthew meant when he said something profound. Recall Matthew, non-senior but long serving 'eyes and ears' since the first moment of Northern Territory self-government, who was asked if he was a 'radical black' in the same year Rowley published his words.

Matthew's interview was full of anecdotes and rich commentary on the public service characters he had known. He said his own profound words over an ordinary cup of tea, without the fresh hot damper he joked we should have been cooking on the fire for his historic storytelling—which he insisted not be conducted in either his office or mine but outside, in the breeze. He said:

> We're the *engine room*, mate. *We're* what's on the ground.

This study has embraced the structural and the subjective in the interviewees' navigation of the expectations and opportunities of representative bureaucracy. It is through the interviewees' accounts of doing representative bureaucracy, and not through representative bureaucracy's time-honoured self-serving account, that we now know how representative bureaucrats create a sense of government.

Meeting Indigenous employment targets: A ménage à trois

The Northern Territory Government continues to urge that the employment of Aboriginal people in the public service matches their proportion in the general population, through the standing invitation for Aboriginal and Torres Strait Islander contributions to the administration of government and the periodic setting of targets.

In 2010, the Commissioner for Public Employment reissued the 2012 target of 10 per cent that had been set by the Generation Plan of Action in 2007. Ten per cent by 2012 must have seemed a modest and achievable aim from the 2010 Indigenous public sector employment level of 8 per cent, just as 10 per cent by 1982 must have seemed modest and achievable to Chief Minister Everingham in 1980. But Indigenous employment had not reached 9 per cent by May 2015, when Chief Minister Adam Giles promised to double the numbers to 16 per cent by 2020 (OCPE 2015: 6–7). This was three years after the return of the Country Liberal Party. Giles's promise repeated former Country Liberal Party Chief Minister Everingham's double-up target of 20 per cent by 1990 and former Labor Party Chief Minister Martin's double-up target of 20 per cent by 2017. Lining up the targets in this way, their glibness is breathtaking. But policy is always aspirational.

Under Chief Minister Giles, the Indigenous Employment and Career Development Strategy 2015–2020 announced the even more ambitious aim that 'Indigenous employees will hold 10 per cent of senior management/executive roles in the NTPS by 2020'. *Senior* Indigenous public servants would form a higher proportion of the Northern Territory Public Service's positions than *Indigenous public servants have ever occupied since Northern Territory self-government.* This was a stretch target indeed.

Chief Minister Giles dedicated $0.5 million to a small Indigenous team to pick up the baton of past efforts, working with a new Commissioner for Public Employment, Craig Allen. In May 2016, Commissioner Allen was passionately committed to building Indigenous employment numbers throughout the Northern Territory Public Service. He believed the Strategy would help him get there. 'When you embark on one of these journeys, you've got to stay the course', he said, 'and there will be detractors' (personal communication, 25 May 2016). Rather than inviting contributions to policy and decision-making, the 2015–2020 Strategy aimed more judiciously, but still ambitiously, at 'a public sector that reflects the Aboriginal and Torres Strait Islander population of the Northern Territory community it serves'. The Strategy recognised that the Northern Territory's Aboriginal and Torres Strait Islander population is an internally mobile and stable labour pool, and that this population constitutes 70 per cent of public service clientele (OCPE 2015: 6). Those implementing the Strategy seemed to be heeding the lessons of the past by taking the targets seriously, encouraging a more honest engagement with Aboriginal and Torres Strait Islander employees, improving attraction and retention and introducing new career strategies.

The first annual progress report for the Indigenous Employment and Career Development Strategy 2015–2020 reported a one per cent increase in Indigenous employment (OCPE 2016). Commissioner Allen attributed this result to the introduction of 'special measures' recruitment, in which an Aboriginal and Torres Strait Islander employee who met the selection criteria was awarded any level job in any role—with no expectation of only serving the Aboriginal and Torres Strait Islander population—and a simplified selection process that encouraged greater numbers of Aboriginal and Torres Strait Islander applicants. Commissioner Allen hoped to be the first Commissioner to achieve the 10 per cent Indigenous employment target. Chief Minister Giles, himself Indigenous, stayed in touch through a reference group of Aboriginal and Torres Strait Islander senior public servants. There were now two groups, one for Darwin and one for Alice Springs. A secondment program between the Northern Territory Government and non-government organisations was being trialled. A four-year investment of $1.35 million was announced by the Minister for Public Employment to support cross cultural awareness, mentoring, performance conversations and to bring Aboriginal and Torres Strait Islander staff together in an annual forum (Styles 2016).

In August 2016 there was a change of government in the Northern Territory, back to Labor. Time will tell if the hospitality towards Aboriginal and Torres Strait Islander senior public servants stays on course and the Northern Territory Public Service achieves its social mirror—and hears Aboriginal and Torres Strait Islander people. But meeting Indigenous public sector employment targets is one of the most confounding challenges for all governments in Australia today, and while the Northern Territory's particular challenge is unique, the Northern Territory Government is not alone in the pressure to announce targets. The Australian Government's National Partnership on Indigenous Economic Participation of 2009–2013 required all the States and Territories to sign up to public sector employment targets to help halve the gap in employment outcomes between Aboriginal and Torres Strait Islander peoples and other Australians within 10 years. The Department of the Prime Minister and Cabinet has responsibility for the next reforms, and through the Employment Parity Initiative 'aims to increase the number of large Australian companies with a workforce reflective of the size of the Indigenous population' (Department of the Prime Minister and Cabinet 2015). In November 2015, the Australian Public Service Commission launched the Australian Government's own Aboriginal and Torres Strait Islander Employment Strategy. The Strategy aims to match the Aboriginal and Torres Strait Islander proportion of the Australian population, increasing Indigenous employee representation across the Commonwealth public sector to 3 per cent by 2018 (Australian Public Service Commission 2016). Progress is being monitored by the Department of the Prime Minister and Cabinet and published on that department's website, as well as in other Australian Government agencies' annual reports.

The history of Aboriginal and Torres Strait Islander employment in the Australian Public Service has its own twists and turns, but there are strong parallels with the Northern Territory experience of unmet targets (see Australian National Audit Office 2014). There are also parallels in the challenge for Aboriginal and Torres Strait Islander public servants to contribute meaningfully in the workplace. Confidential interviews with 34 current and former Commonwealth Aboriginal and Torres Strait Islander public servants in a recent study by Nick Biddle and Julie Lahn found a number of factors with a strong bearing on their decisions to leave. These included Australian Public Service entry programs 'overselling' the ability of Indigenous public servants to make a difference to policy, 'political expediency' overriding their contributions and Indigenous public servants having to be the 'messenger of bad news'. Biddle and Lahn identified lack of career development, limited avenues to respond to racist attitudes and 'being undervalued' among Indigenous public servants' reasons for leaving. As in my research, Biddle and Lahn's interviewees discussed feeling token and wanting to have more influence over policies and programs. The Indigenous sector was a common destination for those who left, and some who left did not rule out returning (Biddle & Lahn 2016).

Some interviewees in my research who had worked for the Australian Government pointed out the similarity of their experiences across governments. Some had found working in Canberra, the national capital, too removed from their communities. Sandy acknowledged her mentoring in Canberra, but she had missed home. Julia observed that her experience as a senior public servant in the regional office of a Commonwealth department had been just like 'the situation in the NT Government at the moment':

> I was never called on once to actually give an Aboriginal perspective … It's like they want to increase Aboriginal people in their service because a lot of their clients are Aboriginal, so they're trying to bring someone with that perspective but it's [Aboriginal people are] the last person [people] that they'll actually ask for.

It is for others to discuss their experiences in the Commonwealth environment. This book is about the relationship between some Aboriginal and Torres Strait Islander people and the government of the Northern Territory of Australia, and I hope it inspires researchers to conduct detailed contextual studies in other times and places.

For now, let's listen again to Sarah, the senior public servant born in the bush whose plea to be heard opened this book. Sarah had something else profoundly important to say:

> Our views, our experience, our knowledge, our understanding, our *relationship* means nothing to the group of non-Indigenous people who's running this show—who's making decisions about Aboriginal people.

Sarah's plea might well be directed to all Australian institutions seeking to become more reflective of the populations they serve.

'Our *relationship*', in Sarah's statement, was the *representative relationship* between Aboriginal public servants and their communities. The relationship is representative because it involves Aboriginal public servants who are present in bringing forth the absent. This rapidly becomes a relationship of representation when Aboriginal public servants are invited, or feel compelled by their jobs, to speak for their people.

In her *employment relationship* with the government, Sarah was asking the government to take into account her relationship with other Aboriginal people.

There is a third relationship. This is the *constituency relationship*. This relationship is between the government and all Aboriginal and Torres Strait Islander Australians. Sarah asked the government not just to have a truer engagement with her but also with remote Aboriginal communities, in the constituency relationship it should have with them. She expected this of herself, and she asked no less of the government. When Sarah questioned 'whether we're just numbers, we're just bums on seats', she was looking to be an important part of the government's relationship with Aboriginal people, and not the unimportant part she felt. Her test of whether the public service could be serious in its dealings with Aboriginal people was whether it could be serious with her. She was not looking to substitute for absent people, but to be acknowledged and allowed to speak as a local Aboriginal person who had been profoundly affected by the past policies of child removal, who was now present. Like many Aboriginal and Torres Strait Islander public servants, Sarah did not want her presence to substitute for the governments' constituency relationship with communities. Rather, as an employee who was also a member of that constituency, she was willing to help government improve that relationship.

Aboriginal and Torres Strait Islander public servants are in all three relationships: they are in the representative relationship with their people, they are in the employment relationship with the government and they are also in the constituency relationship between the government and their people. In this ménage à trois, Aboriginal and Torres Strait Islander people are only too aware of the protocols for daily survival, and government departments could learn much from their navigation of hazardous terrain. Here might be the sum of the interviewees' message to government, and indeed any institution that wants to relate to Aboriginal and Torres Strait Islander Australians: 'You need to ask our people what they think, not just ask us. But we can help you ask them properly.'

The message for theory is the message for government: a bureaucracy can only be truly representative if it remembers who is being represented. Sarah's presence in government was circumstantial, the product of events that started with her removal from a campfire at the age of three. She did not always feel like a public servant. She could not always distance herself from her policy subjects. She always remembered the represented. She would not speak of generic 'remotes', but insisted on being specific. She laid out an encyclopedic knowledge of Northern Territory communities, their traditional ownership and settlement histories. This was her ground. She neither understated nor overstated the personal loss that framed her identity. She simply modelled a process for the government's engagement with her people, and hoped to be treated to engagement of that quality herself. If she wasn't treated to that quality of engagement, she could still speak up for others' right to it. This would ease her conscience for being the one, in her representative relationship, who had a job in government.

To achieve their targets, governments make an invitation to Aboriginal and Torres Strait Islander Australians: enter our institution, self-identify and contribute at all levels across our departments. This research has shown that the invitation is hollow unless government learns to listen to those who try accepting it. Like the very idea of representative bureaucracy, Indigenous public sector employment policies contain no theory of action. Somehow, the presence of Aboriginal and Torres

Strait Islander people means they inject their knowledge and views and—hey presto!—there emerges a government that reflects and understands the people it serves. Indigenous employment policies are long on promise and short on strategy. They do not ask workplaces to examine their norms, understand why people leave or follow where they go. They show surprisingly little curiosity about the experiences of Aboriginal and Torres Strait Islander public servants. Governments in Australia say they want to engage with Indigenous Australians, but miss the texture and meaning of the relationship that is within reach.

I am sometimes asked to give advice about how governments in Australia can do better in meeting the targets for Indigenous public sector employment. Let's take each relationship in turn.

The employment relationship

Meeting targets is not merely a matter of recruiting more entries, but of intercepting the outflow. Indigenous employment targets cannot be achieved while the flow of Aboriginal and Torres Strait Islander employees is as much outbound as inbound. With the movement of people in one door and out another, employment numbers are only kept buoyant by the turnstile ticker effect. The numbers remain steady, but the incumbents are forever changing. The only way to intercept the outflow of employees and allow the numbers to build is for government to learn how to retain Aboriginal and Torres Strait Islander employees. This means acknowledging the tensions of representative bureaucracy. It is not possible to dissolve tensions that are deeply embedded in the structures of government, if those structures cannot be changed. It is better to embrace the mobility of Aboriginal and Torres Strait Islander employees. If the orbit is inevitable and the statistic is the prize, then governments should get on-side. That is, keep the door open for Aboriginal and Torres Strait Islander employees who leave to work in the government's outsourced service-delivery arm, place a value on that work, and thus set up their return. This way, Aboriginal and Torres Strait Islander numbers and contributions will grow.

The invitation to Aboriginal and Torres Strait Islander people to enter the employment relationship should not overuse the word 'representation'. The interviewees would ask government departments to say what they mean: if they mean to seek a population-proportionate number of Aboriginal and Torres Strait Islander employees, say so and say why. If an employee is expected to bring community knowledge into government, check if that is possible and ask for it. If an Aboriginal and Torres Strait Islander person is needed on an interview panel or other committee, be clear what role he or she is to play. If a local solution is needed, invite locals into the conversation. Most importantly, hear what they say.

The representative relationship

The representative relationship is different. The government is not a party to this relationship. Aboriginal and Torres Strait Islander public servants who have accepted the invitation to join the administration of government manage their own relationship with other Aboriginal and Torres Strait Islander people. They know their place in this relationship, and do not necessarily discuss it in the workplace. They will be protecting their relationship with vulnerable people and, like all public servants, will generally be acting mindfully within public service ethics and the terms of their employment. The representative relationship is only revealed under conditions of trust. It may be sturdy, it may be fragile. It should not be disrupted by others. This relationship is a matter for Aboriginal and Torres Strait Islander people. The interviewees said often that their relationships and culture were their business. Their message might go something like this: never assume that the perspective of one Aboriginal or Torres Strait Islander employee is the view of that person's group or of the Indigenous population more generally. Recall Jay's satirical take on colleagues who leaped to the assumption: 'Is *that* what Aboriginal people think?' When he tried to point out the problem, colleagues took *that* to be what Aboriginal people thought!

The representative relationship is of very great value to government, because those who are absent—whether they are looking for a career, or are just unemployed and disaffected—look to those who are present, their role models, as their guide.

The constituency relationship

Finally, to the constituency relationship. During and since the interviews, I have been tested over and again—for my honesty with the interview material, my silence on the identity of interviewees, my willingness to broach difficult subjects like the importance of competency and the misuse of culture, and my commitment to conveying the findings of this research. This book is based on relationships of trust. If I have inadvertently broken any of those with anyone, I may not be told, but my work will have no credibility with the affected Aboriginal and Torres Strait Islander people. The same applies to government departments that invite Aboriginal and Torres Strait Islander people into their workplaces and do not hear what they say, or try having conversations with Aboriginal and Torres Strait Islander employees that those departments should be having with communities. Government may not be told, but it will have no credibility with the affected Aboriginal and Torres Strait Islander people. The message is simple. If the words of 76 Aboriginal and Torres Strait Islander people in the Northern Territory are anything to go by, then attend to the relationship and the rest will follow. The interviewees were clear on this point: Aboriginal and Torres Strait Islander employees would stay in government longer if the government worked harder on its relationship with their communities. A better constituency relationship—the third relationship—will lead to a better employment relationship, a better representative relationship, and better government.

At the very least, governments in Australia should heed Sarah's plea:

> How can you make decisions about Aboriginal people when you can't even talk to the people you've got *here* that are blackfellas?

Even as they leave the public service, there are things Aboriginal and Torres Strait Islander people might want to tell a government department that knows how to ask. Interviewees said time and again that our conversations felt like the exit interview they had never been offered.

The 'missing ingredient' in the policy focus on 'normalising' Indigenous Australians is 'an understanding that Aboriginal conditions of life are not a remote problem to be solved, but an extension of settler conditions of life', concluded Patrick Sullivan in his finely-tuned consideration of Indigenous–government relations in Australia today (2011: 122). That is, government needs the relationship with Aboriginal and Torres Strait Islander people as much as they need the relationship with government. Both parties are already in it. But as we now know, Aboriginal and Torres Strait Islander people are in it twice when they take on the mantle of government.

A conversation starter

This book has situated the political identity of Aboriginal senior public servants in a policy narrative and in a time and place. It has drawn extensively on normative political theory, not to judge Aboriginal senior public servants but as a guide to their working models.

Why is it important to understand how bureaucratic representation works? Finding a balance between contradictory needs and wants is the central dilemma of any political representative. It matters very much to Aboriginal and Torres Strait Islander people who decides the complex and painful matters affecting their people. This is why descriptive representation is important, and this is why descriptive representatives need to be up to the task.

Through the interviews, this book found Aboriginal senior public servants who were neither tokens nor advocates but practising representatives. As representatives, they were good enough in the circumstances. Mindful of their responsibilities as public servants, and seeing themselves as sharing fates with the absent, they used opportunities in the cracks and crevices of daily work to give voice to their people. They stood up for Aboriginal people in the corridors of power. They preferred not to speak in place of the absent, although they did so when necessary. To rise to the complex occasion of administering government, they were prepared to defy political correctness. Most were not content to bring forth the absent by just sitting there: they tried to influence the democratic structure in which they worked, to make it possible for the absent to become more present. This is why they did jobs that made them feel they were failing and worked in bureaucratic cultures that sometimes asked the wrong questions. Indeed, by submitting to the public service criteria of merit and impartiality that inherently did not favour their backgrounds, by risking the disparagement of those for whom the true Aboriginal person is only ever disadvantaged and the committed Aboriginal person is only ever righteously situated outside government, they were more than good enough. If we had the analytic tools, we might cast them as exemplary representatives. They were as good as representative bureaucrats could be.

For a community of people to be a community of shared fate, it needs to have a story that has ethical significance to the community (Williams 2009). If the community believes in the story, it is true. No one else can judge this but the people in the community— in this case, the community of people who are in the representative relationship. Although their place of employment did not do enough to seek out the views of the represented, the relationship between the interviewees and their absent suggests representation. Or at the very least, diversely positioned interviewees had a story to tell that was ethically significant for them and for those they reached. In this community of shared fate, members sought out the interactions that let them believe in their accountability.

In closing, we will avoid the normative political theory and settle for low-lying pragmatism. At the very least, this book has acknowledged Aboriginal and Torres Strait Islander people who are on the side of service provision and not just service recipients. As public servants, the interviewees in this study were more willing and more complicit in government than Aboriginal and Torres Strait Islander people are usually portrayed. They were as quick and discerning as any good policy adviser, and potentially more determined to make a difference.

Recall Rowley said that the first Aboriginal public servants, 'hoping to be received as the representatives of their people must have been dismayed to find themselves cogs in the bureaucratic machine' (Rowley 1978: 207). Some Aboriginal and Torres Strait Islander public servants might feel the opposite, after watching and participating in more than 30 years of unconvincing representative bureaucracy. Hoping to be received as public servants, they might be dismayed to be received as representatives. But let's not generalise, and instead present representative bureaucracy's antithesis by giving voice to the committed individualism of someone who had experienced abandonment by both his community and his public service. Despite his ambition, Louis had not made it to seniority; he found writing hard and only spoke 'very simple English'. He did not see himself as a representative. Indeed, he went on to find a new, more private life elsewhere, in which I hope he is happy. Back in 2007, Louis forswore the idea of representing anyone with a finer use of English than the most celebrated orator, when he said:

> I can't, because I'm only me. And I don't expect anyone else to represent me, either—because I can't find any other Indigenous person like me, that's why.

The interviewees were as diverse and contradictory as any people could and should be.

How compelled are Aboriginal and Torres Strait Islander people, including those who already populate government structures, by the invitations of Indigenous public sector employment? Do they feel they embody the Aboriginal and Torres Strait Islander populations sufficiently to bring the unreachable and non-compliant among them into government?

I suggest that many are not remotely convinced by repeated posturing about their so-called rising numbers. Not all will be persuaded into the tight corners of representative practice by the invitation to contribute to policy and decision-making about their people. They certainly would not all see themselves as representatives, even after reading this book. However, many will continue to be drawn by a sense of history, conscience, ambition or need to participate in the representative bureaucracy of their place. If the hospitality they receive is ambivalent, so be it—they know worse things than invitations that say one thing and mean another. They might reply in kind, meeting ambivalence with ambivalence. Or they might answer with a return invitation to their government and to those who doubt or romanticise them, or don't even notice they're here: take our service seriously. The rest is for Aboriginal and Torres Strait Islander Australians to say.

Bibliography

Aboriginal Development Division (1986). *Aboriginal Development Division programs and activities*, Office of the Public Service Commissioner, Northern Territory Government, Darwin.

Acting Director Office of Aboriginal Liaison (1983). Memorandum to Director-General, Department of the Chief Minister: Proposed changes in role and organisation of the Office, 17 May 1983 [File 86/0106 – Policy, Aboriginal Development]. *NTRS 366/P4 – Department of Community Development, Aboriginal Development Division 1986*, Northern Territory Archives Service, Darwin.

Acting Director Office of Aboriginal Liaison (1984). Memorandum to Acting Deputy Secretary, Department of the Chief Minister: Aboriginal advice to government, 3 December 1984 [File 86/0106 – Policy, Aboriginal Development]. *NTRS 366/P4 – Department of Community Development, Aboriginal Development Division 1986*, Northern Territory Archives Service, Darwin.

Advisory Committee to the PSCNT (1985). Minutes of meeting, Advisory Committee to the Public Service Commissioner on Matters Pertaining to Aboriginals in the N.T.P.S., Public Service Commissioner for the Northern Territory, 13 May 1985 [File AD 85/0019 folios 1–9]. *NTRS 366/P4 – Department of Community Development, Aboriginal Development Division 1976–1986*, Northern Territory Archives Service, Darwin.

Ah Chin W (2006). From strategy to reality: a model for community engagement. *Public Administration Today* Oct–Dec.

Alcoff L (1995). The problem of speaking for others. In Roof J & Wiegman R (eds), *Who can speak? Authority and critical identity*, University of Illinois Press, Urbana.

Austin-Broos D (2003). Places, practices, and things: the articulation of Arrernte kinship with welfare and work. *American Ethnologist* 30 (1): 118–35.

Australian National Audit Office (2014). *Indigenous employment in Australian government entities,* Commonwealth of Australia, Canberra.

Australian Public Service Board (1975). *Statistical bulletin: employment of Aboriginals in the Australian Public Service at 1 October 1974,* Australian Government Publishing Service, Canberra.

Australian Public Service Board (1976). *Statistical bulletin: employment of Aboriginals in the Australian Public Service at 1 October 1975,* Australian Government Publishing Service, Canberra.

Australian Public Service Board (1980). *Statistical bulletin: employment of Aboriginals in the Australian Public Service at 1 October 1979,* Australian Government Publishing Service, Canberra.

Australian Public Service Commission (2016). *Commonwealth Aboriginal and Torres Strait Islander Employment Strategy,* Commonwealth of Australia, Canberra.

Bennett SC (1989). *Aborigines and political power*, Allen & Unwin, Sydney.

Bhabha H (1984). Of mimicry and man: the ambivalence of colonial discourse. *Discipleship: a special issue on psychoanalysis* 28: 125–33.

Biddle N & Lahn J (2016). *Understanding Aboriginal and Torres Strait Islander employee decisions to exit the Australian Public Service,* Working Paper 110, Centre for Aboriginal Economic Policy Research, Australian National University, Canberra.

Bickford S (1999). Reconfiguring pluralism: identity and institutions in the inegalitarian polity. *American Journal of Political Science* 43 (1): 86–108.

Briggs L (2008). Indigenous employment in the APS: address to the Executive Leadership Group Victoria, Australian Public Service Commission, Canberra.

Brough M (2007). House of Representatives Questions Without Notice: Child Abuse, 21 June 2007, Commonwealth of Australia Parliamentary Debates.

Cohen C (1997). Straight gay politics: the limits of an ethnic model of inclusion. In Shapiro I & Kymlicka W (eds), *Ethnicity and group rights – Nomos XXXIX*, New York University Press, New York.

Cole LA (1976). *Blacks in power: a comparative study of black and white elected officials*, Princeton University Press, Princeton.

Commonwealth of Australia (2015). *Closing the gap: Prime Minister's report 2015*, Australian Government, Canberra.

Commonwealth of Australia (2016). *Closing the gap: Prime Minister's report 2016*, Australian Government, Canberra.

Coombs HC (1977). *Australian Government Administration: report of Royal Commission*, Parliamentary Paper 185/1976, Commonwealth Government Printer, Canberra.

Cooper D (1995). *Power in struggle: feminism, sexuality and the state*, New York University Press, New York.

Cowlishaw G (2004). *Blackfellas, whitefellas and the hidden injuries of race*, Wiley-Blackwell, Malden.

Cross Cultural Communication Consultant (1980). Attachment to memorandum from the Director, Aboriginal Liaison Unit to the Director General, Department of the Chief Minister proposing improvements to the Aboriginal Liaison Unit: proposed guidelines for the communication component of the Aboriginal Liaison Unit, Department of Chief Minister 28 April, 1980 [File AD86/0105], *NTRS 366/P4 – Department of Community Development, Aboriginal Development Division 1976–1986*, Northern Territory Archives Service, Darwin.

Dawson MC (1994). *Behind the mule: race and class in African-American politics*, Princeton University Press, Princeton.

Department of External Affairs (1919). *Report of the Administrator for the year ending 30th June 1918*, Government Printer, Canberra.

Department of Territories (1964). *The Northern Territory: annual report for 1962–63*, Government Printer, Canberra.

Department of Territories (1966). *The Northern Territory: annual report for 1964–65*, Government Printer, Canberra.

Department of Territories (1968). *The Northern Territory: annual report for 1965–66*, Government Printer, Canberra.

Department of the Chief Minister (1979). Aboriginal Liaison Unit – functional responsibilities [File AD86/0105], *NTRS 366/P4 – Department of Community Development, Aboriginal Development Division 1976–1986*, Northern Territory Archives Service, Darwin.

Department of the Interior (1971). *The Northern Territory of Australia: annual report for 1969–70*, Government Printer, Canberra.

Department of the Prime Minister and Cabinet (2015). *Employment parity initiative*, Commonwealth of Australia, Canberra, www. dpmc.gov.au/indigenous-affairs/employment/employment-parity-initiative.

Deputy Director-General (1983). Memorandum to the Director-General: Office of Aboriginal Liaison, Department of Chief Minister 7 June 1983 [AD86/0106 – Policy, Aboriginal Development], *NTRS 366/P4 – Department of Community Development, Aboriginal Development Division 1976–1986*, Northern Territory Archives Service, Darwin.

Deputy Director-General & Director Office of Aboriginal Liaison (1981). Aboriginal Affairs and the Northern Territory Government – an assessment of the role of the Office of Aboriginal Liaison, September 1981 [File 11–20 (Part 4)], *NTRS 782/P1 – General Correspondence and Administration files of the Chief Minister (P.A.E. Everingham) 1978–1984*, Northern Territory Archives Service, Darwin.

Deputy PSCNT (Public Service Commissioner of the Northern Territory) (1983). Letter to the Director, Office of Aboriginal Liaison, Office of the Public Service Commissioner 9 November 1983 [86/0106 folio 245], *NTRS 366/P4 – Department of Community Development, Aboriginal Development Division 1986*, Northern Territory Archives Service, Darwin.

Dillon MC & Westbury ND (2007). *Beyond humbug: transforming government engagement with Indigenous Australia,* Seaview Press, West Lakes.

Director Office of Aboriginal Liaison (1983). Memorandum to Acting Deputy Director-General, Department of Chief Minister: Office of Aboriginal Liaison, 11 January 1983 [File 86/0106 – Policy, Aboriginal Development], *NTRS 366/P4 – Department of Community Development, Aboriginal Development Division 1986,* Northern Territory Archives Service, Darwin.

Dovi S (2002). Preferable descriptive representatives: will just any woman, black, or latino do? *American Political Science Review* 96 (04): 729–43.

Dovi S (2006). *Political representation,* plato.stanford.edu/archives/spr2014/entries/political-representation/.

Dovi S (2007). *The good representative,* Blackwell, Oxford.

Dryzek JS (1996). Political inclusion and the dynamics of democratization. *The American Political Science Review* 90 (3): 475–87.

Dryzek JS & Niemeyer S (2008). Discursive representation. *American Political Science Review* 102 (4): 481–93.

Eisenstein H (1996). *Inside agitators: Australian femocrats and the state,* Allen & Unwin, St Leonards.

Everingham P (1978). Letter to Prime Minister Malcolm Fraser, 27 October 1978 [File 84/787, Aboriginal Employment Policy Part 1], *NTRS 366/P4 – Department of Community Development, Aboriginal Development Division 1976–1986,* Northern Territory Archives Service, Darwin.

Everingham P (1979). Memorandum to Director-General: Office of Policy and Planning, 16 February 1979 [File 84/787, Aboriginal Employment Policy Part 1], *NTRS 366/P4 – Department of Community Development, Aboriginal Development Division 1976–1986,* Northern Territory Archives Service, Darwin.

Everingham P (1980). Ministerial Statement: policies for the improvement of Aboriginal communities, Hansard 30 April 1980 [File AD86/0098 folios 1–8], *NTRS 366/P4 – Department of Community Development, Aboriginal Development Division 1976–1986*, Northern Territory Archives Service, Darwin.

Everingham P (1983). Letter to the Hon Clyde Holding, Federal Minister for Aboriginal Affairs, 23 December 1983 [File 11–20 (Part 12)], *NTRS 782/P1 – General Correspondence and Administration files of the Chief Minister (P.A.E. Everingham) 1978–1984*, Northern Territory Archives Service, Darwin.

Foucault M (1988). *The history of sexuality, vol 1* (translated by R Hurley), Penguin Books, UK.

Foucault M (1991). Governmentality. In Burchell G, Gordon C & Miller PM (eds), *The Foucault effect: studies in governmentality, with two lectures by and an interview with Michel Foucault*, Harvester Wheatsheaf, London.

Ganter E (2010). An ambivalent hospitality: Aboriginal senior public servants and the representation of others in Australia's self-governing Northern Territory, PhD thesis, The Australian National University, Canberra, digitalcollections.anu.edu.au/handle/1885/10128.

Ganter E (2011). Representatives in orbit: livelihood options for Aboriginal people in the government of the Australian desert. *Rangeland Journal* 33: 385–93.

Ganter R, Martinez J & Lee GM (2006). *Mixed relations: Asian-Aboriginal contact in North Australia*, University of Western Australia Press, Crawley, WA.

Gerritsen R (1982). Blackfellas and whitefellas: the politics of service delivery to remote Aboriginal communities in the Katherine region. In Loveday P (ed.), *Service delivery to remote communities*, Australian National University North Australia Research Unit, Darwin.

Hatton S (1992). Ministerial statement by the Northern Territory Chief Minister, The Hon Steve Hatton, c. November 1992: a Minister for Aboriginal Development, *Daily Hansard*, Parliament House, Darwin.

Holcombe S (2005). Luritja management of the state. *Oceania* 75 (3): 222–33.

Hood C & Peters G (2004). The middle aging of New Public Management: into the age of paradox? *Journal of Public Administration Research and Theory* 14 (3): 267–82.

Howard MC (1981). *Aboriginal politics in southwestern Australia*, University of Western Australia Press, Nedlands, WA.

Howard MC (1982). Australian Aboriginal politics and the perpetuation of inequality. *Oceania* 53 (1): 82–101.

Human Rights and Equal Opportunity Commission (1997). *Bringing them home: report of the National Inquiry into the Separation of Aboriginal and Torres Strait Islander Children from their Families*, Human Rights and Equal Opportunity Commission, Sydney.

Hunter B (2005). The role of discrimination and the exclusion of Indigenous people from the labour market. In Austin-Broos DJ & Macdonald G (eds), *Culture, economy and governance in Aboriginal Australia*, Sydney University Press, Sydney.

Joint Committee on the NT (1974). Parliamentary inquiry into constitutional development in the Northern Territory: transcript of evidence, 27 August. Canberra.

Juddery B (1978). A vision splendid of a bureaucracy based on merit: contradictory responses to the NT's approaching self-government. *Canberra Times*, 23 June 1978 [Item 22A – NTPS General file]. *NTRS 784/P1 – Departmental Memoranda to the Majority Leader and the Chief Minister (P.A.E. Everingham) 1977–1979*, Northern Territory Archives Service, Darwin.

Karnig AK & McClain PD (1988). Minority administrators: lessons from practice. In Karnig AK & McClain PD (eds), *Urban minority administrators: politics, policy, and style*, Greenwood Press, New York.

Kowal E (2008). The politics of the gap: Indigenous Australians, liberal multiculturalism and the end of the self-determination era. *American Anthropologist* 110 (3): 338–48.

Kowal E (2015). *Trapped in the gap: doing good in Indigenous Australia,* Berghahn Books, New York.

Krislov S (1974). *Representative bureaucracy,* Prentice-Hall, New Jersey.

Kymlicka W (1993). Group representation in Canadian politics. In Seidle FL (ed.), *Equity & community: the charter, interest advocacy, and representation,* Institute for Research on Public Policy, Montreal.

Lahn J (2013). *Aboriginal professionals: work, class and culture,* Working Paper 89, Centre for Aboriginal Economic Policy Research, Australian National University, Canberra.

Langton M (2008). Trapped in the Aboriginal reality show. *Griffith Review* 19.

Larkin S (2013). Race matters: Indigenous employment in the Australian Public Service, PhD thesis, Queensland University of Technology.

Lea T (2008). *Bureaucrats and bleeding hearts: Indigenous health in northern Australia,* University of New South Wales Press, Sydney.

Lippman L (1979). The Aborigines. In Patience A & Head B (eds), *From Whitlam to Fraser: reform and reaction in Australian politics,* Oxford University Press, Melbourne.

Lipsky M (1980). *Street-level bureaucracy: dilemmas of the individual in public services,* Russell Sage Foundation, New York.

Loveday P (1982). Access to services – some social and political complications. In Loveday P (ed.), *Service delivery to remote communities,* The Australian National University North Australia Research Unit, Darwin.

Loveday P (1983). The politics of Aboriginal society. *Politics* 18(1).

Loveday P & Cummings R (1989). Aboriginal Public Servants and role conflict, Unpublished work-in-progress report, The Australian National University North Australia Research Unit, Darwin.

Malloy J (2003). *Between colliding worlds: the ambiguous existence of government agencies for Aboriginal and women's policy,* University of Toronto Press, Toronto.

Manderson D (2008). Not yet: Aboriginal people and the deferral of the rule of law. *Arena* (29/30): 219–72, www.arena.org.au/pdf/journal-29-30/manderson29-30.pdf.

Mansbridge J (1999). Should blacks represent blacks and women represent women? A contingent 'yes'. *Journal of Politics* 61 (3): 628–57.

Mansbridge J (2003). Rethinking representation. *American Political Science Review* 97 (4): 515–28.

Martin D (2003). *Rethinking the design of Indigenous organisations: the need for strategic engagement*, Discussion Paper 248, Centre for Aboriginal Economic Policy Research, The Australian National University, Canberra.

Meier KJ & Hawes DP (2009). Ethnic conflict in France: a case for representative bureaucracy? *American Review of Public Administration* 39 (3): 269–85.

Merlan F (1998). *Caging the rainbow: places, politics, and Aborigines in a north Australian town*, University of Hawai'i Press, Honolulu.

Mitchell T (1999). Society, economy, and the state effect. In Steinmetz G (ed.), *State/culture: state-formation after the cultural turn*, Cornell University Press, Ithaca.

Moran M, Anda M, Elvin R, Kennedy A, Long S, McFallan S, McGrath N, Memmott P, Mulgan R, Stanley O, Sullivan P, Tedmanson D, Wright A & Young M (2009). *Desert services that work: year one research report*, Working Paper 30, Desert Knowledge CRC, Alice Springs, nintione.com.au/sites/default/files/resource/DKCRC-Working-paper-30-Desert-Services-That-Work.pdf.

Moran T (Chair) (2010). *Ahead of the game: blueprint for the reform of Australian Government administration*, Department of the Prime Minister and Cabinet, Canberra.

Moreton-Robinson A (2000). *Talkin' up to the white woman: Indigenous women and feminism*, University of Queensland Press, Brisbane.

Mulgan R (1998). Politicisation of senior appointments in the Australian Public Service. *Australian Journal of Public Administration* 57 (3): 3–14.

Northern Territory Administrator (1949). Circular memorandum to Branch Heads: employment of police trackers and Aboriginal assistants, 15 July 1949, *NAAD F1 1949/408*, Australian Archives, Darwin.

Northern Territory Board of Inquiry into the Protection of Aboriginal Children from Sexual Abuse (2007). *Ampe akelyernemane meke mekarle 'Little children are sacred': report of the Northern Territory Board of Inquiry into the Protection of Aboriginal Children from Sexual Abuse*, Northern Territory Government, Darwin.

Northern Territory Government (2007). *Closing the gap of Indigenous disadvantage: a generational plan of action*, Northern Territory Government of Australia, Darwin, hdl.handle.net/10070/238201.

OAL (Office of Aboriginal Liaison) (1983). Policies, functions and objectives of the Office [of Aboriginal Liaison] – broadly stated, Department of the Chief Minister [File 86/0106, folios 253–276], *NTRS 366/P4 – Department of Community Development, Aboriginal Development Division*, Northern Territory Archives Service, Darwin.

OCPE (Office of the Commissioner for Public Employment) (1997). 1996/97 *Annual report*, Northern Territory Government, Darwin.

OCPE (Office of the Commissioner for Public Employment) (2001). *Review of Aboriginal Employment and Career Development Strategy 1995–2000*, Northern Territory Government, Darwin.

OCPE (Office of the Commissioner for Public Employment) (2002). *Northern Territory Public Sector Indigenous Employment and Career Development Strategy 2002–2006*, Northern Territory Government, Darwin.

OCPE (Office of the Commissioner for Public Employment) (2003). *Northern Territory Public Sector Indigenous Employment and Career Development Strategy 2002–2006: Progress report (1), September 2003*, Northern Territory Government, Darwin.

OCPE (Office of the Commissioner for Public Employment) (2004). *Northern Territory Public Sector Indigenous Employment and Career Development Strategy 2002–2006: Progress report (3), June 2004– December 2004*, Northern Territory Government, Darwin.

OCPE (Office of the Commissioner for Public Employment) (2005). *Northern Territory Public Sector Indigenous Employment and Career Development Strategy 2002–2006: Progress report (4), January 2005–June 2005*, Northern Territory Government, Darwin.

OCPE (Office of the Commissioner for Public Employment) (2006). *Northern Territory Public Sector Indigenous Employment and Career Development Strategy 2002–2006: Progress report (5), July 2005– December 2005*, Northern Territory Government, Darwin.

OCPE (Office of the Commissioner for Public Employment) (2007). *Northern Territory Public Sector Indigenous Employment and Career Development Strategy 2002–2006: Progress report (6), December 2006*, Northern Territory Government, Darwin.

OCPE (Office of the Commissioner for Public Employment) (2008). *2007/08 annual report*, Northern Territory Government, Darwin.

OCPE (Office of the Commissioner for Public Employment) (2009). *State of the service report 2008–09*, Northern Territory Government, Darwin.

OCPE (Office of the Commissioner for Public Employment) (2010). *Northern Territory Public Sector Indigenous Employment and Career Development Strategy 2010–2012*, Northern Territory Government, Darwin.

OCPE (Office of the Commissioner for Public Employment) (2015). *Indigenous Employment and Career Development Strategy 2015–2020*, Northern Territory Government, Darwin.

OCPE (Office of the Commissioner for Public Employment) (2016). *Northern Territory Public Sector Indigenous Employment and Career Development Strategy 2015–2020: Progress report April 2015 to March 2016*, Northern Territory Government, Darwin.

Office of Aboriginal Development (1996). *1995/96 annual report*, Northern Territory Government, Darwin.

Office of Aboriginal Liaison (1980 [1983]). Handwritten notation, 14 November 1983 [File 11–20 (Part 10)], *NTRS 782/P1 – General Correspondence and Administration files of the Chief Minister (P.A.E. Everingham) 1978–1984*, Northern Territory Archives Service, Darwin.

Perkins C (1975). *A bastard like me*, Ure Smith, Sydney.

Peterson N (1993). Demand sharing: reciprocity and the pressure for generosity among foragers, *American Anthropologist* 95 (4): 860–74.

Phillips A (1991). *Engendering democracy*, Polity Press in association with Blackwell, Cambridge.

Phillips A (1995). *The politics of presence,* Clarendon Press, Oxford.

Pitkin HF (1967). *The concept of representation*, University of California Press, Berkeley.

PSCNT (Public Service Commissioner of the Northern Territory) (1978). Minute to Majority Leader: review of Northern Territory Government operations, 3 February 1978 [Item 22 – NTPS General file], *NTRS 784/P1 – Departmental Memoranda to the Majority Leader and the Chief Minister (P.A.E. Everingham) 1977–1979*, Northern Territory Archives Service, Darwin.

PSCNT (Public Service Commissioner of the Northern Territory) (1981). *1980/81 annual report*, Northern Territory Government, Darwin.

PSCNT (Public Service Commissioner of the Northern Territory) (1983). *1982/83 annual report*, Northern Territory Government, Darwin.

PSCNT (Public Service Commissioner of the Northern Territory) (1984). *1983/84 annual report*, Northern Territory Government, Darwin.

PSCNT (Public Service Commissioner of the Northern Territory) (1987). *1986/87 annual report*, Northern Territory Government, Darwin.

Read P (1990). *Charles Perkins: a biography,* Viking, Ringwood.

Rehfeld A (2009). Representation rethought: on trustees, delegates and gyroscopes in the study of political representation and democracy. *American Political Science Review* 103 (2): 214–30.

Richardson HS (2002). *Democratic autonomy: public reasoning about the ends of policy*, Oxford University Press, New York.

Rose N & Miller P (1992). Political power beyond the state: problematics of government. *British Journal of Sociology* 43 (2): 173–205.

Rose NS (1999). *Powers of freedom: reframing political thought,* Cambridge University Press, Cambridge.

Rowley CD (1971). *Aboriginal policy and practice, vol 3, The remote Aborigines,* Australian National University Press, Canberra.

Rowley CD (1976). Aboriginals and the administration: Royal Commission on Australian Government Administration, Appendix 3.1. *Parliamentary Paper 188/1976,* Government Printer of Australia, Canberra.

Rowley CD (1978). *A matter of justice,* Australian National University Press, Canberra.

Rowley CD (1980). Aboriginals and the Australian political system. In Jaensch D & Weller PM (eds), *Responsible government in Australia,* Drummond Publishing on behalf of the Australasian Political Studies Association, Richmond.

Rowse T (2000). *Obliged to be difficult: Nugget Coombs' legacy in Indigenous affairs,* Cambridge University Press, Cambridge.

Rowse T (2001). 'Democratic systems are an alien thing to Aboriginal culture ...'. In Sawer M & Zappalá G (eds), *Speaking for the people: representation in Australian politics,* Melbourne University Press, Carlton South.

Rowse T (2002). *Indigenous futures: choice and development for Aboriginal and Islander Australia,* University of New South Wales Press, Sydney.

Rowse T (2005). The Indigenous sector. In Austin-Broos DJ & Macdonald G (eds), *Culture, economy and governance in Aboriginal Australia,* Sydney University Press, Sydney.

Sabel CF & Simon WH (2011). Minimalism and experimentalism in the administrative state. *Georgetown Law Journal* 100 (1): 53–93.

Sackett L (1983). Michael C Howard, 'Aboriginal politics in southwestern Australia' [book review]. *Oceania* 53 (4): 409–10.

Sanders W (2002). *Towards an Indigenous order of Australian government: rethinking self-determination as Indigenous affairs policy*, Discussion Paper 230, Centre for Aboriginal Economic Policy Research, Australian National University, Canberra.

Sapiro V (1981). When are interests interesting? The problem of political representation of women. *American Political Science Review* 75 (3): 701–16.

Saward M (1992). *Co-optive politics and state legitimacy,* Dartmouth, Brookfield, USA.

Saward M (2006). The representative claim. *Contemporary Political Theory* 5 (3): 297–318.

Saward M (2009). Authorisation and authenticity: representation and the unelected. *Journal of Political Philosophy* 17 (1): 1–22.

Sawer M (1990). *Sisters in suits: women and public policy in Australia,* Allen & Unwin, Sydney.

Sawer M & Zappalá G (2001). *Speaking for the people: representation in Australian politics,* Melbourne University Press, Carlton South.

Scott AK (1985). Two new training initiatives within the NTPS relating to Aboriginals. In Loveday P & Wade-Marshall D (eds), *Economy and people in the north,* The Australian National University North Australia Research Unit, Darwin.

Sherman N (1998). Empathy and imagination. *Midwest Studies in Philosophy* XXII.

Spivak GC (1988). Can the subaltern speak? In Nelson C & Grossberg L (eds), *Marxism and the interpretation of culture,* University of Illinois Press, Urbana.

Steering Committee for the Review of Government Service Provision (2014). *Overcoming Indigenous disadvantage: key indicators 2014,* Productivity Commission, Canberra.

Styles P (2016). *Minister for Public Employment press release: investing in Aboriginal employment and career development,* Northern Territory Government, Darwin.

Sullivan P (2010). *The Aboriginal community sector and the effective delivery of services: acknowledging the role of Indigenous sector organisations*, Working Paper 73, Desert Knowledge CRC, Alice Springs, www.nintione.com.au/resource/DKCRC-Working-paper-73_ Indigenous-sector-oganisations.pdf.

Sullivan P (2011). *Belonging together: dealing with the politics of disenchantment in Australian Indigenous affairs*, Aboriginal Studies Press, Canberra.

Summers A (1986). Mandarins or missionaries: women in the federal bureaucracy. In Grieve N & Burns A (eds), *Australian women: new feminist perspectives*, Oxford University Press, Melbourne.

Taussig MT (1993). *Mimesis and alterity: a particular history of the senses*, Routledge, New York.

Taylor C (1992). The politics of recognition. In Taylor C & Gutmann A (eds), *Multiculturalism and 'the politics of recognition': an essay*, Princeton University Press, Princeton.

Taylor C (2004). *Modern social imaginaries*, Duke University Press, London.

Theobald N & Haider-Markel DP (2009). Race, bureaucracy, and symbolic representation: interactions between citizens and police. *Journal of Public Administration Research and Theory* 19 (2): 409–26.

Thielemann GS & Stewart JJ Jnr (2003). A demand-side perspective on the importance of representative bureaucracy. In Dolan JA & Rosenbloom DH (eds), *Representative bureaucracy: classic readings and continuing controversies*, ME Sharpe, New York.

Thompson FJ (1976). Minority groups in public bureaucracies: are passive and active representation linked? *Administration and Society* 8 (2): 201–26.

Urbinati N (2000). Representation as advocacy: a study of democratic deliberation. *Political Theory* 28 (6): 758–86.

Vemuri R (2007). *Evaluation of the effectiveness and implementation of the NTPS Indigenous Employment & Career Development Strategy 2002–2006: Final report, 29 June 2007*, Charles Darwin University, Darwin.

Wakerman J, Matthews S, Hill P & Gibson O (2000). *Beyond Charcoal Lane. Aboriginal and Torres Strait Islander health managers: issues and strategies to assist recruitment, retention and professional development*, Centre for Remote Health Joint Centre of Flinders University and Charles Darwin University, Alice Springs.

Watson S (1990). The state of play: an introduction. In Watson S (ed.), *Playing the state: Australian feminist interventions*, Verso, London.

Wilenski PS (1986). *Public power and public administration*, Hale & Ironmonger in association with the Royal Australian Institute of Public Administration, Sydney.

Williams MS (1998). *Voice, trust and memory: marginalized groups and the failings of liberal representation*, Princeton University Press, Princeton.

Williams MS (2009). Citizenship as agency within communities of shared fate. In Coleman WD & Bernstein SF (eds), *Unsettled legitimacy: political community, power, and authority in a global era*, University of British Columbia Press, Vancouver.

Wilson B (1998). Police trackers: myth and reality. In Austin T & Parry S (eds), *Connection and disconnection: encounters between settlers and Indigenous people in the Northern Territory*, Northern Territory University Press, Darwin.

Yeatman A (1990). *Bureaucrats, technocrats, femocrats: essays on the contemporary Australian state*, Allen & Unwin, Sydney.

Young IM (1997). Deferring group representation. In Shapiro I & Kymlicka W (eds), *Ethnicity and group rights – Nomos XXXIX*, New York University Press, New York.

Young IM (2000). *Inclusion and democracy*, Oxford University Press, Oxford.

Young IM (2004). Situated knowledge and democratic discussions. In Andersen J & Sim B (eds), *The politics of inclusion and empowerment: gender, class and citizenship*, Palgrave Macmillan, New York.

Index

Note: locators in italics indicate tables, figures or other illustrative material.

CAEPR Research Monograph Series

1. *Aborigines in the economy: a select annotated bibliography of policy relevant research 1985–90*, LM Allen, JC Altman and E Owen (with assistance from WS Arthur), 1991.

2. *Aboriginal employment equity by the year 2000*, JC Altman (ed.), published for the Academy of Social Sciences in Australia, 1991.

3. *A national survey of Indigenous Australians: options and implications*, JC Altman (ed.), 1992.

4. *Indigenous Australians in the economy: abstracts of research, 1991–92*, LM Roach and KA Probst, 1993.

5. *The relative economic status of Indigenous Australians, 1986–91*, J Taylor, 1993.

6. *Regional change in the economic status of Indigenous Australians, 1986–91*, J Taylor, 1993.

7. *Mabo and native title: origins and institutional implications*, W Sanders (ed.), 1994.

8. *The housing need of Indigenous Australians, 1991*, R Jones, 1994.

9. *Indigenous Australians in the economy: abstracts of research, 1993–94*, LM Roach and HJ Bek, 1995.

10. *The native title era: emerging issues for research, policy, and practice*, J Finlayson and DE Smith (eds), 1995.

11. *The 1994 National Aboriginal and Torres Strait Islander Survey: findings and future prospects*, JC Altman and J Taylor (eds), 1996.

12. *Fighting over country: anthropological perspectives*, DE Smith and J Finlayson (eds), 1997.

13. *Connections in native title: genealogies, kinship, and groups*, JD Finlayson, B Rigsby and HJ Bek (eds), 1999.

14. *Land rights at risk? Evaluations of the Reeves Report*, JC Altman, F Morphy and T Rowse (eds), 1999.

15. *Unemployment payments, the activity test, and Indigenous Australians: understanding breach rates*, W Sanders, 1999.

16. *Why only one in three? The complex reasons for low Indigenous school retention*, RG Schwab, 1999.

17. *Indigenous families and the welfare system: two community case studies*, DE Smith (ed.), 2000.

18. *Ngukurr at the millennium: a baseline profile for social impact planning in south-east Arnhem Land*, J Taylor, J Bern and KA Senior, 2000.

19. *Aboriginal nutrition and the Nyirranggulung Health Strategy in Jawoyn country*, J Taylor and N Westbury, 2000.

20. *The Indigenous welfare economy and the CDEP scheme*, F Morphy and W Sanders (eds), 2001.

21. *Health expenditure, income and health status among Indigenous and other Australians*, MC Gray, BH Hunter and J Taylor, 2002.

22. *Making sense of the census: observations of the 2001 enumeration in remote Aboriginal Australia*, DF Martin, F Morphy, WG Sanders and J Taylor, 2002.

23. *Aboriginal population profiles for development planning in the northern East Kimberley*, J Taylor, 2003.

24. *Social indicators for Aboriginal governance: insights from the Thamarrurr region, Northern Territory*, J Taylor, 2004.

25. *Indigenous people and the Pilbara mining boom: a baseline for regional participation*, J Taylor and B Scambary, 2005.

26. *Assessing the evidence on Indigenous socioeconomic outcomes: a focus on the 2002 NATSISS*, BH Hunter (ed.), 2006.

27. *The social effects of native title: recognition, translation, coexistence*, BR Smith and F Morphy (eds), 2007.

28. *Agency, contingency and census process: observations of the 2006 Indigenous Enumeration Strategy in remote Aboriginal Australia*, F Morphy (ed.), 2008.

29. *Contested governance: culture, power and institutions in Indigenous Australia*, J Hunt, D Smith, S Garling and W Sanders (eds), 2008.

30. *Power, culture, economy: Indigenous Australians and mining*, J Altman and D Martin (eds), 2009.

31. *Demographic and socioeconomic outcomes across the Indigenous Australian lifecourse*, N Biddle and M Yap, 2010.

32. *Survey analysis for Indigenous policy in Australia: social science perspectives*, B Hunter and N Biddle (eds), 2012.

33. *My Country, mine country: Indigenous people, mining and development contestation in remote Australia*, B Scambary, 2013.

34. *Indigenous Australians and the National Disability Insurance Scheme*, N Biddle, F Al-Yaman, M Gourley, M Gray, JR Bray, B Brady, LA Pham, E Williams and M Montaigne, 2014.

35. *Engaging Indigenous economy: debating diverse approaches*, W Sanders (ed.), 2016.

36. *Better than welfare? Work and livelihoods for Indigenous Australians after CDEP*, K Jordan (ed.), 2016.

Centre for Aboriginal Economic Policy Research,
College of Arts and Social Sciences,
The Australian National University, Canberra, ACT, 2601

Information on CAEPR Discussion Papers, Working Papers and Research Monographs (Nos 1–19) and abstracts and summaries of all CAEPR print publications and those published electronically can be found at the following website: caepr.anu.edu.au.

www.ingramcontent.com/pod-product-compliance
Lightning Source LLC
Chambersburg PA
CBHW040142270326
41928CB00023B/3321